W9-BZB-760

Educational Resilience in Inner-City America
Challenges and Prospects

Educational Resilience in Inner-City America
Challenges and Prospects

Edited by

Margaret C. Wang
*Temple University Center for Research
in Human Development and Education
and the
National Center on Education
in the Inner Cities*

Edmund W. Gordon
Yale University

LEA LAWRENCE ERLBAUM ASSOCIATES, PUBLISHERS
1994   Hillsdale, New Jersey   Hove, UK

Lawrence Erlbaum Associates, Inc., Publishers
365 Broadway
Hillsdale, New Jersey 07642

Cover design by Mairav Salomon-Dekel

Library of Congress Cataloging-in-Publication Data

Educational resilience in inner-city America : challenges and
   prospects / edited by Margaret C. Wang and Edmund W. Gordon.
      p.   cm.
   Includes bibliographical references and index.
   ISBN 0-8058-1324-1 (alk. paper). — ISBN 0-8058-1325-X (pbk. :
alk. paper)
   1. Education, Urban—United States.   2. Education, Urban—Social
aspects—United States.   3. Socially handicapped children—
Education—United States.   4. Resilience (Personality trait)—
United States.   I. Wang, Margaret C.   II. Gordon, Edmund W.
LC5101.E4   1994
371.96′7′0973—dc20   93-8619
                                                        CIP

Books published by Lawrence Erlbaum Associates are printed on acid-free
paper, and their bindings are chosen for strength and durability.

Printed in the United States of America
10   9   8   7   6   5   4   3   2   1

Contents

Preface

The story of inner-city life in the United States, and the education of its people, is often told as though it were a tragedy; the ending is often predictable and usually dire, highlighting deficiency, failure, and negative trends. The lives of many inner-city children and families across this country are indeed in disorder, and they are floundering, as are the community agencies to which they traditionally turn for help. As with all social problems and the modern morbidities of our time, children and youth in the inner cities are hit hardest. At a time when they should be learning more and developing broader competencies in better schools, the trend is disastrously otherwise. They should be provided with support for healthy development and constructively engaged in stimulating exchanges with the educational and cultural institutions of their community, but they are not.

But this dismal view is only half the picture. U.S. cities are a startling juxtaposition between the despairing and the hopeful, between disorganization and restorative potential. Alongside the poverty and the unemployment, the street fights and the drug deals, are a wealth of cultural, economic, educational, and social resources. Such resources can and should be cultivated and mobilized to enhance the capacity for education in the cities. Often ignored are the ability for adaptation and the resilience that help many who are seemingly confined by circumstance to struggle and succeed "in the face of the odds."

Perhaps more than any other group, educators are expected to shoulder the burden of these odds—the enormous demographic transformations in the cities, the vast reshaping of U.S. families, the upswing in poverty, and the loss of support networks for those in the inner cities. However, educators too often face these seemingly insurmountable odds with very little knowledge or thorough understanding of either the problems of inner-city life or the forces of resilience that can work to alleviate them.

The future of inner-city children and youth hinges on the quality of their schooling and the development of broad competencies that empower them to fully participate in 21st-century America. We must develop strategies and structural changes that will enhance the chances for schooling success of today's students in today's schools. One such strategy is to build on the resilience with which children are empowered to succeed in the face of enormous adversity. Some children show remarkable resilience and develop quite well despite the adversities in their lives. Indeed, many children are strengthened by the challenges they face, and are able to build productive and promising futures for themselves and their families.

This book is an attempt to broaden our understanding of how to magnify the circumstances known to enhance development and education, so that the burden of adversity is reduced and opportunities are advanced for all children and youth, but especially the children and youth of the inner cities who are in at-risk circumstances. The focus is on (a) raising consciousness about the opportunities available to foster resilience among children, families, and communities; and (b) synthesizing the knowledge base that is central to implementing improvements that serve to improve life circumstances and educational opportunities of children and families. This volume is intended for a wide audience of readers, but particularly for those who are in a position to shape public policy and deliver educational and human services.

The orientation of the writers of this volume is that one should be entirely realistic in appraising the life situations and educational opportunities of children and youth, not forgetting for a moment the difficulties, the complexity, and the complex history of the problems they face. However, the ''positives'' that can be made available to foster resilience and success are also emphasized. At the core of the work discussed by the authors is the resilience of children, families, and institutions, and the factors that create the context for such resilience. A central premise of the work of these authors is that the challenges facing children, youth, families, and schools in inner-city America stem from a variety of economic, political, and health problems; furthermore, their solutions are complex and require the application of knowledge and expertise from many disciplines and professions.

The need to draw insight and practical implications from the theoretical and empirical research base of varied disciplines, to improve education in inner-city schools and communities, served as the basic principle in preparing the chapters included in this volume. The book includes 13 chapters, which are organized under three sections: Part I, ''Understanding Resilience''; Part II, ''Research on Resilience: Conceptual and Methodological Considerations'';

and Part III, "Fostering Educational Resilience." Much of the material in this volume was originally presented at an invitational conference sponsored by the National Center on Education in the Inner Cities (CEIC) at the Temple University Center for Research in Human Development and Education (CRHDE). The research reported herein is supported in part by the Temple University Center for Research in Human Development and Education and in part by the Office of Educational Research and Improvement (OERI) of the U.S. Department of Education through a grant to the CEIC at Temple University. The opinions expressed do not necessarily reflect the position of the supporting agencies and no official endorsement should be inferred.

PART I: UNDERSTANDING RESILIENCE

This section of the book includes five chapters. They address the theoretical underpinnings and research insights relating to the general construct of resilience, particularly the fostering of competence and learning success in inner-city children and youth.

Chapter 1, "Resilience in Individual Development: Successful Adaptation Despite Risk and Adversity," by Ann Masten, examines what has been learned about psychological resilience in individuals, and draws implications for fostering resilience. In chapter 2, "Variations in the Experience of Resilience," Edmund Gordon and Lauren Dohee Song provide a descriptive analysis of a reconceptualization of the construct of resilience and a suggested taxonomy. Chapter 3, "Educational Resilience in Inner Cities," is co-authored by Margaret Wang, Geneva Haertel, and Herbert Walberg. They discuss the concept of *resilience* as it has been advanced in developmental psychology, and summarize educationally relevant research consonant with the definition of educational resilience. Chapter 4, "Understanding Resilient Students: The Use of National Longitudinal Databases," by Samuel Peng, describes the databases produced by the National Center for Education Statistics and their potential use by researchers examining the concept of resilience. In chapter 5, the final chapter of this section, "The Americanization of Resilience: Deconstructing Research Practice," Leo Rigsby critically examines the concept of resilience in an attempt to expose the assumptions underlying the concept and the processes and conditions that are assumed to give rise to resilience.

PART II: RESEARCH ON RESILIENCE: CONCEPTUAL AND METHODOLOGICAL CONSIDERATIONS

Four chapters are included in this section. Chapter 6, "On Resilience: Questions of Validity," by David Bartelt, is concerned with the external validity of resilience as it is employed at the levels of individual, family, and city. In chapter 7, "Resilience as a Dispositional Quality: Some Methodological

Points,'' Joan McCord addresses some of the methodological difficulties in-
herent in studying resilience as a quality in people or their environments. Chapter 8, ''Risk and Resilience: Contextual Influences on the Development of
African-American Adolescents,'' by Ronald Taylor, discusses the developmental tasks of adolescents, the environmental risks that confront African-American
adolescents, and evidence of resilience in light of these risks, as well as implications for the education of African-American adolescents. Chapter 9, ''Special Education as a Resilience-Related Venture,'' by Maynard Reynolds,
discusses the potential merits and issues surrounding the joining of resilience
research and theory with the field of special education.

PART III: FOSTERING EDUCATIONAL RESILIENCE

This section includes four chapters that together provide a synthesis and analysis of what we think will work, based on research and practical experience,
to create learning environments in school, home, and community that serve
as protective factors. The chapters in this section focus on innovative ways of
creating such environments.

In chapter 10, ''Effectiveness and Efficiency in Inner-City Public Schools:
Charting School Resilience,'' Lascelles Anderson focuses on the application
of the resilience concept at the organizational level. Chapter 11, ''Understanding
Resilience: Implications for Inner-City Schools and their Near and Far Communities,'' by Jerome Freiberg, examines alterable variables for creating
resilience constructs that build on proactive and additive models, rather than
on individual or collective deficits, and provides an analysis of the directions
for future research on fostering student resilience. Chapter 12, ''Contextualizing
Resiliency,'' by Howard Liddle, examines the potential resiliency of the
resilience construct. His basic premise is that the continued revision or extension of resilience as a concept is a necessary process in sharpening our understanding of fostering resilience as an intervention strategy in working with
children and youth in at-risk circumstances. Chapter 13, ''Organizing for
Responsiveness: The Heterogeneous School Community,'' by Diana Oxley,
presents a conceptual framework and theoretical underpinnings for organizing schools into small units as a strategy for fostering resilience and learning
success of students in large inner-city schools.

Much of the material in this volume was originally presented at an invitational conference held at the Temple University Center for Research in Human Development and Education. Appreciation is expressed to the Office of
Educational Research and Improvement of the U.S. Department of Education for providing the funding support for the conference. Many of our colleagues played critical roles in facilitating the development and production of
this volume. We are most grateful to Dr. Aquiles Iglesias, the Associate Director

of CEIC, for handling the myriad of administrative details to ensure timely production of the initial drafts of papers for discussion. To Kathy Petrich-LaFevre, for her editorial and administrative support in the preparation of this volume. To Don Gordon for his technical editing expertise and his diligence in monitoring the details to bring this volume to fruition, including preparing the subject index. Finally, we wish to extend our deep appreciation to Dr. Oliver Moles and Jackie Jenkins from OERI for their continuing support and guidance.

MCW
EWG

Part I

Understanding Resilience

Resilience in Individual Development: Successful Adaptation Despite Risk and Adversity

Ann S. Masten
University of Minnesota

Resilience in an individual refers to successful adaptation despite risk and adversity. The rationale for examining resilience phenomena rests on the fundamental assumption that understanding how individuals overcome challenges to development and recover from trauma will reveal processes of adaptation that can guide intervention efforts with others at risk. The goal of this chapter is to examine what has been learned about psychological resilience in individuals and to draw implications from that knowledge for fostering resilience.

The study of resilience in individuals is closely tied to the origins of developmental psychopathology, which has become the central integrative framework for the study of psychological problems in children and adolescents (Masten & Braswell, 1991). The studies of resilience and psychopathology are united by this perspective. They represent two sides of the same story: individual differences in the development of human individuals (Masten, 1989). Both focus on variations in adaptation within a developmental perspective.

Resilience, like psychopathology, is judged on the basis of normative patterns of development in normative environmental contexts. If an individual is judged to be "resilient," this implies an evaluation of adaptation (internal, external, or both) and a frame of reference for the evaluation. When similar characteristics of resilient people emerge from cross-cultural studies, it is probably because humans share an evolutionary heritage of capabilities and live in environments that share certain characteristics, as well as because cultures have developed similar expectations for human development and similar values. However, given that individual humans vary in their characteristics, their cultures, and their environments, it is likely that a specific individual may be better suited to one context than to another. It also follows that as environmental conditions change, the vulnerability or resiliency of an individual with respect to that context may change.

Psychological adaptation historically has had two major components: mental functioning and external behavior. Internal health has been described in terms of psychological well-being, internal equilibrium, and ego strength. Internal problems have been described in terms of psychological distress, decompensation, and anxiety. Externally, "good" psychological adaptation has been referred to as competence and social adjustment, whereas "poor" adaptation has been called externalizing symptoms, antisocial behavior, and social maladjustment. Similarly, resilience has been used to refer both to good internal and external adaptation under challenging conditions. Jeanne and Jack Block (1980) for example, have studied "ego-resiliency," an internal concept. In our research on "Project Competence," the focus has been on understanding how effectiveness in the environment is achieved, sustained, or recovered despite adversity (Garmezy & Tellegen, 1984; Masten, 1989). Some studies focus on both aspects of functioning (Werner & Smith, 1982).

In developmental psychopathology, adaptation is judged according to psychosocial milestones called *developmental tasks* (Masten & Braswell, 1991). These broadly defined expectations for human behavior over the course of development have been enumerated by many different authors (e.g., Greenspan 1981; Havighurst, 1972; Sander, 1975; Sroufe, 1979). Erik Erikson's (1963, 1968) "eight ages of man" reflect similar developmental tasks. For example, in the United States and other industrialized societies, lists of developmental tasks in middle childhood usually include school adjustment (attendance, appropriate behavior), academic achievement, peer acceptance, having at least one friend, and moral conduct (following the rules of social organizations such as family, school, and community, for example by not stealing). In adolescence, new tasks become salient, including adjustment to pubertal change, romantic relationships, and a coherent identity. In adulthood, achievements related to earning a living, establishing a family, and performing community service become important.

Major delays or failures in these developmental expectations are often the basis for evaluation of psychopathology. Attaining these expectations despite significant odds or adversities are often the basis for evaluations of resilience.

It is assumed by most developmental psychopathologists that complex and multiple influences, both genetic and environmental, interact and combine in the development of behavior, including psychopathology (Masten & Braswell, 1991). These dynamic combinations are transformed by developmental processes, while at the same time they show coherence or predictability of pattern over time (Sroufe, 1979). Given the nature of development, marked by many multiple, interacting influences and transformations, an individual's behavior over time is often described as a path or trajectory. Similarly, resilience refers to a pattern over time, characterized by good eventual adaptation despite developmental risk, acute stressors, or chronic adversities.

Individuals may come into the world with genetic liabilities or assets that impede or facilitate psychosocial development. Environmental conditions, including the prenatal environment, will influence the development of the individual and the expression of these liabilities and assets. These assumptions are at the heart of the "diathesis-stressor" model of psychopathology (Gottesman, 1974). Environmental conditions include the quality of parenting for a given child, nutrition, fetal alcohol exposure, educational opportunities, the dangers or resources of a community, and many other factors.

INGREDIENTS OF ADAPTATION: A WORKING MODEL

Based on the assumptions of a developmental perspective on resilience and psychopathology, there are a number of major ingredients of adaptation to consider in understanding individual resilience. These include: (a) developmental path or history, which focuses on the competence or psychological functioning of the individual over time; (b) the nature of the adversities faced by the individual; (c) individual and social assets and risks; (d) individual characteristics that function as vulnerability or protective factors; (e) environmental liabilities or protective factors; and (f) the context for adaptation. In addition, one would always keep in mind the dynamic nature of adaptation.

The study of resilience begins with a "diagnosis" of good adaptation despite risk or adversity. This implies assessments, either formal or informal, of a person's competence or internal adaptation. It also implies that environmental conditions are threatening to development.

Psychological studies focus on the psychosocial environment for development and perceived threat, rather than physical threats such as extreme cold or viral infection, although physical processes clearly influence psychological adaptation. Physical adversities that have, or might have, damaged or impaired the organism are usually treated as vulnerabilities or risk factors in this literature, rather than stressors and adversities. Thus, there are studies of children at risk due to prematurity, low birth weight, chronic illness, malnutrition, and so forth (Horowitz, 1989; Kopp, 1983; Masten & Garmezy, 1985).

Psychosocial adversities are psychological stressors. A stressor is an event or experience that can be expected to cause stress in many people, with the potential for interfering with normal functioning. Psychological stress is the experience of an imbalance between the demands impinging on a person and actual or perceived resources available to meet the challenges, an imbalance that at some level disrupts the quality of functioning in the person.

Adversities vary along a number of dimensions. One is severity. Traumatic experiences are adversities of great severity, usually with acute onset, that are beyond the challenges normally encountered in development. Traumatic events or experiences may be natural, as in floods or earthquakes, or created by human design, as in war, torture, or child abuse. Less severe events that still disturb functioning, at least temporarily, in most people, include such experiences as one's home being burglarized or a close friend's moving away. "Daily hassles" also have been studied, although it is not clear to what extent perceived minor aggravations of everyday life reflect personality rather than adversity (Watson, 1988, 1990; Watson & Pennebaker, 1989).

Some events are normative, encountered by virtually everyone in the course of development, such as the death of a parent, moving, or changing schools. Societies often develop rituals to help people cope with normative stressors. Other stressors are non-normative, such as tornadoes or rape. Crisis interventions are often provided for the latter type of stressors.

Stressors also differ in acuteness of onset and duration. Some stressors are acute and short-lived, as in witnessing the murder of a stranger. Others are chronic, either persistent or oft-repeated, as is often the case with family conflict or child maltreatment. In some cases, the event is acute but the consequences are enduring, such as when a tornado destroys one's family or community, or a parent is murdered.

A risk factor is a characteristic of a group of people that is associated with an elevated probability of undesired outcomes, as in a risk factor for delinquency or dropping out of school. Having a biological parent with schizophrenia, for example, elevates the probability of a child eventually having this disorder by about tenfold over the lifetime population risk (Gottesman & Shields, 1982). Risk is a statistical concept, appropriately used for groups but not individuals. Actual outcomes of people in the risk group will vary. Some risk factors, such as poverty or family violence, predict a wide variety of problems. Some children fall into multiple risk groups and may be generally "at risk" for poor developmental outcomes.

Presumably, risk variables reflect unknown causes of problems. If a person in a risk group develops well despite risk status, it is always possible that the key causal influences were not present. Hence, it is "risky" to infer resilience just because an individual from a high-risk group does well.

Assets are the positive counterparts of risk. In some cases, assets are at the opposite end of risk parameters. High socioeconomic status or high intellectual ability may be viewed as advantages based on data that implicates low socioeconomic status and low intellectual ability as risk factors. Other assets, like musical talent or a wonderful grandparent, may facilitate adaptation, but lacking them would not necessarily constitute a risk factor.

Assets and risks are the correlates of competence and psychopathology. Risk factors and assets are directly associated with the quality of adaptation.

Vulnerabilities and protective factors, on the other hand, moderate the effects of risks or adversities on adaptation. These are not direct effects. A vulnerability factor is a characteristic of an individual that makes that person more susceptible to a particular threat to development. Traditionally, the term *vulnerability* is reserved for individual units, most often human individuals, but it can also be used to refer to other systems, as in a "vulnerable family system."

Protective factors have traditionally included either individual or environmental characteristics that facilitate better outcomes in people at risk or exposed to adversity. Thus, as discussed later, both intellectual ability and relationships with competent adults have been described as protective factors. Some authors have used the phrase "resiliency factors" to refer to protective individual characteristics (i.e., psychological antibodies), reserving the phrase "protective factors" for characteristics of the environment that promote resilience. In this discussion, *protective factors* is used as a generic term for moderators of risk or adversity that enhance good outcomes, regardless of whether they lie in the individual, the environment, or in some interaction between the two. The term *resilience* is reserved for the phenomena we are attempting to understand, in order to avoid confusion with the components and processes that may lead to it. The term *resiliency* is not used in this discussion because it has the connotation of a personality trait.

Regardless of the terminology, it should be kept in mind that resilience is a process. Understanding resilience requires delineating how all these ingredients interplay to produce good adaptations despite threatening circumstances.

THREE MAJOR GROUPS
OF RESILIENCE PHENOMENA

Resilience has been used to describe three major classes of phenomena in the psychological literature (Masten, Best, & Garmezy, 1990). The first type occurs in people from high-risk groups who have better-than-expected outcomes (i.e., those who "overcome the odds" against good development). Anecdotes abound of famous or successful people from very disadvantaged backgrounds. Their stories are often surprisingly congruent with more systematic studies of resilient high-risk children. Such studies attempt to identify the predictors of good outcome in high-risk groups.

The second major class of resilience phenomena refers to good adaptation despite stressful experiences. Sometimes the focus of this work is a common stressor, such as divorce. Other times it is a composite of heterogenous stressful life events that have occurred during a recent time period. Studies examine the general effects of stressors on child behavior, and the moderators that seem to enhance or reduce the effects of adversity (vulnerability and protective factors).

The third class includes studies of individual differences in recovery from trauma. By definition, traumatic experiences are expected to reduce the quality of functioning. No one is *invulnerable*, despite use of the term in years past. When stressors are extreme or life-threatening, resilience refers to patterns of recovery.

Several recent reviews have summarized the findings from diverse studies of these various phenomena (Garmezy, 1985; Luthar & Zigler, 1991; Masten et al., 1990; Rutter 1990; Werner, 1990). This overview is therefore quite selective, focusing on longitudinal studies of resilience. Surprisingly, despite the growth of interest in resilience, very few results have been published from longitudinal studies. These studies are diverse in their samples, their strategies for evaluating resilience, and the age range of their assessments.

LONGITUDINAL STUDIES OF RESILIENCE

The "Vulnerable but Invincible" Children of Kauai

One of the most influential studies in the field involved a cohort of children born on Kauai in 1955 and tracked for over 30 years by Werner and Smith (Werner, 1989; Werner & Smith, 1982, 1992). Based on risk factors evident in the first 2 years of life that predicted maladaptive outcomes at 10 to 11 and 18 years of age, about one third of this cohort was designated "high risk" because the children had four or more risk factors. Risk factors included poverty, perinatal stress, family discord, and low parental education. About one third of this high-risk group (10% of the cohort) was identified as resilient because group members had adapted well in childhood and adolescence. As adolescents, these resilient youth were more responsible, mature, achievement motivated, and socially connected than their less competent high-risk contemporaries. Early assessments suggested that these resilient adolescents had a number of early advantages, including good relationships with their caregivers, more attention and less separation from their caregivers, less family conflict, exposure to fewer life stressors, and better physical health.

Resilience in Children of Mentally Ill Parents

Risk defined in terms of mental illness in a parent has also been investigated in longitudinal studies. A number of studies of children "at risk" because of the mental illness of a parent have focused on resilience (e.g., Bleuler, 1984; Fisher, Kokes, Cole, Perkins, & Wynne, 1987; Garmezy & Devine, 1984; Musick, Stott, Spencer, Goldman, & Cohler, 1987; Radke-Yarrow & Sherman, 1990; Watt, 1984). Studies of resilience in adolescence have been rare, however.

In one study, investigators in the St. Louis Risk Research Project (Anthony, 1987; Worland, Weeks, & Janes, 1987) compared resilient adolescents to less adaptive high-risk peers among a sample of offspring of parents with serious mental disorders. Resilience was defined in terms of the mental health of the adolescents, based on a composite of information from adolescents, parents, psychologists, and teachers. Childhood measures of IQ and visual-motor coordination predicted mental health in this high-risk sample.

Other longitudinal studies of children at risk because of mental illness in a parent have observed a considerable degree of normal development among these children, at least in their early years (Masten, 1989; Watt, Anthony, Wynne, & Rolf, 1984). The severity of parent illness and psychosocial disadvantage have been the most powerful predictors of outcome in many of these studies; the quality of the caregiving environment appeared to be the key correlate of better or worse outcomes in the children (Goldstein & Tuma, 1987; Sameroff, Barocas, & Seifer, 1984).

An example of the possible compensatory role of good relationships is provided by the University of Rochester Child and Family Study (Fisher et al., 1987). Competence in 7- and 10-year-old children who were at risk due to mental illness in a mother was rated by parents and teachers. Greater competence was related to less chronic parent illnesses and more positive family relationships. Good relationships with fathers appeared to compensate for mothers who were not warmly engaged in childrearing. Other empirical and case studies of competence in children of mentally ill parents suggest that in addition to good relationships with one parent, supportive relationships with other adult resources and good intellectual functioning in the children may be protective (Bleuler, 1984; Garmezy, 1985).

Economic Hardship and Resilience

Economic hardship and the risks of inner-city life have been the subjects of numerous studies. Several studies have considered the role of families as protective factors under such socioeconomic adversity.

The work of Elder, Caspi, and their collaborators, on the effects of economic hardship on families and child development during the Great Depression, has made a unique contribution to the literature on resilience (Elder, 1974, 1979; Elder, Caspi, & van Nguyen, 1986; Elder, van Nguyen, & Caspi, 1985). They have examined the resilience and vulnerability of the Oakland Growth Study cohort, which included adolescents during the Depression (Elder et al., 1986). Their findings suggest that fathers and mothers each played important and different roles in mediating the effects of economic hardship on adolescents. Vulnerable fathers, who were more affected by economic hardship, often exhibited harsh parenting behavior, and were harsher with less attractive than they were with more attractive daughters. Adolescents who before the

Depression showed inclinations to tantrums and related behavioral problems or irritability, appeared to be more vulnerable to harsh parenting. In families under stress, affectionate mothers appeared to play a protective role with regard to child problems and the effects on children of harsh parenting by fathers.

Conger and Elder are now collaborating to examine the processes by which economic hardship affects farm families and adolescents in Iowa. Initial data from their project suggest that the influence of economic hardship on adolescents is mediated by its effects on parent mood, which in turn influences the marital relationship and the quality of parenting (Conger et al., 1992).

Lewis and Looney (1983a, 1983b) examined family qualities in relation to competence in adolescents for two samples in contrasting situations: White middle- and upper middle-class suburban families, and African-American working-class families living in the inner city. Although the samples were small, the similarities across these competent adolescents and their families were striking. Adolescents from either background who were rated as adapting well were achievement oriented, doing well in school, reflective, involved in a variety of activities, and socially connected. In addition, their families functioned well in many ways. For example, the parents had good marital relationships and shared family leadership. The families were close, yet respected the development of age-appropriate independence. Both groups had connections with extended family, friends, and community.

In another study of families with competent children reared in contrasting situations, interesting differences in parenting have emerged. Baldwin, Baldwin, and Cole (1990) compared two groups of families of equally competent children: one group was predominantly White and living in middle-class neighborhoods; the other group consisted predominantly of African-American and Hispanic families living in high-risk, urban neighborhoods. Families were identified on the basis of the positive cognitive outcomes of their children, defined as better-than-average performances on a combination of IQ tests, achievement tests, and grades in school. The parents in these two samples shared a number of qualities, including warmth and high expectations for achievement and responsible behavior in their children. They also differed in interesting ways. Effective parents rearing children in more dangerous environments were more restrictive and less democratic, monitored their children more closely, and placed a higher value on self-control than did parents in lower risk environments.

Two other important studies have followed adolescents at risk to reveal better-than-expected outcomes in adulthood. Long and Vaillant (1984) examined factors implicated in "escape from the underclass" by following a cohort of boys who served as the control group in a classic study by Glueck and Glueck (1950). These boys came from low-income urban families and were selected on the basis of low to average IQs with no delinquency. At age 47, four groups that differed in initial psychosocial risk were compared. Results indicated a general pattern of upward mobility in this White male cohort, even for the most disadvantaged group. Greater childhood IQ and competence predicted better outcomes. Better intellectual functioning was particularly associated with good outcomes in the two most disadvantaged groups, suggesting a protective effect.

Teenage Mothers

Another important study that revealed positive developmental trajectories focused on adolescent mothers. The "Baltimore Study" of long-range outcomes in disadvantaged African-American adolescent mothers was conducted by Furstenberg, Brooks-Gunn, and Morgan (1987). A cohort of nearly 300 mothers at risk for early childbirth was followed up after 5 and again after 17 years, tracing the life courses of these young women from first pregnancy through adulthood, and documenting the outcomes of their children.

Results indicated varied outcomes in this group of young mothers, providing the opportunity to examine the correlates of more successful outcomes. Women whose families were on welfare during their childhoods, and women who came from large families, had less success in attaining economic stability after their early motherhood. Women whose parents had failed to complete the 10th grade were also more likely to be on welfare than those whose parents were better educated. The authors suggested that family size and parent education were markers in this study of resource and motivational differences.

In the young mothers themselves, learning aptitude and educational aspirations, mediated by school success, appeared to play a substantial role in better outcomes. Educational attainment was linked to restricting further childbearing.

Adolescent outcomes of the children of these teenage Baltimore mothers were also examined. Better academic achievement and behavioral outcomes were found for adolescents whose mothers had not been on welfare the previous 5 years, had attained a high school education, and had only one or two children.

Children Reared in Institutions or Foster Care

Additional risk factors that have been examined in longitudinal studies include institutional and foster care. Two studies, in particular, speak to the issue of resilience, although the focal outcome is adulthood rather than adolescence. Quinton and Rutter (see Rutter, 1990) examined parenting by women reared in institutions. Good outcomes were associated with both current and antecedent protective factors. A supportive spouse, for example, was an important factor for better parenting by these mothers. Positive school experiences also frequently appeared to play a role in the successful life trajectories of these women.

Adult adaptation of foster children was examined by Festinger (1983) in a follow-up study of 277 children placed in foster care in New York City. She compared their outcomes to a national cohort of similar age and gender reported by the Institute for Social Research at the University of Michigan. As a group, the outcomes of the foster care group were more positive than expected, given the risk associated with foster care status. Outcomes in these two groups of young adults were similar in many respects, including health, symptom status, self-evaluations, employment rates, and welfare dependency rates. In addition, the foster care group did not have excessive foster placement of its own children. The foster care group did show some disadvantage in scholastic achievements. Festinger also noted the willingness of this group's members to share their experiences, many of which were positive, inspiring the title of her book: *No One Ever Asked Us*.

Chronic Illness

Resilience is now also being studied longitudinally in adolescents with chronic illnesses such as diabetes (Hauser, Vieyra, Jacobson, & Wertlieb, 1985, 1989). The Adolescent Health and Illness Project (Hauser et al., 1989; Schwartz, Jacobson, Hauser, & Dornbush, 1989) has been examining protective processes in the family and developmental issues in adolescents with diabetes. These investigators have drawn particularly on the risk and resilience paradigm from studies of family communication in children at risk because of mental illness in a parent (e.g., Wynne, 1984). Results should provide important insights into the linkages among the course of chronic illness, development, and protective processes in adolescence.

Delinquency and Criminality

For many years, the focus of longitudinal studies of psychopathology, delinquency, and other problematic outcomes was on risk and pathways to deviance. More recently, however, a broader perspective is emerging in the context of a developmental approach to psychopathology (Masten & Braswell, 1991). More attention is being directed at protective factors that appear to counteract the risks of negative outcomes. Identified protective factors sound a familiar note. For example, Kolvin, Miller, Fleeting, and Kolvin (1988) examined the protective factors associated with less delinquency in the Newcastle Thousand-Family Study initiated in 1947. Deprivation was a risk factor for delinquency, but among the deprived sample, quality of parental care, intellectual ability (with concomitant school achievement), and positive temperamental qualities were predictive of reduced delinquency in adolescence.

Evidence is mounting to suggest that IQ may function as a protective factor with regard to risk and prognosis for conduct problems and aggression (Garmezy & Masten, 1991). Based on their 22-year study of aggression across three generations, Huesmann, Eron, and Yarmel (1987) hypothesized that low intelligence increases the risk of aggressive behavior in early childhood, and that subsequently aggressive behavior interferes with future intellectual development. In a study of a Danish birth cohort, Kandel et al. (1988) found that among children of severely criminal fathers, children who had avoided crime careers had significantly higher IQ scores as adults than those in the same risk group who developed criminal behavior. J. White, Moffitt, and Silva (1989) recently confirmed this finding in a prospective study of a New Zealand birth cohort. In their data, higher IQ was associated with less delinquency in adolescence for both high- and low-risk children; a very high IQ appeared to be particularly protective for high-risk boys in avoiding delinquency.

Recovery From Severe Adversity: Child Maltreatment

Recovery from severe adversity in individual cases, and in studies of larger groups of children, have documented the remarkable human capacity for resilience, as well as its limitations (Masten et al., 1990). Of particular importance for this review are factors associated with better outcomes across studies of children exposed to severe adversity who have been provided a chance for recovery when the adversity ceases. In our recent review of this literature (Masten et al., 1990), we were impressed by the consistency with which familial factors emerged as correlates of better recovery. The quality of care (parenting or surrogate parenting) in the recovery environment is clearly important. An intact central nervous system and general intellectual functioning also consistently emerged as important factors.

In the literature on child maltreatment reviewed by Kaufman and Zigler (1989), maltreated children who become good parents have one or more of the following characteristics: a good relationship with a caregiving adult in childhood, high IQ, special talents, physical attractiveness, social skills, a supportive spouse, current financial security, social supports, strong religious affiliations, positive school experiences, and therapy. This list is congruent with many other reviews of resilience in diverse situations.

CORRELATES OF INDIVIDUAL RESILIENCE

Longitudinal studies, together with data from cross-sectional research, converge to suggest a set of factors that appear to play a significant role in the resilience of individual children and adolescents across diverse situations. These include the following:

- effective parenting;
- connections to other competent adults;
- appeal to other people, particularly adults;
- good intellectual skills;
- areas of talent or accomplishment valued by self and others;
- self-efficacy, self-worth, and hopefulness;
- religious faith or affiliations;
- socioeconomic advantages;
- good schools and other community assets; and
- good fortune.

The processes by which these factors work (the "how question") are not well researched. One exception is Bandura's work on self-efficacy. Bandura (1977, 1982, 1986, 1990) hypothesized a process by which success feeds back to one's view of the self as effective, which in turn enhances the motivation to act in future situations, as well as minimizing counterproductive anxiety and arousal that can be produced by challenges. Action increases the likelihood of success, and the self-efficacy cycle continues. Interventions designed to scaffold achievement by building on small steps with high probability for success probably tap into this system. Bandura's model of self-efficacy is closely related to earlier concepts of the human motivational system geared to mastering the environment (R. White, 1959).

Parents and mentors often come up as key protective factors, and it is probably useful to consider what effective parents and mentors may have in common. Parents and mentors both:

- Make a person feel worthwhile and valued through their consistent nurturing behavior and engender trust in people as resources. Children who are turned off to adults as resources and social references may lose opportunities and valuable sources of information.
- Model competent behavior.
- Provide information and access to knowledge.
- Coach competent behavior, providing guidance and constructive feedback.
- Steer children away from wasteful or dangerous pitfalls, both by advice and by proactive buffering.
- Support the undertaking of new challenges that they feel reasonably confident a young person can handle or can stretch to meet.
- Function as advocates, opening doors.
- Provide opportunities for competence- and confidence-building experiences.

Undoubtedly, there are other ways in which parents and mentors facilitate competence, both generally and for children at risk because of adversity.

Institutions associated with resilience in individuals may work by similar processes (Masten et al., 1990). Schools, for example, not only provide knowledge and teach problem-solving skills, they provide a setting where children can become connected with caring, competent adults. Effective schools usually have high expectations, combined with high positive regard and support (Comer, 1980; Freiberg, Prokosch, Treister, & Stein, 1990; Rutter, Maughan, Mortimore, Ouston, & Smith, 1979). They also provide a variety of opportunities for efficacy-enhancing achievements, either academic or extracurricular. A given school's actions will vary according to context, culture, and the needs of its children. Good schools vary, just as good parents do. However, some of the basic strategies of effective schools may be similar.

In addition to schools, other institutions have occurred across many periods and cultures, presumably due to their power to enhance and protect development for their members. These include the family, kinship ties, religious organizations, community organizations, and governments. They constitute the multiple and overlapping systems in which individual development is embedded (Bronfenbrenner, 1986). The roles of several of these larger systems are the focus of other chapters in this volume.

STRATEGIES FOR FOSTERING INDIVIDUAL RESILIENCE

Although research is limited on how resilience occurs, research findings are congruent with several basic strategies for intervention suggested by the ingredients of adaptation described earlier: (a) reduce vulnerability and risk, (b) reduce stressors and pileup, (c) increase available resources, and (d) mobilize protective processes. More comprehensive efforts would involve multiple strategies.

Reducing Vulnerability and Risk

Reducing vulnerability and risk is a primary prevention strategy. For example, programs to reduce childbirth in early adolescence, and to promote healthy pregnancies and child development, can prevent children from entering a high-risk category, such as very low birth weight, perinatal complications, or being reared by a teenage parent. Organic damage due to prematurity or fetal exposure to alcohol or cocaine can be avoided by successful preventive interventions. Subsequent risks and stressors faced by individual children may have much greater effect if a child's adaptive potential has been reduced by malnutrition, toxic substances, illnesses, accidents, or other preventable risk factors.

Children being reared in poverty in the United States often have multiple risks (Johnson, Miranda, Sherman, & Weill, 1991). Homeless children, for example, often have young single parents on welfare with few job skills and little formal education. They often have little or no health care, including prenatal care for their mothers. They have often lived in unsafe and unhealthy environments. They experience many stressors in the context of very few resources. Not surprisingly, homeless children have elevated risks for chronic illness and other health problems, emotional and behavioral problems, and academic delays (Masten, 1992).

Reducing Stressors and Pileup

The second basic strategy is to reduce exposure to adversity or the piling up of multiple stressors. The shift from junior high school to middle school models in the United States is an example of recent efforts to reduce the concentration of stressors in early adolescence. Research has suggested that the junior high school transition can be quite stressful for young adolescents also contending with the challenges of puberty (Simmons & Blyth, 1987). School-based stressors can be altered, either to eliminate the stressor or reduce the impact. Middle schools often attempt to combine the intimacy and support of elementary school with the academic, athletic, or social opportunities and challenges of secondary school.

Mobility magnet schools are another concept aimed at reducing stressful transitions for children who frequently move. For example, the St. Paul School District in Minnesota established a mobility zone that included six elementary schools in a region with a significant population of poor, mobile families. For a variety of reasons, families frequently moved around within this region and across the boundaries defining residence for a particular school. Before the mobility zone was created, children were required to change schools whenever their residence changed. Subsequently, parents were encouraged to keep their children in the same school until the end of the year, and transportation was provided for this purpose. Magnet schools, district-wide school choice, and open enrollment policies can serve the same goal of stabilizing the school environment for children in highly mobile families.

Low-income families in many urban areas of the United States are confronted on a daily basis with dangers and stressful events occurring in their communities. A recent book about children growing up in war zones included an analysis of life in inner-city Chicago (Garbarino, Kostelny, & Dubrow, 1991). In a study of homeless and very low-income Minneapolis children, fear levels were high in both groups, compared to other urban school children (Ramirez, Masten, & Samsa, 1991). It seems reasonable to believe that improving public safety in these areas would reduce the intensity of stressful life events faced by children growing up in poverty.

There are many other examples of interventions aimed at reducing the level of adversity experienced by children. These include, for example, divorce and custody mediation, user-friendly children's hospitals, and videotaped courtroom testimony in abuse cases. Interventions to reduce the amount of bullying in schools is another example. These efforts follow the lead of parents who, although they do not "protect" their children from appropriate and developmentally enhancing challenges, do proactively try to limit unnecessary and negative experiences.

Increasing Available Resources

The third basic strategy is to increase the availability of resources to children at risk. Resources include people, materials in the environment, and personal resources. A child's personal resources are increased upon learning new social or problem-solving skills (Elias et al., in press). Providing breakfast at school is an example of a material resource that, in turn, may facilitate learning. Tutors, time and attention from teachers, or health clinics in schools are other examples of resources aimed directly at children.

There are also indirect strategies for increasing resources for children at risk. Parents and teachers are key resources for children in a variety of ways. When resources provided to parents and teachers improve their functions as resources to children, children indirectly benefit. Programs to provide income, food, education, job training, or child management skills to parents can increase child resources. Similarly, programs that aid teachers can improve the functions of teachers as resources.

Sometimes the problem is not resource availability in general, but the accessibility of resources to children at risk, such as very low-income children. A variety of barriers may prevent these children or their families from taking advantage of existing resources. Barriers include transportation, language, poor communication by providers of services, incomprehensible rules, cultural insensitivity, and scattered services that are located for the convenience of employees rather than clients. Barriers also can be psychological. Schools that provide free meals for low-income children have found that children will not eat these meals if there is any way for other children, or even teachers, to know the meals are free. Clever strategies have been developed to protect the privacy of this information, and to eliminate possibilities for embarrassment.

For a time, homeless children in the United States were impeded from one of the most basic U.S. resource centers, public school. Barriers to education included residence requirements, immunizations, school records, transportation, and insensitive treatment. Following public consciousness-raising and federal legislation, some of these barriers were reduced or eliminated. The McKinney Act, passed in 1987 by Congress, requires states to "assure that each child of a homeless individual and each homeless youth have access to a free, appropriate public education." Barriers remain, but progress has been made (Masten, 1992).

Mobilizing Protective Processes

The fourth main strategy for fostering resilience is to attempt to mobilize protective processes. Relationships with parents and other adults have emerged in research as key protective factors. However, even before formal research on resilience, there were attempts to foster protective relationships. The Big Brother/Big Sister organizations, for example, attempt to foster better outcomes in children at risk by providing a special relationship. Various types of mentoring programs for high-risk children appear to be springing up across the country in efforts to facilitate relationships that promote the development of competence. The success of these efforts needs to be evaluated, both to test the effectiveness of mentoring programs and to examine the process of mentoring.

Other programs have attempted to improve the quality of parent–child relationships within the family. An experimental program that grew out of research in Minnesota aims to improve the quality of the attachment relationship between mother and infant in order to prevent child abuse and foster competence (Egeland & Erickson, 1990). The Steps Toward Effective, Enjoyable Parenting (STEEP) program was aimed at high-risk, young, poor, single mothers. The intervention began with home visits before the babies were born, continuing biweekly afterward. The intervention also included group meetings of mothers and babies for demonstrations, discussions, and activities designed to improve child care and dyadic intervention. This program is being rigorously evaluated in a controlled study.

Efforts have also been made to foster the mastery motivation system that is closely linked to self-efficacy and self-esteem. Bandura (1990) argued as follows: "The most effective way of developing a strong sense of efficacy is through *mastery experiences*. . . . After people have become convinced they have what it takes to succeed, they persevere in the face of adversity and quickly rebound from setbacks" (p. 327).

Developmental issues must be considered in these efforts. The methods that work with 6-year-olds are unlikely to work with teenagers. Young children may be readily persuaded that their own efforts have resulted in success, by setting up situations that ensure success. The same strategies, if tried with a cognitively more sophisticated adolescent, may backfire. An adolescent may conclude that you doubt his or her efficacy because you are "trying too hard" to convince or ensure him or her of success.

Some of the best-known intervention programs to foster resilience involve all or most of these basic strategies. Head Start programs are multifaceted attempts to provide more direct and indirect resources to very low-income children, and to begin at an early age to scaffold success and build self-esteem. Relationships are also emphasized between parents and staff, between staff and child, and sometimes among parents. Health care and other services are often provided or coordinated by Head Start centers. Other examples are education-focused efforts like the "Comer process," which is designed to boost academic achievement among disadvantaged urban children, particularly children of color (Comer, 1980). Such programs work to build school–parent linkages, improve the quality of teaching, and foster high expectations and morale at school.

Notably lacking in the literature on resilience are studies of the effectiveness of programs designed to foster resilience; noteworthy exceptions are the published evaluations of Head Start (Woodhead, 1988), the Comer program (Comer, 1985), the Rochester Primary Prevention Project (Cowen, Wyman, Work, & Parker, 1990), and evaluations now under way of programs such as Project STEEP and the Beethoven Project in Chicago. Careful evaluations of intervention programs are critically important, not only for judging program effectiveness, but for testing hypothesized protective processes.

A RESEARCH AGENDA

Most recent reviews of psychological resilience have called for research on the processes by which resilience occurs or develops. Evidence has mounted that certain variables are generally associated with better outcomes across diverse adversities and risk groups, yet little is known about how they operate to yield positive developmental pathways.

A better understanding of resilience will depend to a large degree on longitudinal research designs and recent advances in multivariate statistics that allow for the examination of linkages among multiple aspects of the individual and environment over time. These methods include structural equation modeling (Connell, 1987) and pattern analysis (e.g., Magnusson & Bergman, 1990). These methodologies enable investigators to test in longitudinal data sets the hypotheses originally drawn from cross-sectional studies and from case histories of resilient individuals.

A developmental perspective is also crucial to advances in this area, in terms of both conceptualization and assessment. Resilience implies a qualitative evaluation of functioning based substantially on normative expectations for adaptation that vary according to age and environmental context. The markers of good psychosocial development, developmental tasks, change as a function of age and vary across culture. A developmental perspective also leads one to consider short- versus long-term outcomes. A strategy of adaptation that has short-term benefits for survival may have long-term costs for an individual. For example, a child who avoids an abusive caregiver may be temporarily well-served. But if the child continues to avoid all intimate relationships, the developmental consequences may be negative.

Research on resilience may be headed in three different directions. One direction emerging from the literature is the search to identify and specify basic human processes of adaptation that cut across culture and situations. Parenting and self-efficacy, for example, are general human adaptational systems widely studied as vulnerability and protective processes. As work in this area matures, it seems likely that these general systems will be examined more carefully in relation to how they interact with individual differences, environmental context, social and cognitive development, and physiological systems. Studies of twins and siblings may be useful in examining nonshared environmental factors that influence resilience (Plomin & Daniels, 1987).

A second direction for research is much more narrowly focused on unique protective processes that work in specific situations. Until now, the study of "coping" has yielded little payoff, except in specific domains (Garmezy & Masten, 1991). This is probably because the human repertoire of coping responses is very diverse and flexible, optimizing survival in many situations. Thus, specific coping strategies are more likely to be identified in specific situations, such as treatments for leukemia or the transition to junior high school. Studies of unique situational protective processes have the potential for developing interventions for children at risk because of a specific stressor.

Investigators of coping strategies or effective parenting in specific stressful situations should keep in mind that one of the most adaptive characteristics of human behavior is the capacity to tailor a response to the situation. Good parents vary their behaviors according to the strengths and shortcomings of a specific child and their appraisal of the situation. If a family moved from a dangerous urban "war zone" to a relatively safe small town, effective parents would undoubtedly shift their parenting strategies to foster the development of their child in the new situation. Similarly, parenting changes as a child develops.

The third direction is to study intervention programs. Ultimately, the most powerful test of hypotheses about resilience will come from efforts to change the course of development through intervention. These efforts will be most informative when processes as well as outcomes are evaluated.

CONCLUSION

Studies of risk, vulnerability, adversity, and psychopathology provide important knowledge about the etiology of disorder and maladaptation. Studies of protective factors, resilience, and good development despite risk, vulnerability, and adversity can be a window on the processes by which development rights itself or is fostered by "natural" or professional intervention.

Studies of resilience suggest that nature has provided powerful protective mechanisms for human development. Children have a remarkable capacity for adaptation. Only organic illness, damage, and major interference in the early nurturing system appear to permanently affect that capacity (Masten et al., 1990). When motivation, self-esteem, and competence are crushed or dampened by relentless oppression, atrocities, or maltreatment, the capacity for recovery may not be evident. When adversity is relieved and basic human needs are restored, then resilience has a chance to emerge. Rekindling hope may be an important spark for resilience processes to begin their restorative work.

The study of resilience is itself a hopeful enterprise. For too long, investigators focused on vulnerability or maladaptation in children at risk because of psychosocial adversities or risks. Good outcomes were treated as surprises. Now the pendulum has swung to resilience, and there is great enthusiasm for understanding good and poor outcomes in high-risk children. But there is danger in that enthusiasm and optimism; a note of caution is needed.

Resilience encompasses diverse and complex phenomena. Understanding resilience is going to require sustained efforts by many investigators with different perspectives and expertise. Moreover, what works for one child in one situation may not work for a different child in the same situation, the same child in another situation, or the same child at another point in development. Therefore, research designs and intervention efforts will have to allow for the contextual and individualized nature of adaptation as well as human development. Resilience is also dynamic; measures and intervention strategies will have to allow for this quality. Fostering resilience is an attempt to deflect a developmental pathway in a more positive direction.

Finally, in our enthusiasm for competence and achievement in people who overcome great risk or adversity, we must be careful not to overlook internal pain or the possibility that extraordinary effort is being expended to sustain competence. It is also possible for short-term resilience to produce long-term vulnerability or maladaptation. However, with these cautions in mind, the study of resilience holds great promise for understanding human adaptation and promoting psychological development.

ACKNOWLEDGMENTS

Preparation of this chapter was supported in part by grants to the author from the William T. Grant Foundation, the National Institute of Child Health and Human Development through a grant to the Minnesota Center for Research on Developmental Disabilities (P30 HD24051), the National Institute of Mental Health (MH33222), and the Graduate School of the University of Minnesota.

REFERENCES

Anthony, E. J. (1987). Children at high risk for psychosis growing up successfully. In E. O. Anthony & B. J. Cohler (Eds.), *The invulnerable child* (pp. 147–184). New York: Guilford Press.

Baldwin, A. L., Baldwin, C., & Cole, R. E. (1990). Stress-resistant families and stress-resistant children. In J. Rolf, A. S. Masten, D. Cicchetti, K. H. Nuechterlein, & S. Weintraub (Eds.), *Risk and protective factors in the development of psychopathology* (pp. 257–280). New York: Cambridge University Press.

Bandura, A. (1977). Self-efficacy: Toward a unifying theory of behavioral change. *Psychological Review, 84*(2), 191–215.

Bandura, A. (1982). Self-efficacy mechanism in human agency. *American Psychologist, 37*, 122–147.

Bandura, A. (1986). *Social foundations of thought and action.* Englewood Cliffs, NJ: Prentice-Hall.

Bandura, A. (1990). Conclusion: Reflections on nonability determinants of competence. In R. H. Sternberg & J. Kolligan, Jr. (Eds.), *Competence considered* (pp. 315–362). New Haven, CT: Yale University Press.

Bleuler, M. (1984). Different forms of childhood stress and patterns of adult psychiatric outcome. In N. F. Watt, E. J. Anthony, & J. E. Rolf (Eds.), *Children at risk for schizophrenia* (pp. 537–542). Cambridge: Cambridge University Press.

Block, J., & Block, J. H. (1980). The role of ego-control and ego-resiliency in the organization of behavior. In W. A. Collins (Ed.), *Minnesota symposia on child psychology* (Vol. 13, pp. 39–101). Hillsdale, NJ: Lawrence Erlbaum Associates.

Bronfenbrenner, U. (1986). Ecology of the family as a context for human development: Research perspectives. *Developmental Psychology, 22*, 723–742.

Comer, J. P. (1980). *School power.* New York: The Free Press.

Comer, J. P. (1985). The Yale-New Haven Primary Prevention Project: A follow-up study. *Journal of the American Academy of Child Psychiatry, 24*, 154–160.

Conger, R. D., Conger, K. J., Elder, G. H., Lorenz, F. O., Simons, R. L., & Whitbeck, L. B. (1992). A family process model of economic hardship and adjustment of early adolescent boys. *Child Development, 63*, 526–541.

Connell, J. P. (1987). Structural equation modeling and the study of child development: A question of goodness of fit. *Child Development, 58*, 167–175.

Cowen, E. L., Wyman, P. A., Work, W. C., & Parker, G. R. (1990). The Rochester Child Resilience Project: Overview and summary of first year findings. *Development and Psychopathology, 2*, 193–212.

Egeland, B., & Erickson, M. F. (1990). Rising above the past: Strategies for helping new mothers break the cycle of abuse and neglect. *Zero to Three*, 29–35.

Elder, G. H. (1974). *Children of the Great Depression: Social change in life experience.* Chicago: University of Chicago Press.

Elder, G. H. (1979). Historical change in life patterns and personality. In P. B. Baltes & O. G. Brim, Jr. (Eds.), *Life span development and behavior* (Vol. 2, pp. 117–159). New York: Academic Press.

Elder, G. H., Caspi, A., & van Nguyen, T. (1986). Resourceful and vulnerable children: Family influence in hard times. In R. K. Silbereisen & K. Eyferth (Eds.), *Development as action in context* (pp. 167–186). Berlin: Springer-Verlag.

Elder, G. H., van Nguyen, T., & Caspi, A. (1985). Linking family hardship to children's lives. *Child Development, 56*, 361–375.

Elias, M. J., Weissberg, R. P., Hawkins, J. D., Perry, C. A., Zins, J. E., Dodge, K. C., Kendall, P. D., Gottfredson, D., Rotheram-Borus, M. J., Jason, L. A., & Wilson-Brewer, R. (in press). The school-based promotion of social competence: Theory, research, practice, and policy. In R. J. Haggerty & L. R. Sherrod (Eds.), *Stress, coping, and development: Risk and resilience in children.* New York: Cambridge University Press.

Erikson, E. H. (1963). *Childhood and society*. New York: Norton.

Erikson, E. H. (1968). *Identity, youth and crisis*. New York: Norton.

Festinger, T. (1983). *No one ever asked us*. New York: Columbia University Press.

Fisher, L., Kokes, R. F., Cole, R. E., Perkins, P. M., & Wynne, L. C. (1987). Competent children at risk: A study of well-functioning offspring of disturbed parents. In E. J. Anthony & B. J. Cohler (Eds.), *The invulnerable child* (pp. 211–228). New York: Guilford Press.

Freiberg, H. J., Prokosch, N., Treister, E. S., & Stein, T. (1990). A study of five at-risk inner city elementary schools. *Journal of School Effectiveness and School Improvement, 1*(1), 5–25.

Furstenberg, F. F., Brooks-Gunn, J., & Morgan, S. P. (1987). *Adolescent mothers in later life*. New York: Cambridge University Press.

Garbarino, J., Kostelny, K., & Dubrow, N. (Eds.). (1991). *No place to be a child: Growing up in a war zone*. Lexington, MA: Lexington Books.

Garmezy, N. (1985). Stress-resistant children: The search for protective factors. In J. E. Stevenson (Ed.), *Recent research in developmental psychopathology: Journal of Child Psychology and Psychiatry book* (Suppl. 4, pp. 213–233). Oxford: Pergamon Press.

Garmezy, N., & Devine, V. (1984). Project Competence: The Minnesota studies of children vulnerable to psychopathology. In N. F. Watt, E. J. Anthony, L. C. Wynne, & J. E. Rolf (Eds.), *Children at risk for schizophrenia: A longitudinal perspective* (pp. 289–311). Cambridge: Cambridge University Press.

Garmezy, N., & Masten, A. S. (1991). The protective role of competence indicators in children at risk. In E. M. Cummings, A. L. Greene, & K. H. Karraker (Eds.), *Life-span developmental psychology: Perspectives on stress and coping* (pp. 151–174). Hillsdale, NJ: Lawrence Erlbaum Associates.

Garmezy, N., & Tellegen, A. (1984). Studies of stress-resistant children: Methods, variables, and preliminary findings. In F. Morrison, C. Lord, & D. Keating (Eds.), *Advances in applied developmental psychology* (Vol. 1, pp. 231–287). New York: Academic Press.

Glueck, S., & Glueck, E. (1950). *Unraveling juvenile delinquency*. New York: The Commonwealth Fund.

Goldstein, M. J., & Tuma, A. H. (Eds.). (1987). Special section on high-risk research. *Schizophrenia Bulletin, 13*(3).

Gottesman, I. I. (1974). Developmental genetics and ontogenetic psychology: Overdue detente and propositions from a matchmaker. In A. D. Pick (Ed.), *Minnesota symposium on child development* (Vol. 8, pp. 55–80). Hillsdale, NJ: Lawrence Erlbaum Associates.

Gottesman, I. I., & Shields, J. (1982). *Schizophrenia: The epigenetic puzzle*. New York: Cambridge University Press.

Greenspan, S. I. (1981). *Psychopathology and adaptation in infant and early childhood: Principles of clinical diagnosis and preventive intervention*. New York: Cambridge University Press.

Hauser, S. T., Vieyra, M. A. B., Jacobson, A. M., & Wertlieb, D. (1985). Vulnerability and resilience in adolescence: Views from the family. *Journal of Early Adolescence, 5*, 81–100.

Hauser, S. T., Vieyra, M. A. B., Jacobson, A. M., & Wertlieb, D. (1989). Family aspects of vulnerability and resilience in adolescence: A theoretical perspective. In T. F. Dugan & R. Coles (Eds.), *The child in our times: Studies in the development of resiliency* (pp. 109–133). New York: Brunner/Mazel.

Havighurst, R. J. (1972). *Developmental tasks and education* (3rd ed.). New York: Longman.

Horowitz, F. D. (1989, April). .*The concept of risk: A re-evaluation*. Invited address before the Society for Research on Child Development, Kansas City, MO.

Huesmann, L. R., Eron, L. D., & Yarmel, P. W. (1987). Intellectual functioning and aggression. *Journal of Personality and Social Psychology, 52*, 232–240.

Johnson, C. M., Miranda, L., Sherman, A., & Weill, J. D. (1991). *Child poverty in America*. Washington, DC: Children's Defense Fund.

Kandel, E., Mednick, S. A., Kirkegaard-Sorensen, L., Hutchings, B., Knop, J., Rosenberg, R., & Schulsinger, F. (1988). IQ as a protective factor for subjects at high risk for antisocial behavior. *Journal of Consulting and Clinical Psychology, 56*, 224–226.

Kaufman, J., & Zigler, E. (1989). The intergenerational transmission of child abuse. In D. Cicchetti & V. Carlson (Eds.), *Child maltreatment: Theory and research on the causes and consequences of child abuse and neglect* (pp. 129–150). Cambridge: Cambridge University Press.

Kolvin, I., Miller, F. J. W., Fleeting, M., & Kolvin, P. A. (1988). Social and parenting factors affecting criminal-offense rates: Findings from the Newcastle Thousand Family Study. *British Journal of Psychiatry, 152*, 80–90.

Kopp, C. B. (1983). Risk factors in development. In M. M. Haith & J. J. Campos (Eds.), *Mussen's handbook of child psychology: Vol. 2. Infancy and developmental psychobiology* (pp. 1081–1188). New York: Wiley.

Lewis, J. M., & Looney, J. G. (1983a). Competent adolescents from different socioeconomic and ethnic contexts. *Adolescent Psychiatry: Developmental and Clinical Studies, 11*, 64–74.

Lewis, J. M., & Looney, J. G. (1983b). *The long struggle: Well-functioning working class black families.* New York: Brunner/Mazel.

Long, J. V. F., & Vaillant, G. E. (1984). Natural history of male psychological health. XI: Escape from the underclass. *American Journal of Psychiatry, 141*, 341–346.

Luthar, S. S., & Zigler, E. (1991). Vulnerability and competence: A review of research on resilience in childhood. *American Journal of Orthopsychiatry, 61*, 6–22.

Magnusson, D., & Bergman, L. R. (1990). A pattern approach to the study of pathways from childhood to adulthood. In L. N. Robins & M. Rutter (Eds.), *Straight and devious pathways from childhood to adulthood* (pp. 101–115). Cambridge: Cambridge University Press.

Masten, A. S. (1989). Resilience in development: Implications of the study of successful adaptation for developmental psychopathology. In D. Cicchetti (Ed.), *The emergence of a discipline: Rochester symposium on developmental psychopathology* (Vol. 1, pp. 261–294). Hillsdale, NJ: Lawrence Erlbaum Associates.

Masten, A. S. (1992). Homeless children in the United States: Mark of a nation at risk. *Current Directions in Psychological Science, 1*, 41–44.

Masten, A. S., Best, K. M., & Garmezy, N. (1990). Resilience and development: Contributions from the study of children who overcome adversity. *Development and Psychopathology, 2*, 425–444.

Masten, A. S., & Braswell, L. (1991). Developmental psychopathology: An integrative framework. In P. R. Martin (Ed.), *Handbook of behavior therapy and psychological science: An integrative approach* (pp. 35–56). New York: Pergamon Press.

Masten, A. S., & Garmezy, N. (1985). Risk, vulnerability, and protective factors in developmental psychopathology. In B. B. Lahey & A. E. Kazdin (Eds.), *Advances in clinical child psychology* (Vol. 8, pp. 1–51). New York: Plenum.

Musick, J. S., Stott, F. M., Spencer, K. K., Goldman, J., & Cohler, B. J. (1987). Maternal factors related to vulnerability and resiliency in young children at risk. In E. J. Anthony & B. J. Cohler (Eds.), *The invulnerable child* (pp. 229–252). New York: Guilford Press.

Plomin, R., & Daniels, D. (1987). Why are children in the same family so different from one another? *Behavior and Brain Sciences, 10*, 1–60.

Radke-Yarrow, M., & Sherman, T. (1990). Hard growing: Children who survive. In J. Rolf, A. S. Masten, D. Cicchetti, K. H. Nuechterlein, & S. Weintraub (Eds.), *Risk and protective factors in the development of psychopathology* (pp. 97–119). New York: Cambridge University Press.

Ramirez, M., Masten, A., & Samsa, D. (1991, April). *Fears in homeless children.* Paper presented at the biennial meeting of the Society for Research on Child Development, Seattle, WA.

Rutter, M. (1990). Psychosocial resilience and protective mechanisms. In J. Rolf, A. S. Masten, D. Cicchetti, K. H. Nuechterlein, & S. Weintraub (Eds.), *Risk and protective factors in the development of psychopathology* (pp. 181–214). New York: Cambridge University Press.

Rutter, M., Maughan, B., Mortimore, P., Ouston, J., & Smith, A. (1979). *Fifteen thousand hours: Secondary schools and their effects on children.* Cambridge, MA: Harvard University Press.

Sameroff, A. J., Barocas, R., & Seifer, R. (1984). The early development of children born to mentally ill women. In N. F. Anthony, L. C. Wynne, & J. E. Rolf (Eds.), *Children at risk for schizophrenia: A longitudinal perspective* (pp. 482–514). New York: Cambridge University Press.

Sander, L. W. (1975). Infant and caretaking environment: Investigation and conceptualization of adaptive behavior in a system of increasing complexity. In E. J. Anthony (Ed.), *Explorations in child psychiatry* (pp. 129–166). New York: Plenum Press.

Schwartz, J. M., Jacobson, A. M., Hauser, S. T., & Dornbush, B. B. (1989). Explorations of vulnerability and resilience: Case studies of diabetic adolescents and their families. In T. F. Dugan & R. Coles (Eds.), *The child in our times: Studies in the development of resiliency* (pp. 134–156). New York: Brunner/Mazel.

Simmons, R. G., & Blyth, D. A. (1987). *Moving into adolescence: The impact of pubertal change and school context.* Hawthorne, NY: Aldine.

Sroufe, L. A. (1979). The coherence of individual development: Early care, attachment, and subsequent developmental issues. *American Psychologist, 34*, 834–841.

Watson, D. (1988). Intraindividual and interindividual analyses of positive and negative affect: Their relation to health complaints, perceived stress, and daily activities. *Journal of Personality and Social Psychology, 54*, 1020–1030.

Watson, D. (1990). On the dispositional nature of stress measures: Stable and nonspecific influences on self-reported hassles. *Psychological Inquiry, 1*, 34–37.

Watson, D., & Pennebaker, J. W. (1989). Health complaints, stress, and distress: Exploring the central role of negative affectivity. *Psychological Review, 96*, 234–254.

Watt, N. F. (1984). In a nutshell: The first two decades of high-risk research in schizophrenia. In N. F. Watt, E. J. Anthony, L. C. Wynne, & J. E. Rolf (Eds.), *Children at risk for schizophrenia: A longitudinal perspective* (pp. 572–595). New York: Cambridge University Press.

Watt, N. F., Anthony, E. J., Wynne, L. C., & Rolf, J. E. (Eds.). (1984). *Children at risk for schizophrenia: A longitudinal perspective.* Cambridge: Cambridge University Press.

Werner, E. E. (1989). Children of the garden island. *Scientific American, 260*(4), 106–111.

Werner, E. E. (1990). Protective factors and individual resilience. In S. J. Meisels & M. Shonkoff (Eds.), *Handbook of early intervention.* New York: Cambridge University Press.

Werner, E. E., & Smith, R. S. (1982). *Vulnerable but invincible: A study of resilient children.* New York: McGraw-Hill.

Werner, E. E., & Smith, R. S. (1992). *Overcoming the odds: High risk children from birth to adulthood.* Ithaca, NY: Cornell University Press.

White, J. L., Moffitt, T. E., & Silva, P. A. (1989). A prospective replication of the protective effects of IQ in subjects at high risk for juvenile delinquency. *Journal of Consulting and Clinical Psychology, 57*, 719–724.

White, R. W. (1959). Motivation reconsidered: The concept of competence. *Psychological Review, 66*, 297–333.

Woodhead, M. (1988). When psychology informs public policy: The case of early childhood intervention. *American Psychologist, 43*, 443–454.

Worland, J., Weeks, D. G., & Janes, C. L. (1987). Predicting mental health in children at risk. In E. J. Anthony & B. J. Cohler (Eds.), *The invulnerable child* (pp. 185–210). New York: Guilford Press.

Wynne, L. C. (1984). Communication patterns and family relations of children at risk for schizophrenia. In N. F. Watt, E. J. Anthony, L. C. Wynne, & J. E. Rolf (Eds.), *Children at risk for schizophrenia: A longitudinal perspective* (pp. 551–556). New York: Cambridge University Press.

Chapter 2

Variations in the Experience
of Resilience

Edmund W. Gordon
Lauren Dohee Song
Yale University

It might be argued that the scientific study of religious experiences began with William James' descriptive taxonomy, published in 1902 under the title *Varieties of Religious Experiences*. James' study of the various manifestations of religious beliefs and practices provided the basis for a more systematic investigation of the phenomena of religious experiences. Due to the diversity of their expressions, and the lack of a classification system, these experiences had previously resisted scientific study. In this chapter, we attempt to apply to the construct of *resilience* a similar descriptive analysis, one that will hopefully lead to a reconceptualization of the construct and a suggested taxonomy.

In the case of resilience, considerable scientific work has already begun or been completed. However, some of the ambiguities in this work may be attributed to the lack of consensus relative to the domain covered by the construct of resilience, its boundaries, or the categories of adaptive behavior or circumstances included. Similarly, there seems to be little agreement on the specific nature or domain of the various manifestations or conceptions of behaviors to which resilience refers. Consequently, there are numerous forms of behavioral adaptation, human circumstances, and human achievements that are colloquially included in what is referred to in persons as either resilience, stress resistance, invincibility, invulnerability, or recoverability. Persons who somehow functionally adapt to experiential hazards are sometimes referred to as risk defiers, abuse survivors, or ''superkids.''

Although initially used to refer to human characteristics or categories of persons, in recent years resilience has been applied to communities and institutions. In all cases, however, the assumption underlying the construct maintains that disadvantaged conditions and experiential hazards predispose persons to social and psychological pathology, and that avoidance of damage, or recovery, from handicapping circumstances is an atypical human achievement. It is no doubt for this reason that so much attention has been paid to the study of persons who show pathological characteristics, or who are expected to fail.

Many have asserted that the manner in which a research question is conceptualized, and the methodology by which the question is investigated, will influence the resulting findings and constrain the ways in which these findings are interpreted (Gordon, Rollock, & Miller, 1990; Stanfield, 1985; Sullivan, 1984). Nowhere is this assertion more obviously demonstrated than in the study of resilience and related behavioral adaptations. Generally defined as the capacity to overcome, or the experience of having overcome, deleterious life events, the construct implicitly assumes that bad experiences tend to produce disturbed or maladaptive behaviors. This general conception has led to the study of resilience largely in populations marked by social or psychological pathology. The dominant methodologies used have emphasized correlation analysis applied to incidence data, or descriptive case analysis applied to individual instances. This work has been unusually insightful into the phenomenon under study, but it may have limited our understanding and precluded the examination of a wide variety of related and equally important behavioral adaptations.

The recognition that negative life experiences and stressors may play a precipitating role in the development of mental disorders coincided with the genesis of psychiatric practice. However, a systematic study of stressors and their various effects has been undertaken only in the last few decades (Garmezy & Rutter, 1985). One outcome of this development was the recognition that (a) there is a preventive value in re-orienting the study of the concept of risk toward the resilience construct, and (b) there is a need for a more adequate conceptualization of the phenomena of human resilience. Because the current status of resilience can be better understood in the context of related orientations toward stress, and their implications for human development, it may be useful to review some of these before proceeding further.

An early phase in the systematic study of life's stresses may be characterized as having placed "the main emphasis. . . on the demonstration that 'bad' experiences did indeed serve to produce or precipitate psychiatric disturbances" (Rutter, 1985, p. 598). There were two general approaches toward this task: (a) the orientation of developmental psychopathology, and (b) epidemiological studies of "at-risk" populations. As Masten and Garmezy (1985) pointed out, "developmental psychopathology emphasizes a life span developmental approach in tracing the origins, signs, and time course of the disorder" (p. 505). This approach often takes the form of individual case studies. At the same time, developmental psychopathologists and clinical practitioners are interested in identifying both the vulnerability and protective factors that can modify the individual adaptational outcomes of those presumed highly vulnerable to developing some behavioral or psychological pathology.

On the other hand, epidemiological studies of populations at risk tend to focus on the increased likelihood that a certain group or groups of people will at some point manifest a particular disorder. It is important to note that the subject of epidemiological studies is a population or populations rather than an individual, and that unlike vulnerability (as it is generally studied), ''risk'' is mainly a construct that refers to populations. On the other hand, the vulnerability/resilience phenomena tend to refer to individuals. In the past, the epidemiological research on dysfunction and stress tended to be narrowly oriented toward identifying possible risk factors. Like the developmental psychopathologists of that time, the epidemiologists were mostly concerned with identifying those elements, presumed operative in persons or environments, that may dispose them toward psychosocial pathology.

Epidemiological studies have generated an extensive list of potential biological and behavioral risk factors, such as gender, demographic status, social and intellectual resources, genetic history, developmental defects, mobility patterns, and negative or traumatic life events. However, colloquial wisdom suggests that differences in individual outcomes make obvious the need for a better understanding of qualitative and subjective factors associated with these presumably negative factors. This need has led to a greater concern for the context in which these factors are experienced, and to a recognition of the importance of the meaning of the experience to the subject under study. Thus, the second phase of this work, although adhering to the earlier assumptions, has been attentive to existential and phenomenological aspects of life conditions and events.

The third phase of this work is even more troubling to the initial assumptions and conceptions surrounding the construct. The dilemma stems from the almost universal observation that even with the most severe stressors and the most glaring adversities, it is unusual for more than one half of observed individuals to succumb to psychological or social dysfunction (Paykel, 1978; Rutter, 1979). The clinical, conceptual, and empirical works, reflected in these three phases of the systematic study of resilience and related constructs, have led to contemporary studies of the phenomenon.

Although there appears to be a clear history of the study of resilience in the psychiatric and mental health literature, there is little information on it in the developmental psychology and sociology archives. It is unclear why this is so, because conceptually the study of resilience should represent developmental inquiry. Its course has been examined at distinct life stages from infancy to adolescence (Murphy & Moriarty, 1976) as well as more holistically (Werner, 1989; Werner & Smith, 1982). Case and life history analyses have been utilized, but largely to identify correlates of adaptation or maladaptation.

The epigenetic tradition often associated with developmental research is not characteristic of this work. Despite this limitation, the search has resulted in resilience being viewed as a dynamic phenomenon that is affected both by various life circumstances and by the person's characteristics. These life circumstances or mediating factors (see Vygotsky, 1978) of behavioral outcome take a variety of forms, and may have differing results, depending on the context, circumstance, and meaning for the developing person. Thus, a phenomenological perspective has come to characterize more recent investigations of resilience (Chess & Thomas, 1977).

This more contextualist and phenomenological approach to work on resilience has, nonetheless, failed to free the work from the limitations imposed by the initial conceptual orientations. Research continues to be dominated by the search for causal agents, significant events, or combinations of factors that either make for stress or risk-related dysfunction, or enable adaptive resilience or resistance to pathology. Horowitz (1989) cited high-risk infancy, conduct disorders, behavioral teratogenesis (adverse invasive factors), critical periods, and developmental psychopathologies as culpable. Luthar (1991) identified six analytic foci with similar orientations in the research methodologies applied to resilience, including: (a) life events, (b) small events or hassles, (c) specific life stresses, (d) low socioeconomic status (SES), (e) indicators of stress and risk, and (f) outcome measures of maladjustment versus competence. All of these foci reflect the notion that events and experiences that are assigned negative valence constitute experiential hazards, and the notion that these hazards place developing persons at risk. What seems to be missing from this viewpoint is concern with processual analyses of the multiple and interacting forces by which behavior of almost any kind is more likely to be explained. As Sameroff, Seifer, Barocas, Zax, and Greenspan (1987) suggested, there is no definite criterion by which a particular variable is defined as a risk factor, a protective factor, or even as a measure related to the outcome in question. So we have included variables at different levels of organization (individual, familial, and societal) as potential risk or protective factors, and thus incorporated different causal systems that likely affect different developmental processes.

It may well be that the central problem is defining the construct. Instead of a single construct, we may be dealing with a complex of related processes that deserve to be identified and studied as discrete constructs. Consider for example the following notions:

1. Threats to the integrity of behavioral development and adaptation may exist along a continuum, with the degree of threat better defined by existential meaning than by "reality" factors, meaning the criterion by which a force is defined is very much a function of the perspective and attributions of the person or persons living the experience (Gordon et al., 1990).

2. Apparently similar life circumstances and events can be perceived as threats, challenges, opportunities, annoyances, or as any of a wide variety of positive, neutral, or negative forces. The subject's reaction may depend on the actual perception or the connotation permitted by the context in which the phenomenon is experienced (Gordon, 1985).

3. Given differential arousal states and thresholds of responsiveness, apparently similar conditions may result in differential patterns and levels of awareness and reaction in different persons, and at different points in the life of one person (Chess & Thomas, 1980).

4. It may be that abuse, disadvantagement, or even trauma may be of lesser consequence for the behavior of the person experiencing it than is the sense of power or powerlessness that the subject associates with the experience. Even the effect of powerlessness, which we tend to think of as negative, may depend on the aspects of one's life to which it relates and the importance attached to those aspects (Gurin & Epps, 1975).

Such a list may be endless. The point is that the conditions we label as *resiliency, resistance, invincibility*, and so forth, are relative, situational, and attributional. Thus, the assumed meaning of the construct may have greater significance for the researchers who define or investigate it, than for the person or persons who experience it. If you think that I am a "loser," and I think I am a "winner," whose classification is to apply? If you define my status as poverty stricken, and my own experience is that of sufficiency, is my resource availability a high-risk factor? If it is my behavior that we are trying to explain, whose perceived reality is valid as an independent variable?

It is within the context of struggling with issues like these that my colleagues and I have sought to identify correlates of success and failure in the lives of selected persons whom we have judged to be disadvantaged, and to conceptualize and describe developmental processes in which multiple factors interact dialectically to result in functional and dysfunctional adaptations. We have avoided use of the several constructs commonly used in related literature, instead focusing on what we refer to as defiance of negative predictions of success. We feel that this formulation better captures the processual phenomenon we are trying to study.

This work utilizes correlation and life history analyses to identify candidate hypotheses by which the phenomena of success and failure can be explained. Subsequent stages will likely lead into longitudinal, hypothesis-testing studies. Unfortunately, the population does not lend itself to controlled experimentation, although it may be possible to use natural experiments. To date, our work has enabled us to generate a reconceptualization of the developmental processes involved, and several postulates to explain defiance of predictions of failure.

Justine Wise Polier, a children's court judge, once observed that she had never encountered in her court a youth in serious trouble who had experienced a sustained and supportive relationship with a significant adult. It is unlikely that this observation was informed by careful empirical investigation, but it captures the intuitive idea that supportive environments and significant others are important components of successful achievement, particularly in persons at risk of failure. A few social scientists have conducted empirical studies of factors associated with achievement "against the odds." Much of this work has given primary emphasis to the characteristics of environments and circumstance. However, these studies and the investigation reported herein tend to confirm the intuitive judgment of Judge Polier, and further suggest a number of postulates or implicit hypotheses by which we can better explain the phenomenon of "making it against the odds."

POSTULATING DEFIANCE
OF NEGATIVE PREDICTION

The achievement of success or popular designation as a successful person is likely to result from the confluence and interaction of a number of factors referable to the person who succeeds, the environmental context of his or her development, and the situational context in which the achievement occurs. In this study, several of the factors have been identified. They include: (a) the presence of significant others; (b) support for development and learning; (c) a sense of community; (d) models and heroes; (e) opportunity; (f) challenge; (g) various manifestations of developed ability; (h) networking; (i) personality, as reflected in specific response tendencies; and (j) specific environmental influences.

As important as these individual factors are, their impact is viewed as collective, because little evidence exists to support the notion that a significant percentage of the variance in achievement can be accounted for by any one of these variables. It appears that these factors and others interact dialectically and reciprocally to accommodate and influence each other. Furthermore, they appear to be expressed in clusters, in which several factors are associated collectively to produce the dependent variable (educational and/or occupational achievement). Thus, in this study, not all the factors are found in every developmental transaction; or, if present, they are not expressed in the same form across all cases. The collectivity of the factors present in the life of a single subject may best be viewed as causally related to his or her achievement. To understand the relationship from which causation is often inferred requires that one not focus on the presence or absence of specific unitary factors, but examine the nature of the interactions within the collectivity of factors. Success may be conceptualized as the product of the interactions between the person's various characteristics, the characteristics of the environment, and the characteristics of the situation in which both development and achievement can occur.

Personal characteristics include status and individual functional attributes by which the nature of the person and his or her adaptive behavior are described. From our perspective, important measures of status include the following: gender, SES, ethnicity, language, and intelligence quotient. Functional characteristics include measures of: self-concept, drive, cognitive style, temperament, motivation identity, knowledge of dominant culture values, health and nutrition, social competence, life-course organization, and autonomy.

Environmental characteristics refer to material and social phenomena, outside the person, which form part of the context for behavior. Physical objects, other people, ambient conditions, and social structures are examples of components in this category. It is thought to be the "press" of these environmental characteristics that influences behavior. Environmental press, then, is the influence of a phenomenon. As early as 1938, Murray identified environmental press as the power to positively or negatively affect the well-being of the subject. *Alpha press* exists objectively for a person, and is generally represented by the consensus perception of objective reality held by participants. *Beta press* involves the individual's subjective perception of the phenomenon and its idiosyncratic meaning. Beta press need not be congruent with the Alpha press, and may not reflect the objective reality, but for purposes of the individual it may have to be regarded as real. Thus, there is a range of differential perceptions about the "true" state of reality.

Situational constraints are somewhat more elusive, but by no means unimportant. They are metaphenomena, in the sense that they include the characteristics of persons and their environments but are more than the summation of the two. Situations are the products of personal, environmental, and social interactions, and are highly susceptible to attribution. Situations may also have their alpha and beta presses. Situational constraints are defined by the limits and opportunities provided by the objective and existential context in which the behavior originates and is expressed. The impact of situational constraints is implicit in patterns of access, challenge, control, demand, expectation, opportunity, reinforcement, and threat.

Because success is a product of interactions that are dynamic and dialectical, it appears fallacious to assert that "success" is a function of a specific factor or pattern of interactions. A specific achievement of success is probably best thought of as reflecting the deliberate or fortuitous orchestration of a pattern of interactions idiosyncratic to success in that individual. In the search for correlates of success, commonalities were noted in the clustering of the factors, as well as in the patterning of the interactions across subjects. These observations provide the bases for the following inventory of propositions that has been generated by this work.

INVENTORY OF PROPOSITIONS

Epigenetic Phenomenon

Although success at any given time may result from the cumulative effect of
a number of factors, any given achievement may be associated with the confluence of factors at a particular point, and under a given set of circumstances.
Implicit in this proposition is the notion that there is no fixed and essential
pattern of achievement in persons at high risk of failure. These are only examples of cumulative experiences that may lead to success among persons for whom
the factors that initiated movement toward a particular kind of achievement
emerged (possibly by chance) at a crucial (in terms of their development) moment. This proposition is consistent with Freedman's (1969) conclusion that
much of the variance in "the process of work establishment" can be attributed to chance and the widely held conclusion that behavioral effects are cumulative, even though their products appear episodically.

Parallel and Hierarchical Networking

Parallel or peer networking is more likely to be found in the career development of women defiers of negative predictions, and hierarchical networking
is more likely to be found in the career development of male defiers. Because
relatively few females are in high-status positions, and because of the greater
emphasis on individual effort and achievement by males, there tends to be much
more mutual assistance and collective boosting of the "sister." In the cases
of several male subjects, hierarchical networking is seen with a higher status
person who opens the door and otherwise mediates the movement of the
"brother." Also, when parallel networking occurred among males, it served
as a social function that operated to deter rather than facilitate achievement.
In several of our male respondents, the effort was to overcome the negative
drag of the parallel network, whereas in several of the female respondents, the
parallel network provided support (moral or material) for upward movement.

Noncritical Periods

The timing of the appearance of success or its precursors is not age-bound.
Influential factors may occur at any point in the life span, but tend not to be
significant after the fourth decade. In the studied population, a mix of temporal patterns was found that revealed career development for the 26 African-
American respondents. Some respondents evolved at an early age (pre-teen),
a career path that greatly increased the chance of success. Others, it was found,
"stumbled" onto or were placed on the track at later points in their lives. For

instance, one respondent was obviously on an antisocial and potentially destructive path until his late 30s, when events and circumstances moved him
in a more socially productive and acceptable direction. Another was on a
collision course with authority figures. It was interesting to note, however,
that many of the same behaviors were transposed from one goal direction
to another. Implied in this experience is the possibility that the nature of an
effort may not be as important as is the social acceptability of the goal toward which it is directed. In addition, it appears that optimal periods for development in specific domains may be a more useful notion than "critical
periods."

Goal Choice

Human effort and the factors surrounding it are not sufficient for achievement, but their presence is necessary. What may determine the effectiveness
of effort in influencing achievement, are the goals toward which these efforts
and factors are directed. It may well be that what is regarded as failure, or
a lack of success, may reflect a mismatch between personal goals and social
norms. Discussing unsuccessful peers and siblings with respondents revealed
that many persons have been working just as hard as were the respondents,
or spending a comparable amount of time and energy, toward goal attainment
that is endogenously functional but dysfunctional in terms of the dominant culture. We found little achievement without effort, but the magnitude of energy
deployment, and the fact of effort expended, did not adequately explain
achievement.

Support for Development

Age- and situation-specific supports for learning and development (generated
by oneself or others) are essential to the development of negative prediction
defiers. At all levels of development, resources and supports for learning and
development are required; the availability of such resources appears to be essential. For subjects in the present study, the homes of respondents either had
the necessary resources, or they were acquired from other sources. In the case
of one subject, his mother would borrow books and beg school supplies from
the local doctor. Later she negotiated summer employment in order to pay
for college tuition. She exchanged laundry services for the local doctor's service as mentor to her son. At every level of development, appropriate supports
and resources were made available to him. This postulate finds support in the
work of Wolf (1966) and Mercer (1973), who argued that where appropriate
supports for learning are available, the achievement patterns of low-status pupils
are not significantly different from those of higher status pupils.

Autonomy

The autonomous/maverick type is more likely to be a defier of negative prediction than the more conservative and conforming personality. Several respondents seemed particularly capable of "swimming upstream." One subject was able to withdraw from gang activity at the appropriate times to go to the museum or library. Another subject resisted the temptation to use his illegal winnings to join his friends "on the town," instead saving his money to buy real estate. Whether they withstood peer pressure in order to do more goal-directed activities, or to reject the overt or covert predictions of failure, a frequent pattern encountered among the subjects was that of the loner or autonomous person who could separate him or herself in order to pursue personal achievement-oriented behaviors. This capacity to "march to the beat of a different drummer" appears to be a significant component of success for the study group of defiers.

This self-directedness may be related to the notion of field independence/dependence (Witkin, Moore, Goodenough, & Cox, 1977). What seems to be involved is the capacity to fix one's sights and chart one's course without excessive dependence on exogenous forces, often despite them. The importance of this characteristic in the population studied may be a function of the limited number and quality of exogenous factors that point toward success. In a population where achievement in traditional ways is the mode, autonomy may be dysfunctional for success. In situations where variance from the modal behavior is required, autonomy may be essential.

Significant Others

A meaningful relationship with a "significant other" is an almost universal factor in the career development of defiers of negative predictions. Significant others function as models, guides, providers, and mentors in support of the development of defiers. In this study, parents, teachers, guidance counselors, ministers, friends, or peers were often found to fill such roles. It would appear that autonomous individual effort, although important, may not be sufficient to overcome the odds without the support of a significant other. The experience of accountability to, or identification with, another person is viewed as a universal factor in human development. For persons at high risk of failure, it may well be necessary.

Personal Characteristics

The capability for autonomous, deliberate action, and the sense that such action is efficacious, is a characteristic often seen in this population. This characteristic is reflected in the capacity to act independently in the purposeful deployment of energy, and the belief that effectuating change is not only possible, but rewarding. Counterproductive forces include the inability to make decisions, weaknesses in the focused deployment of energy, and doubt concerning the value of the effort. Whether in early childhood, adolescence, or in the young adult years, upward mobility was enhanced when this cluster emerged and took focus. This cluster may represent the essence of the sense of power that Coleman et al. (1966) found accounted for the second largest proportion of variance in school achievement, following home background. Where this feeling or sense of power was present, school achievement tended to be high in low-income and middle-income children, as well as in African-American and European-American children.

Personal Attributions and Existential State

Reality (consensual) factors are important determinants of career development, but the personal perceptions that adhere to specific factors are often of equal or greater power in determining life course outcomes. Objects, conditions, events, persons, and situations have objective characteristics. When there is consensus concerning these characteristics, they are also called factors of reality. These factors also have their special meanings and personal perceptions, which combine to influence the subject's existential state. The subjective, personal attribution and existential state is often the determining factor, rather than the objective or consensus designation. Three of the respondents referred to their families as poor, but said, ''we never thought of ourselves as poor.'' This is interpreted to mean that, despite a limited income and scarce resources, the management of their lives and resources was such that they never felt they had to act and feel like the traditional poor. It is thought that this attribution and the existential state were more influential in their development than the consensual judgment that they were, in fact, poverty stricken.

These attributional phenomena can attach to any and all of a person's experiences. They may be specific to a person, or common to a group of persons. They are nonetheless thought to influence the manner in which an individual reacts to the experience. This attribution phenomenon may partly explain why the same stimulus or condition may be responded to differently by different persons. For one type of person, the experience is threatening and diminishing of effort; for others, it is challenging of effort; for others, a stimulus may be perceived as rewarding. For a fourth group, it may be perceived as neutral or punitive. Much of what we see in the lives of the subjects in this study cannot be understood without paying attention to these personal attributions and existential states.

Positive Response to Constraints

Constraining and negative factors do not necessarily depress development. They sometimes operate as catalytic agents of resistance, or of more constructive responses. For reasons that have not as yet been definitively explained, disadvantagement is not consistently associated with negative effort or outcomes. In many instances, misfortune, rejection, discrimination, deprivation, and racism are responded to as challenges to defy the implicit negative prediction. Subjects spoke of "showing them they are wrong," or "proving that I am as good as they are," or having to demonstrate to oneself the fallacy of inferior status designation. This phenomenon of productivity and achievement in the face of adversity has many examples in human history. Pines (1979) referred to such examples as "superkids," whereas Garmezy (1976) identified such youngsters as "invulnerables."

Belief Systems and Religion

Although belief in oneself (self-concept) and belief that something is worth doing and can be done (efficacy) are important, a system of belief that extends beyond self appears to be strongly associated with achievement against odds favoring failure. Although a system of belief may be a generic characteristic in humans, or specific to the population studied, it was observed that most of the subjects in this study had strong belief systems. More than half of the subjects said they followed strong religious beliefs that played important roles in their lives. A belief system seems to provide anchorage and stability in the face of faith-challenging experiences. When questioned about religion, most of the subjects expressed the sense of community, direction, and fellowship typically associated with African Americans, and a traditional affiliation with religiosity. In addition, several subjects revealed belief in a deity with powers beyond those available to humans. Thus, the belief system phenomenon may both internally and externally influence the success of the achievement process.

SOME METHODOLOGICAL PROBLEMS

The basic intent of this study was to further the body of research on occupational and educational attainment processes for high-risk, low-status African Americans. The major theme guiding the inquiry was the effort to qualitatively describe the life course organization of events among a group of 26 African Americans who have "made it despite the odds." Although retrospective data collection has its weaknesses (inaccuracy, reliance on memory, and omission of significant events), it also has certain strengths (vivid portrayals and historical reports of important events). Hence, a qualitative perspective was employed in order to describe the context in which a group of at-risk persons overcame barriers to achieve success.

Interview data were used as the basis for conducting life history analyses in an effort to discover elements of theory grounded in the career development of 26 African-American men and women whose life chances were considered at high risk of failure because of their ethnic and income status in the child-to-young-adult period. According to Strauss and Glaser (1967), "grounded theory" is to be found in the systematic relationships and their resulting postulates that are buried in naturally occurring events and circumstances. By documenting and analyzing such conditions, circumstances, and events, propositions are generated and hypotheses ultimately developed. Thus, this inquiry began with some notions of the relationships (possibly causal) by which the defiance of negative prediction for success in selected African-American men and women could be explained. Those notions guided the inquiry; some were confirmed through the experiences of the respondents. Others were not strongly supported; still others became obvious in the course of the inquiry.

In *Toward the Discovery of Grounded Theory*, Strauss and Glaser (1967) stated that an examination of naturally occurring data that aims to uncover elements of theory that may be grounded there, carries with it a great likelihood of reporting the preconceived notions of the inquirers. This problem is not limited to this kind of qualitative and generative research. Even in highly controlled experimental work, the notions and questions that drive the investigation can also influence the data generated, and the findings which result. To accommodate this broad problem, at least partly, interview procedures emphasized open-endedness and the freedom of the respondents to offer supplementary and tangential information that was not specifically solicited. In a related study, presently in the design stage, the authors will give detailed attention to multiple sources of information, and to anticipated differences in socialization experiences and life space perceptions as they impact on self and other perceptions. Such context analysis procedures broaden the inquiry, provide multiple perspectives, and are likely to provide a richer body of data with which to work.

In contrast to validation research, this study sought not to test hypotheses, but rather to lay a base for the generation of hypotheses. Although it might be useful to provide definitive answers to questions concerning career development in the population under study, and the phenomena of defiance or resilience, it is more important, at the current stage of our knowledge, to generate better descriptive data from which taxonomies and hypotheses can be developed. From such data and hypotheses, more useful explanatory variables can be identified, and the observed intervariable relationships can be used to generate more advanced theories concerning approaches to the study of human development. Combining the complexities of career development in the general population with the special conditions and problems likely to be encountered by African Americans, an insufficient knowledge base exists for testing the complex hypotheses about life course processes among persons at high risk of failure.

The refinement of ethnographic research in recent years and the increased respect that it has received have, along with recognition of the many limitations of highly quantitative research, resulted in the wider use of qualitative research. When the task is to identify data trends or the nature and strength of relationships between variables, or to parcel out the contribution of specific variables to the variance in a set of data, quantitative methods serve quite well. But when the task is to describe the dynamic blending of variables that produce a particular result, or to explain a phenomenological transaction, quantitative procedures are of little use. In fact, there are presently no systematic procedures for serving these latter purposes.

The approach suggested here involves using descriptive and relational statistical analysis to reflect the nature of the population, and then exploring the qualitative analysis of the ethnographic data to identify and justify our inferences. The interaction of these two kinds of data enhances the capacity of both to inform explanation. In later stages of the research program, when larger samples are utilized, the advantages of integrating qualitative and quantitative data sets, in order to study development in populations of defiers, will become clear. With testable hypotheses, appropriate quantitative techniques can be used to test their validity. Better models of the dialectical interaction of multiple variables can potentially provide concepts by which resilience in development can be better understood.

In the tradition of the social sciences, the research design of this study sought to identify the component variables by which the life histories of specific subjects developed. The classification of these factors enables them to be more efficiently manipulated conceptually. However, when human behavior is reduced to its component parts, there is the risk of losing its functional flow and meaning. To compensate for such loss, in this approach we sought to generate postulates and to collapse much of the descriptive data into summary case histories. These case histories capture the functional flow of human behavior. In the context of the cases, sequence, directionality, intent, circumstances, relationships, and values are more easily perceived as they are experienced in the process of living. The prose of these cases is more in the tradition of anthropological studies, where the task is to capture, as in a photograph, the experience and meaning of a "for instance." Again, it is in the integration of two ways of knowing—the artistic and the scientific—that attention is paid to the complex circumstances and processes by which persons who might be expected to fail build success into their lives.

CONCLUSION

Studies like this, which seek to describe aspects of select human lives, and to generate postulates to explain outcomes, lack definitiveness and precision. The population size, selection criteria, and the use only of self-reported life history data, make the findings more suggestive than conclusive. Nonetheless, many of the postulates reflect informed, intuitive, if not colloquial, wisdom, and may be relevant for the work of counselors, educators, parents, and policymakers as they seek to facilitate optimal development in disadvantaged youth at high risk of failure.

There is much to be learned or reinforced. These workers need to know that disadvantaged status and discriminatory treatment must be eliminated, but until they are, there is much that at-risk persons and those who work with them can do to overcome the odds against success. For those who do not recognize the crucial nature of their roles in the lives of young people, the function of significant others as models, mentors, and nurturant supporters merits attention.

In addition, we cannot draw enough attention to the problems created by the tendency to mislabel and prejudge persons who do not meet "standard" models in their developmental characteristics. Development is an epigenetic process, in which each accomplishment is influenced by prior events and circumstances. The lives that we have studied indicate that intervening events and circumstances can change life chances that were previously judged as negative or nonproductive. Although the characteristics of developing persons are important determinants of the course of development, the interaction of those characteristics with environmental circumstances and conditions is ultimately determinant. Even when human characteristics are immutable, the interactions are still manipulable. Those who intervene as parents, friends, or professionals can be guided in such manipulations by the Inventory of Propositions generated here to explain the defiance of negative predictions of success in populations at high risk of failure.

A wide variety of factors operate to influence the achievement of success in persons against whom the odds are stacked. No single factor can be identified which is necessary or sufficient to produce success. Persons who achieve success against the odds appear to do so through deliberate and fortuitous orchestrations of many personal, environmental, and situational factors. However, to improve the life chances for success for a particular person, it would be logical to consider emphasizing several of the factors explicitly addressed in the propositional inventory above, or implicitly identified in the case material. Persons whose lives are representative of many of these factors are probably more likely to be successful than those in whom such factors are absent.

Some behavior and conditions appear to enable individuals to compete more efficiently than others. However, competition to succeed may be the insurmountable problem, since if a competition has winners there must also be losers. Seeking to better understand how some members of the population at high risk of failure succeed despite the odds, and examining what has worked for them, may not provide meaningful solutions to the broader problem of mass underdevelopment and failure in the low-status populations of society. Many African Americans are struggling to succeed, and failing, but many are struggling only to survive. Moreover, in a society such as ours, structured so that many must fail in order that a few succeed, even orchestrating the life conditions and experiences of all persons to improve the likelihood of success would not eliminate failure. There is not room at the top of society for everyone.

During the early 1960s, at the height of the concern for reducing the number of school dropouts, one observer shocked an assembled group with the question, What will our society do if we succeed in keeping all of our young people in school, and insuring that they are all well educated and successfully prepared to function in the labor force? What will our society do with successive generations, if 100% or even 90% are winners? Are we prepared to absorb and make meaningful places for universal participation in the fulfillment of the "American Dream"? Is it not more likely that, faced with high proportions of winners, society would change the criteria of success to ensure that only a few of these achievers would actually win and most would still lose?

Although these are difficult questions to answer, Berg's (1970) investigations into the role of testing and other selection procedures in employment indicate that they may hint at the truth. Artificial barriers are established, in order to create a pool of potential employees who exceed entry requirements for the job and have certain socially preferred characteristics. Nonetheless, there appears to be no humane and rational alternative but to strive to make life chances for success broadly available to high-risk populations. As one observes the contributions, the models, the quality of life, and the personal satisfaction of the African-American men and women in this study who have made it against the odds, one certainly cannot avoid counseling that their struggles and successes be emulated, especially by those young adults who would otherwise be predicted to fail.

REFERENCES

Berg, I. (1970). *Education and jobs: The great training robbery*. New York: Praeger.

Chess, S., & Thomas, A. (1977). *Temperament and development*. New York: Brunner/Mazel.

Chess, S., & Thomas A. (1980). *The dynamics of psychological development*. New York: Brunner/Mazel.

Coleman, J. S., Campbell, E., Hobson, C., McPartland, J., Mood, A., Weinfeld, F., & York, R. (1966). *Equality of educational opportunity*. Washington, DC: U.S. Government Printing Office.

Freedman, M. K. (1969). *The process of work establishment*. New York: Columbia University Press.

Garmezy, N. (1976). *Vulnerable and invulnerable children: Theory, research and intervention*. New York: American Psychological Association.

Garmezy, N., & Rutter, M. (1985). Acute stress reactions. In M. Rutter & L. Hersov (Eds.), *Child and adolescent psychiatry: Modern approaches*. Oxford: Blackwell.

Gordon, E. W. (1985). Social science knowledge and minority experiences. *The Journal of Negro Education, 54*(2), 117–133.

Gordon, E. W., Rollock, D., & Miller, F. (1990). Coping with communicentric bias in knowledge production in the social sciences. *Educational Researcher, 19*(3).

Gurin, P., & Epps, E. (1975). *Black consciousness, identity and achievement*. New York: Wiley.

Horowitz, F. D. (1989, April). *The concept of risk: A reevaluation*. Invited address to the Society for Research in Child Development, Kansas City, MO.

James, W. (1902). *The varieties of religious experience: A study in human nature*. New York: Random House.

Luthar, S. S. (1991). Vulnerability and resilience: A study of high risk adolescents. *Child Development, 62*, 600–616.

Masten, A. S., & Garmezy, N. (1985). Risk, vulnerability and protective factors in developmental psychology. In B. B. Lahey & A. E. Kazdin (Eds.), *Advances in child clinical psychology* (pp. 1–52). New York: Plenum Press.

Mercer, J. (1973). *Labelling the mentally retarded*. Berkeley, CA: University of California Press.

Murphy, L., & Moriarty, A. (1976). *Vulnerability, coping and growth from infancy to adolescence*. New Haven, CT: Yale University Press.

Murray, H. A. (1938). *Explorations in personality*. New York: Oxford.

Paykel, E. S. (1978). Contributions of life events to causation of psychiatric illness. *Psychological Medicine, 8*, 245–253.

Pines, M. (1979). Superkids. *Psychology Today*, 53–63.

Rutter, M. (1979). New findings, new concepts, new approaches. *Child Development, 50*, 283–305.

Rutter, M. (1985). Resilience in the face of adversity: Protective factors and resistance psychiatric disorder. *British Journal of Psychiatry, 147*, 598–611.

Sameroff, A. J., Seifer, R., Barocas, R., Zax, M., & Greenspan, S. I. (1987). Intelligence quotient scores of 4-year-old children: Social environmental risk factors. *Pediatrics, 79*, 343–350.

Stanfield, J. (1985). The ethnocentric bias of social knowledge production. *Review of Research in Education, 12*.

Strauss, A., & Glaser, B. (1967). *Toward the discovery of grounded theory: Strategies for qualitative research*. Chicago: Aldine.

Sullivan, E. (1984). *Critical psychology: An interpretation of the personal world*. New York: Plenum Press.

Vygotsky, L. S. (1978). *Mind in society*. Cambridge, MA: Harvard University Press.

Werner, E. E. (1989). Children of the garden island. *Scientific American, 260*(4), 106–111.

Werner, E. E., & Smith, R. S. (1982). *Vulnerable but invincible: A study of resilient children*. New York: McGraw-Hill.

Witkin, H. A., Moore, C. A., Goodenough, D. R., & Cox, P. W. (1977). Field-dependent and field-independent cognitive styles and their educational implications. *Review of Educational Research, 47*, 1–64.

Wolf, M. M. (1966). The measurements of environments. In A. Anastasi (Ed.), *Testing problems in perspective* (pp. 491–503). Washington, DC: American Council on Education.

Chapter 3

Educational Resilience in Inner Cities

Margaret C. Wang
Geneva D. Haertel
Temple University Center for
Research in Human Development and Education

Herbert J. Walberg
University of Illinois at Chicago

As the decade of the 1990s unfolds, the nation's attention has been captured by the plight of children and families in a variety of risk circumstances, and by the urgency for interventions that foster resilience and life chances of all children and youth. Problems of great severity exist for many children, youth, and families, particularly those in at-risk circumstances, such as the inner-city communities. The quality of life available to children and families in these communities is threatened by a perilous set of modern morbidities that often involve poverty, lack of employment opportunities, disorderly and stressful environments, poor health care, children born by children, and highly fragmented patterns of service. In responding to such challenges, researchers are focusing on factors that strengthen the resources and protective mechanisms for fostering healthy development and learning success of children and youth.

This chapter has two purposes. The first is to provide a synthesis of findings from three disparate research bases that conceptually are closely linked: (a) the psychological characteristics of resilient school-aged children; (b) characteristics of effective schools, instructional methods, and teacher behaviors that foster learning success among students considered "at risk"; and (c) features that contribute to collaborative interventions integrating family and community resources that effectively serve the developmental and learning needs of children and youth. The second purpose is to discuss their implications for fostering educational resilience of children in at-risk circumstances.

The concept of resilience is discussed as a productive construct that relates psychological characteristics of at-risk children to features of schools, families, and communities that foster resilience and schooling success. In the context of this chapter, *educational resilience* is defined as the heightened likelihood of success in school and in other life accomplishments, despite environmental adversities, brought about by early traits, conditions, and experiences. Furthermore, because a particular interest of educational theorists and practitioners is in alterable variables that are important to learning and improvements in educational practice, the focus of discussion in this chapter is on potentially malleable conditions within communities, homes, student peer groups, schools, and classrooms.

RESILIENCE: A PRODUCTIVE CONSTRUCT

Since the 1970s, developmental psychopathology (Cicchetti, 1990) has grown rapidly as a scientific discipline. It has provided an integrative framework for understanding maladaptation in children and adolescents. Topics of concern have included the roles of risk, competence, vulnerability, and protective factors. Each of these topics has been related to the onset and course of development of psychopathology.

Many of the contributions to the field of developmental psychopathology have been made by distinguished researchers in clinical psychology, psychiatry, and child development. These researchers provided early information documenting the phenomenon of psychosocial resilience in diverse, at-risk populations (Rolf, Masten, Cicchetti, Nuechterlein, & Weintraub, 1990). Among the at-risk populations studied are (a) children with family histories of mental illness (Goldstein, 1990); (b) children of divorced parents (Wallerstein, 1983; Watt, Moorehead-Slaughter, Japzon, & Keller, 1990); (c) children exposed to high levels of maternal stress (Pianta, Egeland, & Sroufe, 1990); (d) children addicted to drugs (Newcomb & Bentler, 1990); (e) children born at medical risk (O'Dougherty & Wright, 1990); (f) children exposed to family violence (Straus, 1983); (g) children exposed to early parental death (Brown, Harris, & Bifulco, 1986); and (h) children in poverty (Garmezy, 1991).

These studies, and many others, led to a new developmental model of psychopathology that addresses both vulnerability and resistance to disorders and spans the years from infancy through adulthood. The findings demonstrate that some children escape adversity without lasting damage. They provide a rich theoretical and empirical basis for new programs of educational research that can identify ways to foster and sustain the learning success of many at-risk students.

The contribution of studies of atypical, pathological, or psychopathological populations is clear. Using results from the study of children who are at risk but able to "beat the odds," however, allows researchers to expand upon the developmental principles on which the theories of developmental psychopathology are based. Studies of at-risk populations, including those who "beat the odds," identify the many pathways that lead from childhood to adulthood. These studies identify which factors are most important to healthy development, for example, physical, socioemotional, cognitive, and environmental.

A New "Vocabulary of Risk"

As developmental psychopathology established itself as a new discipline, a vocabulary of risk emerged. Constructs such as vulnerability, protective factors, adaptations, and competence have provided the conceptual tools for ground-breaking work; they clarified and furthered our understanding of factors that enable individuals to successfully overcome adversities and challenges in development and learning. Within this exciting new field of study, the construct of "resilience" emerged.

Rutter (1990) defined *resilience* as the "positive pole of the ubiquitous phenomenon of individual differences in people's response to stress and adversity" (p. 181). Masten, Best, and Garmezy (1990) referred to the resilience phenomenon as the "capacity for or outcome of successful adaptation despite challenging or threatening circumstances" (p. 425). They further noted that resilience concerns "behavioral adaptation usually defined as internal states of well-being or effective functioning in the environment or both. Protective factors moderate the effects of individual vulnerability or environmental hazards so that the adaptational trajectory is more positive than would be the case if the protective factor were not operational" (p. 426).

The field of prevention, where researchers and practitioners work to eliminate or at least to delay the onset of problems such as alcohol and drug abuse, teenage pregnancy, delinquency, and school dropout, also employs this new vocabulary. These researchers and practitioners identify and describe "protective factors" and methods for building resilience in children and youth.

The Critical Role of Activity in Resilience

Why has the construct of resilience received so much attention over the past decade? The answer to this question is found in prospective studies that focus on individuals believed to be at high risk for developing particular difficulties: children exposed to neonatal stress, poverty, neglect, family violence, war, physical handicaps, and parental mental illness. These studies provide rich databases from longitudinal studies that span several decades of new research aimed at identifying the processes underlying adaptation, successful trajectories, and pathways from childhood to adulthood.

As researchers gained insight into the risk factors that promoted the onset of a disorder, a puzzling but consistent phenomenon began to surface. Although a certain percentage of children in high-risk circumstances developed psychopathologies, a larger percentage did not develop disorders and became healthy and competent adults (Garmezy, 1991; Rutter, 1966, 1987; Watt, Anthony, Wynne, & Rolf, 1984). The often-reported statistic that only one out of four children born to alcoholic parents will become alcoholic (Benard, 1991) is a case in point.

The active role of the individual has been identified as an important factor in surviving stressful circumstances (Rutter, 1990). Individuals' responses to stressful circumstances vary, and what they do is the critical factor in whether they emerge successfully. Passivity in the face of adversity rarely provides the necessary information for an individual to develop strategies that can be useful in stressful conditions. The activity of resilient individuals serves as a self-righting mechanism that provides feedback that can be used to identify productive strategies in order to emerge unscathed from adversity.

Characteristics of Resilient Children

Resilient children, described by Garmezy (1974) as working and playing well and holding high expectations, have often been characterized using constructs such as locus of control, self-esteem, self-efficacy, and autonomy. A profile of resilient children that has emerged from the work of the Western Regional Center for Drug-Free Schools and Communities (Benard, 1991) includes such descriptors as strong interpersonal skills, a capacity to be responsive to others, a high level of activity, and flexibility. Resilient children were observed to perceive experiences constructively; they maintain healthy expectations, set goals, and have a clear sense of purpose about their future agency in controlling their own fate.

One construct that has shed some light on childhood resilience is "learned helplessness" (Seligman, 1975). Resilient children, as described in the research literature, rarely exhibit the passive behaviors associated with learned helplessness. Benard (1991) concluded that resilient children's high expectations, belief that life has meaning, goal direction, personal agency, and interpersonal problem-solving skills coalesce into a particularly potent set of personal attributes. These attributes reduce the propensity of resilient children to exhibit the debilitating behaviors associated with learned helplessness. Seligman's (1991) book, *Learned Optimism*, reviews research on the value of positive belief systems for life success. Although he did not address resilience directly, the behaviors and beliefs he described are in concert with empirical findings on the psychosocial characteristics of children who overcame life adversities (i.e., resilient children).

A second line of research that sheds light on the psychosocial processes that promote resilience considers the coping mechanisms that individuals employ during stressful life events. Chess (1989) identified "adaptive distancing" as the psychological process whereby an individual can stand apart from distressed family members and friends in order to accomplish constructive goals and advance his or her psychological and social development. Adaptive distancing may be only one of a family of coping mechanisms that individuals employ as they successfully adapt to stressful events. Future research on resilience may provide empirical evidence of the types of coping mechanisms that resilient individuals employ.

Rutter (1990) and Chess and Thomas (1990) identified some of the adverse temperamental behaviors that children exhibit that can irritate caregivers and make the children targets of hostility. These behaviors include low regularity in eating and sleeping behaviors, low malleability, negative mood, and low fastidiousness. These attributes reduce a child's likelihood of receiving positive attention from adults. Even temperament, malleability, predictable behavior, mild-to-moderate emotional reactions, approaching rather than withdrawing from novel situations, and a sense of humor are attributes that protect children and produce affection and support from adults. Children in stressful life circumstances who have an easy temperament are more likely to receive the social support necessary for surviving adverse life events. Being female and in good health are two attributes that have also been associated with resilient children (Benard, 1991). Overall, social competence, good problem-solving skills, independence, and a clear sense of purpose are the critical attributes of resilient children (Masten, Best, & Garmezy, 1990; Masten, Morison, Pelligrini, & Tellegen, 1990).

These attributes were also noted in the findings from a study of high-achieving students from economically disadvantaged homes in urban schools. Using the National Education Longitudinal Study (NELS) database (U.S. Department of Education, 1988), Peng, Lee, Wang, and Walberg (1991) conducted a study to identify unique characteristics and experiences of urban students of low socioeconomic status (SES) whose combined reading and mathematics test scores were in the highest quartile on a national norm (i.e., resilient students). They found that 9.2% of low SES urban students were in this category. These students had self-concepts and educational aspirations and felt more internally controlled than nonresilient students. They also interacted more often with their parents and were more likely to attend schools where learning is emphasized and students are encouraged to do their best.

Characteristics of Schools That Foster Student Resilience

Effective schools are powerful environments. Students can acquire resilience in educational environments that foster development and competence in achieving learning success. Effective educational practices have constituted a major research front since the mid-1970s (Cruickshank, 1990). School effectiveness has both macrolevel and microlevel dimensions. The macrolevel factors encompass the total school environment and related extraschool variables.

Microlevel factors emphasize the effectiveness of classroom instruction, including replicable patterns of teacher behaviors and student achievement. Both school- and class-level effectiveness have been heavily researched.

Many definitions of effective urban schools have emerged from the extant research bases. The Carnegie Foundation for the Advancement of Teaching (1988) advanced a definition of an effective urban school based on 15 criteria. These criteria, expressed as questions, are listed here:

- Does the school have clearly defined goals?
- Does the school evaluate the language proficiency of each student? What evidence is there that students are developing their communication skills, both oral and written?
- What are the number and types of books being read by students?
- Does the school have a core curriculum for all students? What is the general knowledge of students in such fields as history, geography, science, mathematics, literature, and the arts? Is such knowledge appropriately assessed?
- What is the enrollment pattern among the various educational programs at the school? Specifically, what is the distribution between remedial and academic courses?
- Is the school organized into small units to overcome anonymity among students and provide a close relationship between each student and a mentor?
- Are there flexible scheduling arrangements at the school?
- Is there a program that encourages students to take responsibility for helping each other learn and helps make the school a friendly and orderly place? How well is it succeeding?
- What teaching innovations have been introduced during the preceding academic year? Are there programs to reward teachers who exercise leadership?
- Does the school have a well-developed plan of renewal for teachers and administrators?
- Is the school clean, attractive, and well equipped? Does it have adequate learning resources such as computers and a basic library? Can the school document that these resources are used by students and teachers to support effective learning?
- Are parents active in the school and kept informed about the progress of their children? Are there parent consultation sessions? How many parents participate in such programs?
- Does the school have connections with community institutions and outside agencies to enrich the learning possibilities of students?

- What are daily attendance and graduation rates at the school?

- What changes have occurred in the dropout rate, in students seeking post-secondary education, and in students getting jobs after graduation? What is being done to improve performance in these areas?

The program features included in these criteria on effective urban schools are plausible. Indeed, it might be difficult to defend the idea that they are desirable only for urban schools. They appear, in fact, to correspond well with an extensive content analysis of approximately 200 research reviews of effective educational policies and practices that apply to schools in general (Wang, Haertel, & Walberg, 1990). One of the challenges for research on urban schools, and indeed schools in general, is to identify ineffective policies and practices. From the point of view of scientific parsimony and educational efficacy, such research might frugally hypothesize that effective policies transcend location, ethnic group, social class, subject matter, grade level, and so on. The burden of proof might then be placed on showing convincing differential policies (i.e., those that work consistently well in some settings but consistently poorly in others).

Among the most perplexing questions in designing innovative, research-based intervention programs for improving students' learning outcomes has been the relative importance of the multiplicity of distinct and interactive influences on student learning. Findings from a recently completed synthesis on variables important to learning document the multidimensional nature of school effectiveness (Wang, Haertel, & Walberg, in press). Results indicate that the proximal variables, such as student cognitive and metacognitive processes, classroom management techniques, teacher–student interactions, and the home environment, had a stronger and more pervasive impact on school learning than distal variables, such as school and district policies, demographic characteristics, and state policies and programs.

Studies of effective teaching provide a rich source of data on the microlevel variables that contribute to school effectiveness. Since the 1980s, a number of research syntheses were published that identified effective instructional practices (Reynolds, 1982; Slavin & Madden, 1989; U.S. Department of Education, 1986; van de Grift, 1990; Wang et al., 1990; Williams, Richmond, & Mason, 1986). The consistent characteristics that have emerged include degree of curriculum articulation and organization; maximized learning time; high expectations for student achievement; opportunity to respond; degree of classroom engagement; and student participation in setting goals, making learning decisions, and engaging in cooperative learning.

Many characteristics of effective schools emphasize the importance of a sense of student ''involvement'' and ''belonging'' that reduces feelings of alienation and disengagement. The more ways that a student feels attached to teachers, classmates, the school, and the instructional program, the more likely that participation in school functions as a protective shield against adverse circumstances. Student engagement and participation in school and classroom life promote self-esteem, autonomy, positive social interactions, and mastery of tasks. These positive outcomes have been shown to enhance life satisfaction and general well-being among urban teenagers (Maton, 1990).

Only a few studies have provided direct evidence on whether a particular set of school characteristics is effective in fostering resilience among students in inner-city schools. Many of the earlier studies conducted on effective schools found high levels of multicollinearity between desirable school characteristics and the SES characteristics of the communities being served (Stringfield & Teddlie, 1991). Characteristics of more effective schools were often associated with schools serving students from well-to-do neighborhoods. Some interesting alterable variables, however, have emerged from recent studies of the effects of urban schools.

In Phase III of the Louisiana School Effectiveness Study, for example, 16 schools of varying SES levels were studied (Teddlie, Kirby, & Stringfield, 1989). These schools were classified as positive and negative outliers. Positive outlier schools were those that scored above their predicted achievement levels, whereas the negative outlier schools performed below their predicted achievement levels. The study documented variance in school, principal, and teacher activities within all SES levels. Greater achievement was obtained at schools that devoted a high percentage of time to tasks that made educational sense. The atmosphere was friendly in the schools that were performing at higher than expected levels of achievement, but principals and teachers protected the time spent on academic tasks and ensured that students' academic programs were well coordinated. Principals were very engaged in school events, remained active in the selection and retention of their faculties, valued high academic achievement, and supported the library in the life of the school. Teachers who achieved higher levels of academic attainment employed teaching methods that involved planning, clearly specified management and disciplinary rules, active teaching of higher order thinking skills, and providing direct instruction when appropriate. In successful schools, they also held high academic expectations.

Maughan (1988) used a multilevel, fixed-effects research design in a 3-year study of school experience and psychosocial risk in 50 multiethnic junior high schools. The findings demonstrate that schools that were successful with socially and economically disadvantaged students enjoyed strong leadership, faculty input on decision making, *esprit de corps* among staff, and strong parental involvement. Effective schools were described as having physically and emotionally pleasant surroundings. Classrooms were well managed, and instruction was stimulating. Children had a strong voice in choosing the kinds of instructional activities and classes in which they participated. These successful schools functioned effectively for both boys and girls, as well as across ethnic groups and social classes.

These findings were also noted in a study by Peng, Weishew, and Wang (1991). Using the NELS database (U.S. Department of Education, 1988), they identified inner-city schools that had high achievement scores despite their disadvantaged circumstances (i.e., resilient schools that "beat the odds"). The resilient schools in their study were found to be more orderly and structured than the low-achieving inner-city schools. Parents of students from the resilient schools held higher educational expectations for their children.

There is an optimism among educational researchers and practitioners about the possibility of implementing what is known from research and practical wisdom. When effectively implemented, effective strategies can shield children from the adversity that abounds in inner-city environments. In his compelling book, *Fifteen Thousand Hours*, psychiatrist Michael Rutter (1979a) argued that a school ethos of high expectations protects students against the debilitating effects of adversity. He found an important relationship between a school's characteristics and children's behavior problems. Problem behaviors decreased in schools designated as successful, and increased in unsuccessful schools. Variations in the rates of disruptive behavior were related to the ethos of the schools themselves. Thus, children living under conditions that are not supportive of psychosocial well-being may experience their school as a force for good or bad depending on the ethos of the school itself.

The review of research prepared by Benard (1991) also stressed the role that high expectations play in the development of resilience. Based on results of six major research studies, Benard reported that schools "that establish high expectations for all kids—and give them the support necessary to achieve them—have incredibly high rates of academic success" (p. 11).

How a school remains effective is a question that has not received much attention. One of the disappointments of the school effectiveness movement has been the inability to maintain improved performance from year to year (Freiberg, 1989). Good and Brophy (1986) expressed this concern in reviewing the school effectiveness literature: "the study of stability presents major technical and conceptual problems to those who study schools as organizational instructional units" (p. 587). Freiberg (1989) cited the work of Dworkin (1987) and Murnane (1975), who cautioned that variables associated with effective schools may differ in urban settings because student populations are very mobile—sometimes expanding, other times shrinking, but always changing. The positive effects of successful schools are amplified over time.

Research efforts to determine how schools become effective and how they maintain their effectiveness require recognition of the multidimensional nature of school effectiveness. Research on school effects, teaching practices, community and family influences, and student and teacher characteristics must be examined in order to understand how inner-city schools can support high performance and resilience in their students. The intimate and informed relations among students, their peers and families, and educators in private (especially parochial) schools, smaller schools, and schools of choice, may explain their appeal and apparent achievement advantages (Boyd & Walberg, 1990; Coleman & Hoffer, 1987; Fowler & Walberg, 1991).

Characteristics of Communities That Foster Resilience

Designing successful educational programs also requires examining the institutions that effectively provide for the education, health, and human services needs of local communities. The role of these institutions needs to be studied to determine if they prevent or facilitate the cycle of ''at-risk-ness'' that adversely affects development and learning.

Benard (1991) identified three characteristics of communities that foster resilience. These characteristics are: availability of social organizations that provide an array of resources to residents; consistent expression of social norms so that community members understand what constitutes desirable behavior; and opportunities for children and youth to participate in the life of the community as valued members. Hill, Wise, and Shapiro (1989) emphasized the role of communities as key contributors in the revitalization of failing urban school systems. Hill, Wise, and Shapiro believe that troubled urban school systems can only recover when the communities that they serve unite in decisive efforts to improve their performance.

One of the clearest signs of a cohesive and supportive community is the presence of social organizations that provide for healthy human development (Garmezy, 1991). Health-care organizations, child-care services, job training opportunities, religious institutions, and recreational facilities are only some of the myriad of social organizations that serve human needs. In communities where there is a large, well-developed, and integrated network of social organizations, there are fewer social problems (Miller & Ohlin, 1985).

Communities that hold and express standards for good citizenship provide protective mechanisms for residents. This is recognized most clearly in studies that explore the importance of cultural norms on student alcohol and drug use (Bell, 1987; Long & Vaillant, 1989). Nettles (1991) analyzed the effectiveness of community-based programs available to African-American youth. She found that school-based clinics are only partially effective in reducing risk. Community-based programs that fostered resilience provided more social support and adult aid, gave concrete help on tasks, and provided opportunities for students to develop new interests and skills.

The role of religion and faith has also been identified as a protective factor for at-risk students. Masten, Morison et al. (1990) identified both the beliefs based on abstract relationships with religious protective figures and the concrete relationships with members of the religious community as protective factors. Religious beliefs are helpful across ethnic groups and social classes, and provide standards and expectations to guide children's behavior.

Urban communities often lack a well-integrated network of social organizations for children and youth. The services provided by these organizations are often compartmentalized and fragmented. In their analysis of the impact of social policies on the quality of human resources available to African-American youth, Swanson and Spencer (1991) emphasized the dual importance of finding ways to reduce risk and making opportunities and resources available in order to break the negative chain reactions associated with adversity. Because schools have the most sustained contact with children and their families, public education officials should take into consideration, when designing their school improvement programs, the potential benefits of coordinating and integrating children's services across school and community organizations (Holtzman, 1991; Kirst & McLaughlin, 1990; National Center on Education in the Inner Cities, 1990).

Some promising new modes of cooperation are already being explored around the country. New coordinating agencies have been created in some cities, for example, out of the offices of city mayors and councils, working toward the coordinated involvement of businesses, labor unions, health-related resources, social agencies, and schools. But a number of these programs are quite new and are still seeking basic funding, leadership, and mechanisms for effective communication (Wang, 1991). Nevertheless, there is an emerging pattern of program design considerations across these new community enhancement models (National Center on Education in the Inner Cities, 1990). They include the following:

- Services needed by children, youth, and their families should be provided in a continuing fashion without artificial discontinuities. This suggests an important vertical coordinating function or coordination through time, as well as horizontal or cross-agency coordination.

- Definite strong provision must be made for staff to coordinate efforts across agencies. Such coordination requires time and effort.

- Agencies, including schools, must be ready to respond to leadership from various sources, not just the traditional "in-house" officer.

- There should be readiness to conduct services or programs in a variety of settings, going beyond traditional arrangements.

- Services are unlikely to be used unless there is very good communication concerning them. Basic information about programs must be spread in every community, and steps must be taken to inspire trust and confidence in the personnel and agencies involved.

- Opportunities should be sought to incorporate all kinds of community resources, including university resources and expertise in building community-school connections, especially through projects of a broad multidisciplinary and multiprofessional nature.

FOSTERING RESILIENCE: A NEW DIRECTION
IN EDUCATIONAL RESEARCH AND DEVELOPMENT

Research on resilience, in general, and on identifying ways to foster resilience, in particular, has generated new approaches to studying and designing innovative interventions. This new research focuses not only on identifying causes of risk and adversity, but on understanding the protective mechanisms that reduce risk and enhance success of all students.

To date, few researchers have studied the development and education of children and youth in at-risk circumstances, such as the inner-city or poor rural communities, using a research model that searches for educational risk and protective factors. A better understanding of the lives and educational potential of children and youth in the inner cities, for example, can be achieved in part by studying resilient children and the role of the family, schools, and communities in fostering resilience among children in at-risk circumstances.

The Role of the Family in Fostering Resilience

The quality of the caregiving environment is central to the development of resilience. In examining the impact of the environment on resilience, the role of the family is a logical starting place. Parents and families provide the first protective agents in the child's environment (Masten, Best, & Garmezy, 1990). Masten et al. noted that parents:

> nurture mastery motivation and self-esteem as well as physical growth. Parents provide information, learning opportunities, behavioral models, and connections to other resources. When these transactional protective processes are absent or are severely limited for prolonged periods, a child may be significantly handicapped in subsequent adaptation by low self-esteem, inadequate information or social know-how, a disinclination to learn or interact with the world, and a distrust of people as resources. (p. 438)

Studies of at-risk families seek to identify barriers that impede the development of children and features of the caregiving environment that fosters resilience.

Fostering resilience in children requires family environments that are caring and structured, hold high expectations for children's behavior, and encourage participation in the life of the family. These characteristics are among the protective factors that can foster resilience (Benard, 1991). Most resilient children have at least one strong relationship with an adult (not always a parent), and this relationship diminishes risks associated with family discord. Receiving care and affection is critical throughout childhood and adolescence, but particularly during the first year of life (Rutter, 1979b; Werner & Smith, 1982).

Rutter (1990) documented the importance of good parent–child relationships in a review of data from short-term prospective studies, intergenerational studies of high-risk populations, and studies involving retrospective recall of adults. Results from all these studies provide evidence that secure and supportive personal attachments early in life make it likely that individuals will be protected against adversity in later life. Positive social relationships throughout life also provide benefits. Positive, intimate relationships correlate with a positive self-concept and can enhance the individual's worth within the social network.

The impact of caring and support is exemplified in Rutter's (1979b) study of discordant families. Of children from discordant families, 75% exhibited conduct disorders when they failed to have a positive relationship with either parent, as compared to 25% when children maintained a good relationship with at least one parent. In their review of studies of competence under stress, Masten, Best, and Garmezy (1990) provided evidence that family instability and disorganization predicted school disruptiveness. Children whose families had a history of marital instability and frequent moves were more often rated as disruptive by peers and teachers. However, in contrast to these conclusions, there is some evidence that the stress produced in discordant families can be mitigated. Benard (1991) found that even though divorce produces stress, the availability of social support from family and community can reduce stress and yield positive outcomes.

A topic of research that has received more attention recently is the impact of mobility on children's lives. Recent statistics provided by the U.S. Department of Commerce (1987) documented that 19% of the nation's school-aged children move in a single year. Lash and Kirkpatrick (1990) reported that some of these moves are the result of parents' seasonal jobs (e.g., migrant farm workers), some reflect job or military transfers, and others are due to divorce and financial instability. Migration has shown to be a serious and pervasive risk factor for student learning among poor and minority children, as revealed by two large national surveys (Long, 1975; Straits, 1987). Moving generally keeps children of lower SES from attaining their normally expected achievement and grade level.

The effect of mobility is particularly large in one case. Moving from a community of lower SES to one of higher SES often results in substantial grade retardation of lower SES children (although it does not appear to affect middle SES children as much or at all). Early grade retardation is important, because it forecasts further retardation, poor achievement, and dropping out—a phenomenon known as the ''Matthew effects'' (Walberg, 1984; Wang, 1990).

Perhaps the most pressing problems facing children and families in at-risk circumstances, such as the inner cities, are the problems faced by the adolescents in the community—behavior problems, substance abuse, academic underachievement, and teenage pregnancy. The intervention literature strongly suggests that these problems cannot be addressed without direct involvement of the family (Benard, 1991; Liddle, 1991). The solution to many of these problems lies within the family.

Garmezy (1985) established the importance of several family-related variables in protecting children against adversity. These variables include family cohesion, family warmth, and the absence of discord. A supportive family environment is critically important to the development of resilience. In addition to holding high expectations of children (i.e., that they will succeed in school and become good citizens in their community), households that are structured and employ consistent discipline, rules, and regulations produce better outcomes among children from at-risk families (Bennett, Wolin, & Reiss, 1988). Masten, Morison et al. (1990) related poor household maintenance and housekeeping to disruptiveness in school.

Benard (1991) pointed to the importance of children's participation in family and household activities in fostering resiliency. Benard cited the work of Werner and Smith (1982), who emphasized the value of assigned chores, caring for brothers and sisters, and the contribution of part-time work in supporting the family. These behaviors help establish that children can truly contribute and improve their circumstances. Helping behaviors on the part of children enhance their self-esteem and ultimately foster resilience.

Family Involvement With Schools.   The importance of family involvement in enhancing children's school performance has been consistently documented (Chan, 1987; Epstein, 1984; Moles, 1982). Families' involvement has been found to facilitate increased communication between schools and homes. The active participation of family members in students' learning has improved student achievement, increased school attendance, decreased student dropouts, decreased delinquency, and reduced pregnancy rates. These results are present regardless of racial, ethnic, or social class membership (Peterson, 1989).

A series of research syntheses reported by Graue, Weinstein, and Walberg (1983) and Iverson and Walberg (1982) provided strong evidence that school-based family involvement programs work, and that there is a significant correlation between school achievement and features of the home environment. Furthermore, parents who participate in family involvement programs were found to feel better about themselves and were more likely to enroll in courses that advance their own education (Flaxman & Inger, 1991). However, based on data drawn from the NELS study of eighth graders in 1988 (U.S. Department of Education), Peng and Lee (1991) found that direct parental involvement and assistance are not as important as the availability of learning opportunities, frequent parent–child conversations, and higher education expectations. Furthermore, they found that having more family rules without complementary support does not relate to higher achievement.

Educational intervention programs designed to involve family members are also significantly more effective than programs aimed exclusively at students

(Walberg, 1984; Weikart, Epstein, Schweinhart, & Bond, 1978). A research study on direct parental involvement was conducted by Comer (1986) in a low-performing school that ranked 32 out of 33 in New Haven, Connecticut. Using strategies for parent involvement over several years, the same school, populated by at-risk students, improved its rank to 3 out of 26 schools. Similar results have been attained with other low-performing schools. Comer attributed results to the success of management teams involving parents, parent-developed workshops, parent involvement in tutoring programs for children, and parents' assisting teachers in planning classroom activities.

Epstein (1987) developed a theory of family–school connections after recognizing four important microsystems that impact the development of children, families, peer groups, schools, and neighborhood/communities. The degree of overlap among these microsystems represents the extent to which they share values, goals, and understandings of the social and cultural processes governing everyday life. The greater the overlap among domains, the more common their cultures and structures. Generally, there is some evidence and strong logic behind an argument that the greater the overlap among microsystems, the more consistent their joint impact on the developing person. When the home, the school, peers, and the larger community are working together, the greater their impact is in a consistent direction.

Several types of family involvement programs are being implemented by schools across the country. Some programs involve families directly in school management and "choice" and encourage parents' actual presence in the school. Others are focused on training families in communication skills and helping their children to develop good study habits and high expectations. Still others focus on family resource and support programs. These programs provide a host of direct services to families and children. They may involve home visits, job training, career counseling, health care, mental health, and social support services (Wang, Haertel, & Walberg, 1992).

The Role of Teachers in Fostering Resilience

The importance of external support systems as protective mechanisms that enable children to cope under adverse conditions has been stressed in the literature on childhood resilience. Teachers can play an important role in reducing stress by providing the positive supports needed by children in adverse conditions. The contribution of teachers has been documented in the words of the children of Kauai who took part in Werner's (1989) longitudinal study of the long-term effects of prenatal and perinatal stress. Of the 142 high-risk children identified in her study, 72 beat the odds and became competent, successful adults. Describing these resilient children as "easygoing" and "even-tempered," teachers praised the students' problem-solving abilities and competence in reading. The school became a home away from home for the children; it was a refuge from a chaotic home life. Favorite teachers became role models in whom the children confided when their own family was threatened by dissolution.

The value of teachers providing concern and support is also described by Benard (1991), who quoted Noddings (1988):

> At a time when the traditional structures of caring have deteriorated, schools must become places where teachers and students live together, talk with each other, take delight in each other's company. My guess is that when schools focus on what really matters in life, the cognitive ends we now pursue so painfully and artificially will be achieved somewhat more naturally. . . . It is obvious that children will work harder and do things—even odd things like adding fractions—for people they love and trust. (p. 32)

In their study of public and private high schools, Coleman and Hoffer (1987) pointed to the role of caring and engaging teachers in helping high school students develop the values and attitudes necessary for persevering in their schoolwork and achieving high grades. They stressed the importance of the personal relationships among teachers and students—sustained, intergenerational, intimate relationships of moderate intensity that support students' academic and social endeavors.

A major risk factor that contributes to learning problems encountered by students, particularly in inner-city schools serving students from diverse ethnic and cultural backgrounds, is the disconnection between schooling experience and family life. Among some of the most critical facilitating factors ameliorating this problem of disconnection are teachers' sensitivity to student diversity and their ability to provide learning experiences that are responsive to individual differences. Effective teachers serve to reduce vulnerability and stress and use a variety of strategies to ensure the personal and academic competence of their students.

Students bring to the learning situation a diversity of cultural and language backgrounds and prior knowledge. These differences may be important sources of variation on how and what students learn. How students interact with the classroom and school environment and the demands for school learning can limit or enhance the students' access to learning resources and, therefore, learning success. Effective teachers play an important mediating function in minimizing "risk" or vulnerability and maximizing resources that can serve to enhance student development and promote resilience.

Campione and Armbruster (1985) pointed out that children with excellent comprehension skills usually relate new information to their personal experiences. Differences in prior knowledge may be the product of cultural differences. These differences may be important sources of variation in students' strategy use and in their learning outcomes. Students from culturally diverse backgrounds may not only have difficulty accessing background knowledge, they may also have knowledge deficits. They may not be able to access prerequisite prior knowledge without help from teachers. This lack of background knowledge is sometimes remediated by using culturally relevant texts and materials. Palincsar and Klenk (1991) recommended that teachers use universal themes with which all students can identify as a method to make new content more easily accessible. Effective teachers who are familiar with the types of background experiences students bring to the classroom not only select materials that are culturally relevant, but make it easier for the students to relate to their classroom experience and to access their prior knowledge.

Recently, Ogbu (1992) identified several ways that teachers can help at-risk children with cultural and language difficulties perform in school. He recommended that teachers learn about students' cultural backgrounds and use the knowledge to organize their classrooms and instructional programs. Teachers can gather information about the cultural backgrounds of at-risk students through observing students' behaviors, asking students and their families questions about their cultural practices, conducting research on ethnic groups in the school setting, and reviewing published research on children from different cultural groups. The information teachers gather can then be used to design and implement instructional programs, to help students get along with each other, and to improve communication among school staff and students' families. In all cases, however, recognition of cultural diversity, which can foster resilience, must be based on actual knowledge of different cultural groups and how these cultures differ from the mainstream culture. According to Ogbu, teachers can increase the success of interventions by recognizing whether the cultural frame of reference of an at-risk minority is oppositional to the cultural frame of reference of mainstream U.S. culture. Without taking these differences into account, teachers will be less able to increase learning and self-esteem among at-risk students. If at-risk students are immersed in a culture that has an oppositional framework to the mainstream culture, they may be less inclined to communicate with school personnel and peers from different ethnic groups and are likely to participate less fully in the life of the school.

Teachers who are effective in responding to student diversity also acknowledge the importance of individual difference variables in their planning and interactions with students. They use a variety of strategies in creating classroom learning environments that maximize each student's opportunities for learning success (Corno & Snow, 1986; Wang, 1990; Wang & Walberg, 1985). Following is a list of some of the methods identified by Corno and Snow (1986) that teachers use to adapt instruction to student differences to ensure the learning success of every child.

- Manipulate classroom organizational structures, such as the use of short-term, nonstigmatizing groups, learning centers, and reward structures.

- Vary the use of materials that present new information and support problem solving, including varying the amount of time spent on reviewing previously learned materials, the number of examples used to provide further explanation and illustration, the use of summaries, points of emphasis, and modeling.

- Vary the types of support materials used, including aides, peer tutoring, a variety of media, and other methods.

- Vary the amount of instructional support and available time for learning to accommodate the needs of the individual student.

- Vary the level, form, and number of questions asked. Ask more higher order questions so that students must go beyond the material they were presented.

- Vary the nature and amount of reinforcement given for correct answers, as well as the level of information provided when a student gives an incorrect answer.

- Enhance the students' use of inquiry processes by implementing ''inductive teaching'' strategies.

- Vary the ways information is presented during instruction to prompt students to give their own examples of new principles or content learned.

- Facilitate students' use of self-regulating techniques, such as self-monitoring or self-reinforcement, by providing a variety of problem-solving opportunities in the classroom instruction/learning process.

The role of instructional mediation has been identified as an important resource for students, particularly those from diverse cultural backgrounds and/or those requiring greater-than-usual instructional support. Different instructional activities place different cognitive demands on students and can alter their information-processing burden. Learning complicated material is difficult and requires a variety of mental resources, including cognitive processing of the new information and metacognitive activity. Instruction mediates student cognition. As instruction bears more of the information-processing burden, a student's general intellectual abilities are less critical. Little instructional mediation provides many opportunities for students to discover more principles and concepts themselves. An example of more instructional mediation might involve the use of teachers modeling cognitive skills. In this case, the teacher provides a model of expert performance, giving novice learners an opportunity to see how new problems are solved. Examples of teachers modeling powerful thinking strategies include teachers thinking aloud as they read a text, talking aloud as they solve a mathematics problem, and allowing students to watch them plan and revise an essay (Means & Knapp, 1991).

Expert scaffolding is another technique that has been shown to be effective in enabling students to handle a complex task by the teacher providing guided practice (Collins, Brown, & Newman, 1990). Both the use of mediated instructional techniques and expert scaffolding have been found particularly effective with students with special needs or those otherwise considered to be at risk (Corno & Snow, 1986; Feurstein, 1980; Means & Knapp, 1991).

In addition to providing supportive instruction, effective teachers serve to foster resilience by finding ways to promote self-concept and self-responsibility for active learning (Wang & Palincsar, 1989). As Bandura (1977, 1982) explicated in his cognitive theory of self-efficacy or perceived self-competence, self-efficacy is best promoted through mastery of new experiences. When students become convinced they are instrumental in their learning success, they work harder to overcome difficulties.

Students develop information about their own efficacy from several sources, including memories of similar past experiences; watching peers, teachers, and others master a task; attending to their own level of motivation and interest in the task; and persuasion and exhortation by others (Winne, 1991). These sources help students develop expectations for their own success. Teachers can foster resilience by providing students with opportunities to set realistic expectations, and by helping them master new experiences. Teachers who work to develop their students' ability to be active learners help strengthen students' ability to overcome adversity.

The role of mentoring has evolved during the past decade and many school reformers believe it to be a powerful intervention. This belief is based in part on the work of researchers such as Lefkowitz (1986), who highlighted the role of caring adults in fostering resilience. Lefkowitz reported that the majority of 500 at-risk youths identified a caring adult as contributing strongly to their success. Mentoring programs in schools have been developed to address problems such as school dropouts, school-to-school transitions, school-to-work transitions, drug and alcohol use, teen pregnancy and parenting skills, and family literacy (Benard, 1992). Typically, these programs have involved not only teachers, but a variety of school personnel and community members. Nevertheless, in schools, teachers play a key role in providing empathic support to pupils and in assisting students to set achievable goals; these are two behaviors involved in successful mentoring. Although many educators have regarded mentoring as a successful intervention that can contribute to programs designed to break the cycle of disadvantage, Benard (1992) cautioned that the long-term effectiveness of planned mentoring programs has not yet been established. The effectiveness of spontaneous mentoring versus planned mentoring needs to be further explored. However, teachers are in frequent contact with students and along with other adults in the school environment can be encouraged to be supportive and caring to students, and thus promote resilience.

The Role of Peer Support in Fostering Resilience

The academic achievement of at-risk students is the product not only of a child's intellectual ability, but also the school's climate and the social support networks available from families. Clark (1991) stated that after the family, peers are the most important source of support. Social support networks from peers provide children and adolescents with a sense of being valued, cared for, and loved. These support networks not only facilitate the development of an individual, but serve as a protective shield against stress. Peers, family, and the school support system can all provide protection.

Coleman and Hoffer (1987) described how students in boarding schools are supportive of their friends when their families disengage. Another strong support for the influence of peers is that the use of cooperative learning strategies is the single most effective school-based intervention for reducing alcohol and drug use (Bangert-Downs, 1988). Similarly, Watt et al. (1990) provided evidence that children of divorced parents find respite from stressful home situations through an external social network that allows them to distance themselves from stressed parents ("adaptive distancing"). The school performance of children of divorce is affected by the peer social network in which they participate, more so than the school performance of children from intact homes. Children of divorce find companionship, love, self-esteem, and care from school friends to a greater degree than children from intact homes.

Research also suggests that peers have a significant impact on a student's self-perceived academic competence and attitude toward school. Cauce (1986) found that the peer group's attitude toward school was a significant predictor of grades, achievement test scores, value placed on being a good student, and perceived competence. Patchen (1982) also found that students with peers who valued high achievement spent more time on homework, finished more of their homework assignments, attended school more regularly, were tardy less often, and missed class without permission fewer times.

Peers exert significant influence on students. Opportunities to interact with students who have high achievement motivation, positive attitudes toward school, and a positive academic self-concept are beneficial to students who are considered at risk or who require special or compensatory education programs. Mentoring programs, cooperative learning programs, cross-age tutoring, use of small learning groups, and extracurricular activities provide mechanisms for children and youth to develop positive peer relationships and stronger support networks that serve as a protective process to foster resilience.

CONCLUSION AND DISCUSSION

The meaning of the term *resilience* offers a provocative challenge to educational researchers and practitioners. In a single word, it can suggest several useful notions and priorities. For educators, the term *resilience* suggests the potential benefits of early experience; the need to mitigate adverse subsequent circumstances; and the importance of educationally important and alterable risk and protective factors in communities, homes, peer groups, schools, and classrooms. For educational researchers, it offers the intriguing hypothesis that early alterable (possibly sustained) conditions fortify students to persist successfully through inevitable and endemic difficulties.

The construct of resilience has been studied for nearly two decades by psychiatrists, clinical psychologists, developmental psychologists, and other mental health professionals. Originally, their research focused on identifying the characteristics and attributes of children who were resilient. Over time, the focus of this research shifted to determining the protective mechanisms and processes that foster resilience.

A parallel development emerged in educational research in the 1980s. Researchers began to recognize that, like children who beat the odds in the developmental psychopathology database, some schools have been more effective in achieving higher levels of learning success of their students than would be expected, given their multiple risk factors. These schools had high achievement gains despite serving impoverished families and communities with multiple adversities and few resources.

Much of the recent research, however, focuses on the influence of ethnicity and SES of at-risk students on their learning and school achievement, as well as ways that at-risk populations differ from the mainstream. Lee, Winfield, and Wilson (1991), for example, found family characteristics to be an important differentiating factor between low- and high-achieving African-American students. Using the National Assessment of Educational Progress (NAEP) data sets (U.S. Department of Education, 1991), they found that higher achieving African-American students tend to come from higher social classes, and a higher proportion of higher achieving students have working mothers. In addition, these students are twice as likely, compared to their low-achieving counterparts, to attend Catholic schools (10% vs. 5%), and are somewhat more likely to come from urban areas.

Although schools make significant efforts to "remediate" or "compensate" for poor academic performance, many at-risk students still experience serious difficulties in achieving learning success. They need better help than they are now receiving. The prototypical remedial or compensatory education program often contributes to children's learning problems. As noted by Wang, Reynolds, and Walberg (1988), substantial evidence shows that students may actually receive inferior instruction when schools provide them with specially designed programs to meet their greater-than-usual learning needs. In many cases, selecting and tracking students for instruction in "specially designed" programs, based on certain perceived student differences, involves delivering radically different and not always appropriate content to some students (Allington & Johnston, 1986; Haynes & Jenkins, 1986; Oakes, 1986). There is a tendency to neglect fundamental content in these special programs, and to provide less instruction in higher order, advanced skills. For example, students with special needs are most likely pulled out of the regular reading classroom and receive drills in phonics, word attack skills, and vocabulary, whereas advantaged students are exposed to reading instruction that emphasizes comprehension and related higher order thought processes.

Similar experiences occur in mathematics instruction for low-achieving students and those considered at risk of failing or dropping out of school. Comprehension, problem solving, and higher order reasoning are less often emphasized in the instruction of these children. Classroom observational studies document that these students experience less instruction on higher order skills than their advantaged counterparts (Oakes, 1986). Furthermore, teachers tend to underestimate what students with special needs or those considered at risk can do. They tend to delay the introduction of more challenging work and not provide students with a motivating context for learning (Knapp & Turnbull, 1990).

Research studies on resilience should focus on the complex interrelationships that characterize the development and functioning of resilient individuals, and interventions that foster such patterns of resilience. Lewis (1991) pointed to the need for a paradigm shift, away from research focusing on a single precipitating event and toward a focus on the interaction of a multitude of factors influencing behavior. Research should also take into account the context of the individual (ecological models), rather than ignore the context; use relative terms to describe behaviors, rather than traits or characteristics; specify underlying mechanisms that promote resilience, rather than identify a list of attributes of resilient children; and provide interpretation, including personal reflections, on the part of the children being followed, rather than depend only on objective assessments.

The rich research bases of developmental psychopathology and effective instruction and school effects can help identify educational practices that inspire and sustain achievement of all students, including and especially those considered to be at risk. The research bases can also help identify school/community connections that serve to mobilize resources, promote positive attitudes and behavior that strengthen the enabling role of families, and ensure student learning success. These lines of research point to characteristics of successful inner-city schools; the process by which unsuccessful inner-city schools are turned around; ways to create protective mechanisms and resources in inner cities to ensure student outcomes; and analysis of the schools' programs, climate, ethos, teachers, and other salient features, to determine biological, psychological, and environmental sources on resilience (National Center on Education in the Inner Cities, 1990).

New research that addresses the concern of factors influencing educational resilience and ways to foster educational resilience is beginning to emerge. It can develop a better understanding of student diversity by studying children who perform at the margins of achievement, and using sophisticated statistical techniques such as data envelopment analysis to identify efficient and effective schools. Along with research on resilient children and schools, there has also been an increase in research on the role of communities in fostering competence and resilience. New research studies aiming to better understand the ecology of cities point to the many factors—economic, political, and sociological—that influence inner-city educational outcomes. Attention is also being paid to ways to coordinate school and community services in order to make a more integrated network of resources and protective mechanisms available to children and their families.

Considerable educational research on school learning and other educational outcomes is consonant with the concept of resilience advanced in studies of developmental psychopathology. In the absence of definitive research, however, it may be reasonable for educators to focus on the implications of intervention studies that will provide direct evidence for understanding educational resilience and the mechanisms for fostering it. It seems imperative and urgent for researchers to probe the validity and extent of the idea over extended periods of time. By definition, resilience implies longitudinal studies of critical segments of the life course.

ACKNOWLEDGMENTS

The research reported in this chapter was supported in part by the Temple University Center for Research in Human Development and Education (CRHDE) and in part by the Office of Educational Research and Improvement (OERI) of the U.S. Department of Education through a grant to the National Center on Education in the Inner Cities (CEIC) at Temple University. The opinions expressed do not necessarily reflect the position of the supporting agencies and no official endorsement should be inferred.

REFERENCES

Allington, R. L., & Johnston, P. (1986). The coordination among regular classroom reading programs and targeted support programs. In B. I. Williams, P. A. Richmond, & B. J. Mason (Eds.), *Designs for compensatory education: Conference proceedings and papers* (Vol. 6, pp. 3–40). Washington, DC: Research and Evaluation Associates.

Bandura, A. (1977). Self-efficacy: Toward a unifying theory of behavioral change. *Psychological Review, 84*(2), 191–215.

Bandura, A. (1982). Self-efficacy mechanism in human agency. *American Psychologist, 37*, 122–148.

Bangert-Downs, R. (1988). The effects of school-based substance abuse education. *Journal of Drug Education, 18*(3), 1–9.

Bell, P. (1987). Community-based prevention. In *Proceedings of the National Conference on Alcohol and Drug Abuse Prevention: Sharing knowledge for action*. Washington, DC: NICA.

Benard, B. (1991). *Fostering resiliency in kids: Protective factors in the family, school and community*. Portland, OR: Northwest Regional Educational Laboratory.

Benard, B. (1992). *Mentoring programs for urban youth: Handle with care*. Portland, OR: Northwest Regional Educational Laboratory.

Bennett, L., Wolin, S., & Reiss, D. (1988). Cognitive, behavioral, and emotional problems among school-age children of alcoholic parents. *American Journal of Psychiatry, 145*(2), 185–190.

Boyd, W. L., & Walberg, H. J. (1990). *Contemporary educational issues series of the National Society for the Study of Education*. Berkeley, CA: McCutchan.

Brown, G. W., Harris, T. O., & Bifulco, A. (1986). The long-term effects of early loss of parent. In M. Rutter, C. E. Izard, & P. B. Read (Eds.), *Depression in young people* (pp. 251–296). New York: Guilford Press.

Campione, J., & Armbruster, B. (1985). Acquiring information from texts: An analysis of four approaches. In J. Segal, S. Chipman, & R. Glaser (Eds.), *Thinking and learning skills: Relating instruction to research* (Vol. 1, pp. 317–359). Hillsdale, NJ: Lawrence Erlbaum Associates.

Carnegie Foundation for the Advancement of Teaching. (1988). *An imperiled generation: Saving urban schools*. Princeton, NJ: Author.

Cauce, A. (1986). Social networks and social competence: Exploring the effects of early adolescent friendships. *American Journal of Community Psychology, 14*, 607–628.

Chan, Y. (1987). *Parents: The missing link in educational reform*. Prepared statement presented before the House Select Committee on Children, Youth, and Families, Indianapolis, IN.

Chess, S. (1989). Defying the voice of doom. In T. Dugan & R. Coles (Eds.), *The child in our times* (pp. 179–199). New York: Brunner Mazel.

Chess, S., & Thomas, A. (1990). Continuities and discontinuities in temperament. In L. Robins & M. Rutter (Eds.), *Straight and devious pathways from childhood to adulthood* (pp. 205–220). New York: Cambridge University Press.

Cicchetti, D. (1990). A historical perspective on the discipline of developmental psychopathology. In J. Rolf, A. S. Masten, D. Cicchetti, K. H. Nuechterlein, & S. Weintraub (Eds.), *Risk and protective factors in the development of psychopathology* (pp. 2–28). New York: Cambridge University Press.

Clark, M. (1991). Social identity, peer relations, and academic competence of African-American adolescents. *Education and Urban Society, 24*(1), 41–52.

Coleman, J. S., & Hoffer, T. (1987). *Public and private high schools: The impact of communities*. New York: Basic Books.

Collins, A., Brown, J. S., & Newman, S. (1990). Cognitive apprenticeship: Teaching students the craft of reading, writing, and mathematics. In L. B. Resnick (Ed.), *Knowing, learning, and instruction: Essays in honor of Robert Glaser* (pp. 453–494). Hillsdale, NJ: Lawrence Erlbaum Associates.

Comer, J. P. (1986). Parent participation in the schools. *Phi Delta Kappan, 67*(6), 442–446.

Corno, L., & Snow, R. E. (1986). Adapting teaching to individual differences among learners. In M. C. Wittrock (Ed.), *Handbook of research on teaching* (3rd ed., pp. 605–629). New York: Macmillan.

Cruickshank, D. R. (1990). *Research that informs teachers and teacher educators*. Bloomington, IN: Phi Delta Kappan Educational Foundation.

Dworkin, A. G. (1987). *Teacher burnout in the public schools: Structural causes and consequences for children*. Albany: State University of New York Press.

Epstein, J. L. (1984, April). *Effects of parent involvement on change in student achievement in reading and math*. Paper presented at the annual meeting of the American Educational Research Association, New Orleans, LA.

Epstein, J. L. (1987). Toward a theory of family-school connections: Teacher practices and parent involvement. In K. Hurrelmann, F. Kaufmann, & F. Losel (Eds.), *Social intervention: Potential and constraints* (pp. 121–136). New York: W. De Gruyler.

Feurstein, R. (1980). *Instrumental enrichment: An intervention program for cognitive modifiability*. Baltimore: University of Maryland.

Flaxman, E., & Inger, M. (1991). Parents and schooling in the 1990s. *The ERIC Review, 1*(3), 2-6.

Fowler, W. J., & Walberg, H. J. (1991). School size, characteristics, and outcomes. *Educational Evaluation and Policy Analysis, 13*, 189-202.

Freiberg, H. J. (1989). Multidimensional view of school effectiveness. *Educational Research Quarterly, 13*(2), 35-46.

Garmezy, N. (1974, August). *The study of children at risk: New perspectives for developmental psychopathology.* Paper presented at the 82nd annual meeting of the American Psychological Association, New Orleans, LA.

Garmezy, N. (1985). Stress resistant children: The search for protective factors. In J. Stevenson (Ed.), *Recent research in developmental psychopathology: Journal of Child Psychology and Psychiatry book* (Suppl. No. 4, pp. 213-233). Oxford, England: Pergamon Press.

Garmezy, N. (1991). Resiliency and vulnerability to adverse developmental outcomes associated with poverty. *American Behavioral Scientist, 34*(4), 416-430.

Goldstein, M. J. (1990). Factors in the development of schizophrenia and other severe psychopathology in late adolescence and adulthood. In J. Rolf, A. S. Masten, D. Cicchetti, K. H. Nuechterlein, & S. Weintraub (Eds.), *Risk and protective factors in the development of psychopathology* (pp. 408-423). New York: Cambridge University Press.

Good, T. L., & Brophy, J. E. (1986). School effects. In M. C. Wittrock (Ed.), *Handbook of research on teaching* (3rd ed., pp. 570-602). New York: Macmillan.

Graue, M. E., Weinstein, T., & Walberg, H. J. (1983). School-based home instruction and learning: A quantitative synthesis. *Journal of Educational Research, 76*, 351-360.

Haynes, M. C., & Jenkins, J. R. (1986). Reading instruction in special education resource rooms. *American Educational Research Journal, 23*(2), 161-190.

Hill, P. T., Wise, A. E., & Shapiro, L. (1989). *Educational progress: Cities mobilize to improve their schools.* Santa Monica, CA: Rand Corporation, Center for the Study of the Teaching Profession.

Holtzman, W. H. (1991, August). *Psychology in the school of the future: Community renewal, family preservation and child development.* Paper presented at the annual convention of the American Psychological Association, San Francisco, CA.

Iverson, B. K., & Walberg, H. J. (1982). Home environment and school learning: A quantitative synthesis. *Journal of Experimental Education, 50*, 144-151.

Kirst, M. W., & McLaughlin, M. (1990). Rethinking policy for children: Implications for educational administration. In B. Mitchell & L. L. Cunningham (Eds.), *Educational leadership and changing contexts of families, communities, and schools: The eighty-ninth yearbook of the National Society for the Study of Education* (Part 2, pp. 69-90). Chicago: University of Chicago Press.

Knapp, M. S., & Turnbull, B. J. (1990). *Better schooling for the children of poverty: Alternatives to conventional wisdom. Vol. 1: Summary.* Washington, DC: U.S. Department of Education.

Lash, A. A., & Kirkpatrick, S. L. (1990). *New perspectives on student mobility* (Contract No. R117E80041). Washington, DC: Office of Educational Research and Improvement, U.S. Department of Education.

Lee, V. E., Winfield, L. F., & Wilson, T. C. (1991). Academic behaviors among high-achieving African-American students. *Education and Urban Society, 24*(1), 65-86.

Lefkowitz, B. (1986). *Tough change: Growing up on your own in America.* New York: The Free Press.

Lewis, E. M. (1991). *Risk and resiliency: A theoretical review.* Unpublished manuscript.

Liddle, H. A. (1991). Engaging adolescents in family systems therapy: Some early phase skills. In T. Nelson (Ed.), *101 interventions in family therapy* (pp. 389-398). New York: Haworth.

Long, L. H. (1975). Does migration interfere with children's progress in school? *Sociology of Education, 45*, 369-381.

Long, J. V. F., & Vaillant, G. (1989). Escape from the underclass. In T. Dugan & R. Coles (Eds.), *The child in our times* (pp. 200-213). New York: Brunner Mazel.

Masten, A. S., Best, K. M., & Garmezy, N. (1990). Resilience and development: Contributions from the study of children who overcome adversity. *Development and Psychopathology, 2*, 425-444.

Masten, A. S., Morison, P., Pelligrini, D., & Tellegen, A. (1990). Competence under stress: Risk and protective factors. In J. Rolf, A. S. Masten, D. Cicchetti, K. H. Nuechterlein, & S. Weintraub (Eds.), *Risk and protective factors in the development of psychopathology* (pp. 236–256). New York: Cambridge University Press.

Maton, K. (1990). Meaningful involvement in instrumental activity and well-being: Studies of older adolescents and at-risk urban teenagers. *American Journal of Community Psychology, 18*(2), 297–320.

Maughan, B. (1988). School experiences as risk protective factors. In M. Rutter (Ed.), *Studies of psychosocial risk: The power of longitudinal data* (pp. 200–220). London: Cambridge University Press.

Means, B., & Knapp, M. S. (Eds.). (1991). *Teaching advanced skills to educationally disadvantaged students* (Final Report, Contract No. LC89089001). Washington, DC: U.S. Department of Education.

Miller, A., & Ohlin, L. (1985). *Delinquency and community: Creating opportunities and controls.* Beverly Hills, CA: Sage.

Moles, O. C. (1982, November). Synthesis of recent research on parent participation in children's education. *Educational Leadership, 40*(2), 44–47.

Murnane, R. J. (1975). *The impact of school resources on the learning of inner-city children.* Cambridge: Ballinger.

National Center on Education in the Inner Cities. (1990). *Center for education in the inner cities: A technical proposal.* Philadelphia, PA: Temple University Center for Research in Human Development and Education.

Nettles, S. M. (1991). Community contributions to school outcomes of African-American students. *Education and Urban Society, 24*(1), 132–147.

Newcomb, M., & Bentler, P. (1990). Drug use, educational aspirations, and involvement: The transition from adolescence to young adulthood. *American Journal of Community Psychology, 14*(3), 303–321.

Noddings, N. (1988, December 7). Schools face crisis in caring. *Education Week*, p. 32.

Oakes, J. (1986). Tracking, inequality, and the rhetoric of school reform: Why schools don't change. *Journal of Education, 168*, 61–80.

O'Dougherty, M., & Wright, F. S. (1990). Children born at medical risk: Factors affecting vulnerability and resilience. In J. Rolf, A. S. Masten, D. Cicchetti, K. H. Nuechterlein, & S. Weintraub (Eds.), *Risk and protective factors in the development of psychopathology* (pp. 120–140). New York: Cambridge University Press.

Ogbu, J. U. (1992). Understanding cultural diversity and learning. *Educational Researcher, 21*(8), 5–14.

Palincsar, A. S., & Klenk, L. J. (1991). Learning dialogues to promote text comprehension. In B. Means & M. S. Knapp (Eds.), *Teaching advanced skills to educationally disadvantaged students* (Final Report, Contract No. LC89089001, pp. 21–34). Washington, DC: U.S. Department of Education.

Patchen, M. (1982). *Black–White contact in schools: Its social and academic effects.* West Lafayette, IN: Purdue University Press.

Peng, S. S., & Lee, R. M. (1991). *Home variables that make a difference: A study of 1988 eighth graders.* Unpublished manuscript, Temple University Center for Research in Human Development and Education, Philadelphia, PA.

Peng, S. S., Lee, R. M., Wang, M. C., & Walberg, H. J. (1991). *Resilient students in urban settings.* Unpublished manuscript, Temple University Center for Research in Human Development and Education, Philadelphia, PA.

Peng, S. S., Weishew, N., & Wang, M. C. (1991). *High-achieving schools in disadvantaged communities: What are their attributes?* Unpublished manuscript, Temple University Center for Research in Human Development and Education, Philadelphia, PA.

Peterson, D. (1989). *Parent involvement in the educational process.* Urbana, IL: ERIC Clearinghouse on Educational Management, University of Illinois. (ED 312 776)

Pianta, R. C., Egeland, B., & Sroufe, L. A. (1990). Maternal stress and children's development: Prediction of school outcomes and identification of protective factors. In J. Rolf, A. S. Masten, D. Cicchetti, K. H. Nuechterlein, & S. Weintraub (Eds.), *Risk and protective factors in the development of psychopathology* (pp. 215–235). New York: Cambridge University Press.

Reynolds, M. C. (1982). *Foundations of teacher preparation: Responses to Public Law 94-142.* Washington, DC: American Association of Colleges for Teacher Education.

Rolf, J., Masten, A. S., Cicchetti, D., Nuechterlein, K. H., & Weintraub, S. (Eds.). (1990). *Risk and protective factors in the development of psychopathology.* New York: Cambridge University Press.

Rutter, M. (1966). *Children of sick parents: An environmental and psychiatric study* (Maudsley Monograph No. 16). London: Oxford University Press.

Rutter, M. (1979a). *Fifteen thousand hours.* Cambridge, MA: Harvard University Press.

Rutter, M. (1979b). Protective factors in children's responses to stress and disadvantage. In M. W. Kent & J. E. Rolf (Eds.), *Primary prevention of psychopathology. Vol. 3: Social competence in children* (pp. 49–74). Hanover, NH: University Press of New England.

Rutter, M. (1987). Parental mental disorder as a psychiatric risk factor. In R. E. Hales & A. J. Frances (Eds.), *American Psychiatric Association annual review* (Vol. 6, pp. 647–663). Washington, DC: American Psychological Association.

Rutter, M. (1990). Psychosocial resilience and protective mechanisms. In J. Rolf, A. S. Masten, D. Cicchetti, K. H. Nuechterlein, & S. Weintraub (Eds.), *Risk and protective factors in the development of psychopathology* (pp. 181–214). New York: Cambridge University Press.

Seligman, M. (1991). *Learned optimism.* New York: Pocket Books.

Slavin, R., & Madden, N. (1989). What works for students at risk: A research synthesis. *Educational Leadership, 46,* 4–13.

Straits, B. C. (1987). Residence, migration, and school progress. *Sociology of Education, 60,* 34–43.

Straus, M. (1983). Ordinary violence, child abuse and wife beating: What do they have in common? In D. Finkelhor, R. Gelles, G. Hotaling, & M. Straus (Eds.), *The dark side of families: Current family violence research* (pp. 213–234). Beverly Hills, CA: Sage.

Stringfield, S., & Teddlie, C. (1991). Schools as affecters of teacher effects. In H. C. Waxman & H. J. Walberg (Eds.), *Effective teaching: Current research* (pp. 161–179). Berkeley, CA: McCutchan.

Swanson, D. P., & Spencer, M. B. (1991). Youth policy, poverty, and African-Americans: Implications for resilience. *Education and Urban Society, 24*(1), 148–161.

Teddlie, C., Kirby, P., & Stringfield, S. (1989). Effective versus ineffective schools: Observable differences in the classroom. *American Journal of Education, 97*(5), 221–236.

U.S. Department of Commerce. (1987). *Geographic mobility: 1985* (Current Population Reports, Series P20, No. 420). Washington, DC: U.S. Government Printing Office.

U.S. Department of Education. (1986). *What works: Research about teaching and learning.* Washington, DC: Author.

U.S. Department of Education. (1988). *National education longitudinal study.* Washington, DC: Author.

U.S. Department of Education. (1991). *National assessment of educational progress: The nation's report card.* Washington, DC: Author.

van de Grift, W. (1990). Educational leadership and academic achievement in elementary education. *School Effectiveness and School Achievement, 1,* 26–40.

Walberg, H. J. (1984). Families as partners in educational productivity. *Phi Delta Kappan, 65,* 397–400.

Wallerstein, J. (1983). Children of divorce: The psychological tasks of the child. *American Journal of Ortho-Psychiatry, 53*(2), 230–243.

Wang, M. C. (1990). Programs that promote educational equity. In H. C. Waxman, P. Baptiste, J. Anderson, & J. Walker de Felix (Eds.), *Leadership, equity, and school effectiveness.* Newbury Park, CA: Sage.

Wang, M. C. (1991, August). *The School of the Future: A demonstration project in four Texas cities with financial and technical support of the Hogg Foundation for Mental Health.* Presentation at the annual convention of the American Psychological Association, San Francisco, CA.

Wang, M. C., Haertel, G. D., & Walberg, H. J. (1990). What influences learning? A content analysis of review literature. *Journal of Education Research, 84*(1), 30–43.

Wang, M. C., Haertel, G. D., & Walberg, H. J. (1992, October). *The effectiveness of collaborative school-linked services.* Paper presented at the CEIC School/Community Connections Conference, Leesburg, VA.

Wang, M. C., Haertel, G. D., & Walberg, H. J. (in press). Toward a knowledge base for school learning. *Review of Educational Research.*

Wang, M. C., & Palincsar, A. S. (1989). Teaching students to assume an active role in their learning. In M. C. Reynolds (Ed.), *Knowledge base for the beginning teacher* (pp. 71–84). Oxford, England: Pergamon Press.

Wang, M. C., Reynolds, M. C., & Walberg, H. J. (1988). Integrating the children of the second system. *Phi Delta Kappan, 70*(3), 248–251.

Wang, M. C., & Walberg, H. J. (Eds.). (1985). *Adapting instruction to individual differences.* Berkeley, CA: McCutchan.

Watt, N. F., Anthony, E. J., Wynne, L. C., & Rolf, J. (Eds.). (1984). *Children at risk for schizophrenia: A longitudinal perspective.* New York: Cambridge University Press.

Watt, N. F., Moorehead-Slaughter, O., Japzon, D. M., & Keller, G. G. (1990). Children's adjustment to parental divorce: Self-image, social relations, and school performance. In J. Rolf, A. S. Masten, D. Cicchetti, K. H. Nuechterlein, & S. Weintraub (Eds.), *Risk and protective factors in the development of psychopathology* (pp. 281–304). New York: Cambridge University Press.

Weikart, D. P., Epstein, A. S., Schweinhart, L., & Bond, J. T. (1978). *The Ypsilanti Preschool Curriculum Demonstration Project: Preschool years and longitudinal results.* Ypsilanti, MI: Monographs of the High/Scope Educational Research Foundation.

Werner, E. (1989, April). Children of the garden island. *Scientific American*, pp. 107–111.

Werner, E., & Smith, R. (1982). *Vulnerable but invincible: A longitudinal study of resilient children and youth.* New York: Adams, Bannister, & Cox.

Williams, B. I., Richmond, P. A., & Mason, B. J. (1986). *Designs for compensatory education: Conference proceedings and papers.* Washington, DC: Research and Evaluation Associates.

Winne, P. H. (1991). Motivation and teaching. In H. C. Waxman & H. J. Walberg (Eds.), *Effective teaching: Current research* (pp. 295–314). Berkeley, CA: McCutchan.

Chapter 4

Understanding Resilient Students: The Use of National Longitudinal Databases

Samuel S. Peng*
National Center for Education Statistics,
U.S. Department of Education

BACKGROUND AND PURPOSE

Studies of child development and learning have often revealed that many children from stressful environments thrive unexpectedly well in school and career development (Rolf, Masten, Cicchetti, Nuechterlein, & Weintraub, 1990; Rutter, 1984, 1990; Werner, 1989). This phenomenon, known as resilience, has drawn increasing attention from educational researchers as a viable new discipline that might enhance our understanding of at-risk students and help us find ways to mitigate the effect of risks and adversities. As Winfield (1991) noted, ''In order to move beyond simply identifying and categorizing youth at risk, the focus must necessarily shift to understanding the notion of resilience. . . . The critical issues for policy and instruction center around identifying the protective processes and mechanisms that reduce risk and foster resilience'' (p. 7).

Resilience is, however, a complex construct. Studies have found that some individuals are more resilient than others to adverse environments. These individuals have tendencies that enable them to adeptly resist negative influences with little external assistance, and to easily win the affection of others that results in greater opportunities for learning (Werner & Smith, 1982). Studies also have found that vulnerable children with support networks of parents, grandparents, neighbors, or relatives are able to escape from adversities without lasting harm (Werner & Smith, 1982). Furthermore, research has found that students from economically distressed families tend to do better in schools where learning

---

*The opinions expressed in this chapter are the author's. No endorsement from the U.S. Department of Education should be inferred.

is emphasized and teachers encourage students to do their best (Peng, Lee, Wang, & Walberg, 1992). Thus, studies of resilience require comprehensive, longitudinal, and integrated data about families, schools, and their communities.

Such comprehensive data are difficult to obtain, particularly data with a national perspective. They take time and resources to collect, and resources may be a problem for many researchers. Thus, researchers may need to look for existing national databases and make creative use of them. In recent years, the National Center for Education Statistics (NCES) of the U.S. Department of Education has produced several rich national databases about students and their families and schools. These databases offer valuable resources for researchers to examine the concept of resilience.

The purpose of this chapter is to describe these databases and to illustrate their potential use in identifying resilient students and related factors. The chapter is structured into three major sections: (a) the nature of the databases, (b) their potential use in resilience studies, and (c) an illustration of the analytic use of a national database.

NATIONAL DATABASES

NCES has provided a number of student-based data systems for public use (Nelson, 1991). Among them are two longitudinal studies: High School and Beyond (HS&B) and the National Educational Longitudinal Study of 1988 (NELS:88). Figure 4.1 shows the time span by year in school and age for these two data systems.

High School and Beyond

HS&B involved two cohorts of participants, sophomores and seniors in 1980. A national probability sample of 1,015 high schools was drawn, and up to 36 sophomores and 36 seniors were randomly selected in each school for the study. The realized sample sizes were about 30,000 sophomores and 28,000 seniors. The base-year data were collected from these students in 1980. The first follow-up survey, conducted in 1982, reduced the sophomore sample to 27,000 students and the senior sample to 12,000 students. The second follow-up survey further reduced the sophomore sample to 15,000 students. Additional follow-up surveys were conducted in 1986 for both cohorts, and in 1992 for the sophomore cohort.

In the base-year survey, students were asked to take a series of cognitive tests and to complete a questionnaire that tapped information about student background and school experience. A sample of parents from both cohorts was

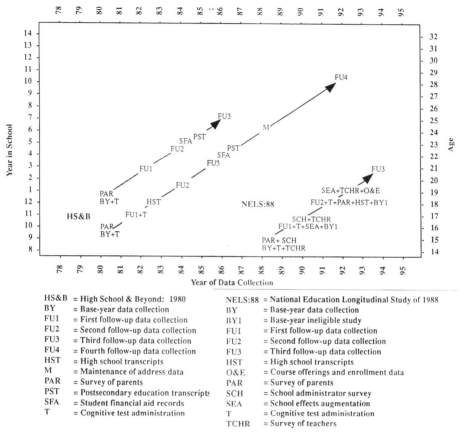

FIG. 4.1.   Research design for HS&B and NELS:88 (*Source:* Ingels et al., 1990, Figure 1-2, p. 4).

also asked to fill out a parent questionnaire that provided information about home environment. In addition, teachers provided comments on the sampled students through the use of a check list, and a school official provided information about school programs. In the first follow-up survey, the entire sophomore sample was retested in their schools, and special efforts were made to track transfers, dropouts, and early graduates. Moreover, additional educational experience in secondary schools over 2 years was collected for the sophomore cohort. In the subsequent second and third follow-up surveys, students were asked to provide information about their educational, occupational, and personal development and related factors. Persistent tracking and follow-ups of nonrespondents yielded a high completion rate, more than 90% in each wave of data collection. Detailed information about this database is presented in the *Data File User's Manual* (National Center for Education Statistics, 1987).

National Education Longitudinal Study of 1988

NELS:88 is more comprehensive than HS&B in content coverage and student populations. It began with an eighth-grade student cohort with planned follow-ups at 2-year intervals. The base-year survey was completed in 1988 with a national sample of 24,599 eighth graders from 1,052 participating schools. Like HS&B, NELS:88 collected background information and educational experience from students and their parents through a questionnaire survey. It also collected data about the characteristics and programs of schools attended by the sampled students. Moreover, students were asked to take curriculum-based achievement tests in reading, mathematics, science, and social studies, and each student was rated by two teachers.

Similar data were collected from the sampled students who were still in school 2 and 4 years later, in 1990 and 1992, in the first and second follow-up surveys. Students were retested at both times to measure academic growth. For those who dropped out of school, a separate questionnaire was used to collect information about their occupational and personal development and related factors. Like HS&B, NELS:88 had a high response rate, more than 90% in each survey. Detailed information about the design of the study can be found in the NELS:88 student component *Data File User's Manual* (Ingels, Abraham, Karr, Spencer, & Frankel, 1990).

POTENTIAL USE OF HS&B AND NELS:88 DATA IN RESILIENCE STUDIES

Both HS&B and NELS:88 have provided comprehensive data that are useful for addressing issues of resilience. Specifically, they are useful for exploring various constructs of resilience and formulating hypotheses for in-depth field studies to identify factors that foster resilience.

Exploring Constructs of Resilience

Resilience reflects an individual's successful coping with stressful environments. Such environments may be defined in terms of family in poverty (e.g., low income, unemployment), unstable family (e.g., single parent), low parental education, and economically deprived communities (e.g., inner city, a high percentage of students in free or reduced-price lunch or in Chapter 1 programs). HS&B and NELS:88 have data on such variables and allow researchers to examine the impact of the different stresses and difficulties faced by students.

HS&B and NELS:88 also have rich data on student characteristics and performance. In addition to demographic variables such as gender, age, and race-ethnicity, there are measures of students' self-concept, locus of control, life goals, attitudes toward learning, educational aspirations, and career aspirations. There are also measures of grade point average, achievement test scores, problem behaviors (e.g., use of drugs and alcohol, trouble with the law), misbehavior (e.g., tardiness, unexcused absences), courses taken in high school, classroom behaviors as rated by teachers, educational attainment (e.g., dropping out, completion of high school, entering college, completion of college, etc.), and employment status. Using these variables, different ways of measuring student successes can be explored. For example, some may define resilience on the basis of academic achievement. Others may define resilience on the basis of successful completion of high school, attainment of post-high school education, gainful employment, and/or family formation.

Furthermore, the longitudinal nature of the databases allows researchers to observe sustained positive behaviors, or a consistent success, over a period of time. For example, one may define a resilient student as one who maintains high achievement from the 8th through the 12th grades, because both the HS&B sophomore cohort and NELS:88 have test scores at multiple points in time. One may also define a resilient student as one who resided in an inner city with a broken family and in poverty but completed high school and proceeded to achieve higher education, gainful employment, and a normal family. Similarly, one may define a resilient student as one who maintains stable employment over several years after high school graduation.

Identifying Factors of Resilience

HS&B and NELS:88 include data on parents, families, peers, schools, teachers, and communities that can be used to identify potential factors of resilience. Specifically, the following data are available:

1. Measures of peer network, including friends' educational plans and peers' self-perceptions.

2. Family support and home environment, including parent education, occupation, and income; family composition (e.g., both parents, single parent, etc.); family size; communication with parents; learning materials at home; parental assistance in schoolwork; parents' educational expectations for children; learning activities at home; educational attainment of siblings and other family members; family rules for study and TV watching; child supervision after school; and predominant language used at home.

3. School and teacher supports, including school climate, course requirements, remedial programs, school socioeconomic status (SES; percentage of students in free or reduced-price lunch program), percentage racial-ethnic minority, percentage language minority, extra-class activities, counseling services, instructional practices, and teacher relationships with students.

4. Community characteristics, including urbanization (rural, suburban, urban) and economic conditions (e.g., percentage of students in free or reduced-price lunch or in Chapter 1 programs, percentage of parents unemployed).

Data on these variables provide a basis for testing relationships between environmental factors and student resilience. These relationships may shed some light on the protective process of individuals at risk, and they may formulate additional hypotheses to be tested with in-depth observational data that are generally not obtained by a large national survey.

AN ILLUSTRATION

The following example illustrates one use of the base-year survey data of NELS:88 in studying student resilience, involving student attributes, family support, school environment, and community type. The purpose of the analysis is to examine the differences in resilience rates under various environments, which in turn provide a basis for formulating hypotheses about the varying environmental impacts on fostering resilience. The process and results of the analysis are described here.

Variable Specifications

Resilience.   Previous studies have found that students from families of low SES are most likely to have low achievement scores and a high dropout rate; thus, low SES is frequently considered a major factor for students at risk. As SES in this study is a composite measure of family income, parental education, parental occupation, and household items, low SES reflects several or all of the following conditions: low income, low parental education level, low level of occupation, and few household items. In comparison to other students, students with a low SES background may feel deprived because of limited resources available at home. Also, because they are also more likely to live in a less friendly community, they are subject to more negative influences and face more challenges and difficulties. Nevertheless, some students with such backgrounds still performed very well in school; their combined reading and mathematics scores placed them in the highest quartile of all students. These students were considered resilient in this analysis.

Student Attributes.   These were measured by a composite consisting of educational aspirations, self-esteem, and the locus of control. A higher self-esteem score means a more positive and optimistic personality or attitude, and a higher score on the locus of control means more self-control and self-reliance. These three scores were each standardized first, using the population mean and standard deviation. Then they were summed with educational aspirations and the locus of control, both having a weight of 2, and self-esteem, having a weight of 1. The weighted sum of these scores divided by 5 was the composite measure of student attributes. The choice of weights was based on the findings of a study by Peng et al. (1992) that educational aspirations and the locus of control are twice as important as self-esteem in relation to student achievement. It was assumed in this study that students with a high score on this composite were more goal-oriented and self-reliant and internally stronger than students with a low score, and therefore more resistent to negative influences.

Family Support.   Family support was measured by a composite of the following four components: conversation with parents, learning materials at home, parental educational expectations for children, and learning activities provided by parents. Each of these components was a composite derived from a set of related items (see Peng & Lee, 1992). Each component measure was standardized with the population mean and standard deviation. The average of these scores, with educational expectations and conversation with parents having a weight of 2, and the other two components a weight of 1, was the measure of family support. A high score on this variable means the family is highly supportive.

School Environment.   This variable was measured by a simple composite of two items: whether teachers encouraged students to do their best, and whether learning was emphasized in school (Peng, Weishew, & Wang, 1991). Again, the component scores were standardized with the population mean and standard deviation. A high score on this variable indicates the school is highly supportive of student learning.

Community Type.   Communities were classified into three types: urban, suburban, and rural. An urban community is a large central city; a suburban community is the area surrounding a central city, within a county constituting the Metropolitan Statistical Area (MSA); and a rural community is the area outside of the MSA.

Analysis Procedure

In this analysis, resilience rates were computed for students with different attributes and family and school backgrounds in the three different types of communities. As mentioned earlier, the analysis involved only low SES students, and those students with achievement scores in the fourth (highest) quartile were classified as resilient students. Student attributes, family support, and school environment were all grouped into two categories: high and low, using the population mean as the criterion. Students with scores above the mean were in the high group; others were in the low group.

Resilience rates by student attributes, family support, school environment, and community type were calculated. In this calculation, sampling weights were used to obtain unbiased estimates, because students were selected with unequal probabilities. Sampling weights are the inverse of selection probabilities, adjusted for nonresponse (see Ingels et al., 1990).

Results of Analysis

Table 4.1 presents results for all possible combinations of student attributes, family support, and school environment categories (i.e., models) in each community type. The resilience rates range from 3% for urban students with low attributes and low family and school supports to 34% for suburban students with high attributes and high family and school supports. The results reveal a clear pattern that confirms previous research findings: Individual attributes and the family, school, and community factors, as well as the different combinations of these factors, all suggest differential impacts on student resilience rates.

The results of this analysis offer a practical basis for forming hypotheses for future research on the process of fostering resilience. Several hypotheses about the process of fostering resilience are discussed here.

> Hypothesis 1: Students with high personal attributes have a high resilience rate even when their family and school supports are low. These students are also more likely to be resilient than students with low attributes under similar circumstances.

This hypothesis is primarily based on the comparison between Models 1 and 5 (4.11% vs. 12.79% resilience rate). Model 1 denotes students who were low in student attributes as well as family and school support, while Model 5 denotes students with high student attributes but low family and school support. High student attributes in Model 5 may not necessarily be the product of school and family factors, because both school and family are low in their support to students. Model 5 students are likely to be those "lucky" ones that are able to thrive even in a very adverse environment. This indicates the presence of individual differences in dealing with adversary circumstances, and the importance of certain individual characteristics in protecting students from an environment's negative influence.

This hypothesis is also based on the differences between Models 6 and 2, Models 7 and 3, and Models 8 and 4—all suggest that students with high personal attributes have higher resilience rates than students with low attributes

TABLE 4.1

Percentage of Low Socioeconomic Students With Combined Reading
and Mathematics Scores in the Fourth Quartile of the Population

	Attribute			Sample Size			Percentage		
Model	Student	Family	School	Urban	Suburban	Rural	Urban	Suburban	Rural	Average
1	Low	Low	Low	899	977	1,195	3.01	4.90	4.43	4.11
2	Low	Low	High	377	504	619	3.93	6.22	5.08	5.08
3	Low	High	Low	224	285	257	7.34	14.44	16.58	12.79
4	Low	High	High	131	176	125	12.21	14.19	17.03	14.48
5	High	Low	Low	385	453	443	6.80	12.63	18.94	12.79
6	High	Low	High	219	236	242	11.46	16.93	20.62	16.34
7	High	High	Low	473	555	499	15.54	28.17	24.38	22.70
8	High	High	High	345	370	279	24.47	33.80	31.85	30.04
Average							10.60	16.41	17.36	14.79

Source: Base-year data of the National Education Longitudinal Study of eighth graders in 1988 (NELS:88), the National Center for Education Statistics, U.S. Department of Education.

when family, school, and community environments are considered. These comparisons also suggest that students with high personal attributes will greatly benefit from school and family support. As shown by the difference between Models 6 and 2 and between Models 8 and 4, students with high attributes can benefit more significantly from schools than students with low attributes, probably because they are more likely to use the learning opportunities and resources available in the school.

Questions of interest for future research are: What are the typical personal attributes of resilient students? Can such personal attributes as sunny personalities, high self-esteem, and a strong sense of identity and goal orientation, be nurtured by educational programs and/or by certain types of family practices? Answers to these questions will be valuable for finding ways to foster student resilience.

Hypothesis 2: Family support has a stronger impact on students than school environment in fostering resilience.

This hypothesis is based on the comparisons between Models 3 and 2, and between Models 7 and 6. Both Models 3 and 7 denote students with high family but low school support, while Models 2 and 6 denote students with low family but high school support. The percentages of resilient students are 12.79 versus 5.08 and 22.7 versus 16.34, respectively, for these two comparisons. Several other comparisons also reveal the pattern of the differential impact of family and school on resilience. For example, the difference in resilience rate between Models 1 and 2 (i.e., school effect) is smaller than the difference between Models 1 and 3 (i.e., family effect). Similarly, the difference in resilience rate between Models 3 and 4 (i.e., school effect) is smaller than the difference between Models 2 and 4 (i.e., family effect).

Findings on this hypothesis will further confirm the importance of families in bringing up healthy children who can benefit greatly from schools. Such findings will certainly not be new to researchers, but they will further support the effort for parental education as an effective way to improve the nation's education. Without strong family support, the effect of school is limited or greatly reduced. Thus, we need to know more about the kind of family characteristics and practices that foster resilience, so that we can develop programs to help parents become effective.

Hypothesis 3: Among students of similar attributes, the resilience rate is highest when both family and school are supportive.

This hypothesis is based on the patterns shown by the data, that Model 4 students have higher percentages than students in Models 1, 2, and 3, and that Model 8 students have higher percentages than students in Models 5, 6, and 7. Both Models 4 and 8 have high family and school supports. These patterns suggest that family and school jointly have a greater influence on students than either one independently, within each type of community, suggesting it is important for schools and families to be congruent in their educational expectations and practices. The incongruence between the school and the family is a major problem in the education of inner-city schools. Solving this problem could improve student learning.

Hypothesis 4: Vulnerable students (i.e., students with low personal attributes) could be successful in learning if their family and/or school were supportive.

This hypothesis is based on the comparison between Model 1 and Models 2, 3, and 4. The resilience rates increased from 4.11%, when both family and school supports were low (Model l), to 14.48% when those supports were high (Model 4). The pattern is consistent across community types.

Findings on this hypothesis would be very encouraging and welcome, because they would indicate that vulnerable students are not beyond help. A major challenge to educators is finding ways to help families and schools become more supportive to these students.

Hypothesis 5: Students with similar personal attributes and family and school support perform better in suburban and rural communities than in urban ones.

This hypothesis is based on the comparisons within each model and across models among the three community types. As shown in the row total (i.e., across models), the resilience rates are 16.41%, 17.36%, and 10.6%, respectively, for students in the suburban, rural, and urban communities. A similar pattern exists in each row (i.e., within a model) to suggest that certain characteristics in rural and suburban communities are helping students. What then are the characteristics of a community that helps foster resilience? Do suburban and rural communities foster resilience more because they have more homogeneous or consistent social and cultural norms than urban communities, so that their students understand better what constitutes desirable behavior, as suggested by the Western Regional Center for Drug-Free Schools and Communities (1991)? Or is it because they have fewer negative influences, temptations, and distractions that create additional stresses on students? Findings on this hypothesis will further confirm the value of studies of community characteristics, and they may reveal the kind of resources needed for helping children in urban communities.

ACCESS TO NATIONAL DATABASES

The national databases have been released for public use in several formats for mainframe computers and personal computers (PCs). They can be obtained from NCES in computer tapes, diskettes, or CD ROMs in SAS, SPSS or AS-CII forms. The data files have been well documented and explained. For more information, one can write to Longitudinal Studies Branch, the National Center for Education Statistics, 555 New Jersey Avenue, NW, Washington, DC 20208-5654.

REFERENCES

Ingels, S. J., Abraham, S. Y., Karr, R., Spencer, B. D., & Frankel, M. R. (1990). *Data file user's manual: National Educational Longitudinal Study of 1988*. Washington, DC: National Center for Education Statistics, U.S. Department of Education.

National Center for Education Statistics. (1987). *High School and Beyond 1980 sophomore cohort third follow-up (1986): Data file user's manual*. Washington, DC: U.S. Department of Education.

Nelson, D. D. (1991). *Programs and plans of the National Center for Education Statistics*. Washington, DC: U.S. Government Printing Office.

Peng, S. D., & Lee, R. M. (1992, April). *Home variables, parent-child activities, and academic achievement: A study of 1998 eighth graders*. Paper presented at the annual meeting of the American Educational Research Association, San Francisco, CA.

Peng, S. S., Lee, R. M., Wang, M. C., & Walberg, H. J. (1992, April). *Resilient students in urban settings*. Paper presented at the annual meeting of the American Educational Research Association, San Francisco, CA.

Peng, S. S., Weishew, N., & Wang, M. C. (1991). *High-achieving schools in disadvantaged communities: What are their attributes?* Unpublished manuscript, Temple University Center for Research in Human Development and Education, Philadelphia, PA.

Rolf, J., Masten, A. S., Cicchetti, D., Nuechterlein, K. H., & Weintraub, S. (Eds.). (1990). *Risk and protective factors in the development of psychopathology*. New York: Cambridge University Press.

Rutter, M. (1984, March). Resilient children. *Psychology Today*, pp. 57–65.

Rutter, M. (1990). Psychosocial resilience and protective mechanisms. In J. Rolf, A. S. Masten, D. Cicchetti, K. H. Nuechterlein, & S. Weintraub (Eds.), *Risk and protective factors in the development of psychopathology* (pp. 181–214). New York: Cambridge University Press.

Werner, E. (1989, April). Children of the garden island. *Scientific American*, pp. 107–111.

Werner, E., & Smith, R. (1982). *Vulnerable but invincible: A longitudinal study of resilient children and youth*. New York: Adams, Bannister, & Cox.

Western Regional Center for Drug-Free Schools and Communities. (1991). *Fostering resiliency in kids: Protective factors in the family, school and community*. Portland, OR: Northwest Regional Education Library.

Winfield, L. F. (1991). Resilience, schooling, and development in African-American youth, a conceptual framework. *Education and Urban Society, 24*(1), 5–14.

Chapter 5

The Americanization of Resilience:
Deconstructing Research Practice

Leo C. Rigsby
Temple University

This chapter critically examines the concept of *resilience* (Masten, chapter 1, this volume) with the aim of laying out some assumptions underlying the concept and the processes and conditions that are assumed to give rise to resilience. First, the concept is placed in the broader cultural context of the emphasis on individualism and mobility striving that has characterized U.S. society. Next the origins and uses of the term in social science and public policy are examined. A number of cautions are drawn for research and policy from this discussion. The final section of the chapter discusses some specific directions for theory development and research on resilience processes.

INDIVIDUALISM AND MOBILITY STRIVING
IN AMERICAN CULTURE

Resilience is a quintessentially U.S. concept. It has roots in the U.S. hero myth commemorated in books and stories by Horatio Alger in the latter half of the 19th century. Downs (1971) described the theme as follows:

> A typical Alger plot centers around a teenage boy, nearly always fatherless [read from a single-parent home for the present context], who must make his way in a great city against heavy financial and social odds. Often he has to support a widowed mother, whose little home or farm is about to be seized by a ruthless

banker or village squire because she has fallen behind on her mortgage payments. Whatever the situation, the boy must rely upon himself to solve the problem and to get ahead in the world. The theme is reflected in such titles as *Sink or Swim, Strive and Succeed, Shifting for Himself, Helping Himself, Facing the World, Do and Dare, Struggling Upward*, and *Risen from the Ranks*. The requisites for success are piety, courage, thrift, alertness, punctuality, morality, hard work, and all the related virtues. (p. 42)

Americans seek to understand success in terms that magnify the agency of the striving spirit of the individual. Resilience also has roots in the U.S. quality first noted by Alexis de Tocqueville (1969) in the middle 1800s: "The first thing that strikes one in the United States is the innumerable crowd of those striving to escape from their original social condition. . . . Every American is eaten up with longing to rise. . . . All are constantly bent on gaining property, reputation, and power" (p. 627). We revere those who overcome the odds and who, through sheer determination, manage to rise above their origins to achieve personal fame or fortune. Above all, we admire success. We demand ambition and upward striving from all who would fulfill the requirements to be American.

Turner (1960) argued that the themes of upward striving and individual agency are contained in the "organizing folk norm which defines the accepted mode of upward mobility" (p. 856) for the mass educational system of the United States. In the article that began a tradition of research on this subject, Turner compared the guiding norms governing the British educational system with those governing the U.S. educational system. He argued that "contest mobility norms" characterize U.S. education, and the terms he used in his description bear great similarities to those used by Downs (1971) and de Tocqueville (1969):

> *Contest mobility* is a system in which elite status is the prize in an open contest and is taken by the aspirants' own efforts. While the "contest" is governed by some rules of fair play, the contestants have wide latitude in the strategies they may employ. (p. 856)

> Victory must be won by one's own efforts. The most satisfactory outcome is not necessarily a victory of the most able, but of the most deserving. The tortoise who defeats the hare is a folk-prototype of the deserving sportsman. Enterprise, initiative, perseverance, and craft are admirable qualities if they allow the person who is initially at a disadvantage to triumph. (p. 857)

Drawing from these images of the mythology or folk norms underpinning common understandings of our society, and especially of the connections of education to ultimate socioeconomic achievement, we can isolate some underlying assumptions:

1. everyone can and should strive to "get ahead," to improve their standing (it is left implicit that this will entail surpassing others, not improvement for everyone)

2. the arena of competition for getting ahead is open, fair, and accessible to all (no structural impediments for groups defined by race, gender, culture, etc.)

3. the competition for getting ahead is structured like a continuing game in the sense that there are few points of "no return," one can always get oneself together and reenter the competition

4. disadvantages that affect one's chances of success are individual and can be overcome with individual effort.

SOCIAL SCIENCE USES OF RESILIENCE

Similar assumptions undergird our conceptions of resilience. Masten (chapter 1, this volume) suggests that resilience as a social science concept originates in studies of developmental psychopathology. She states that *resilience* and *psychopathology* represent opposing possibilities for individual human development. In the United States we value and celebrate "resilience" and recoil from failure or defeat. Our commitment to achievement and success is so strong that we sometimes label lack of success "pathology."[1]

Although the concept of resilience has increasing currency in the social science literature, a number of debates about its usefulness remain. We problematize the concept and, in doing so, question its potential contributions to a progressive research tradition[2] focused on human development. This analysis draws primarily on Masten (chapter 1, this volume). Even though this chapter explicitly represents work in progress, it focuses on, and makes familiar, a number of critical issues found in other studies.

According to Masten, "resilience in an individual refers to successful adaptation despite risk and adversity" (p. 3). Resilience has been used to understand adaptations in at least three contexts. Resilient individuals are those who

---

[1] Masten (chapter 1, this volume) is explicit in her discussion about the normative character of the terms *resilience* and *pathology*.

[2] The term *research tradition* has been used by Laudan (1977) to designate very broad theoretical/empirical enterprises that give direction to a number of theories and efforts at theory assessment. His definition is as follows: "A research tradition is a set of general assumptions about the entities and processes in a domain of study, and about the appropriate methods to be used for investigating the problems and constructing the theories in that domain" (p. 81). Summarizing important post-Kuhnian developments in the philosophy of science, Laudan argued that research traditions may be progressive (grow, increase in content, solve new problems, exhibit new instances of corroboration) or degenerate (stagnate, fail to solve new problems, fail to resolve theoretical inconsistencies, fail to add new content).

have achieved success even though: (a) they are members of high-risk groups for whom adaptive success is given low probabilities, such as children from deprived, minority neighborhoods with high levels of unemployment and homelessness; (b) they have endured stressful experiences, such as children from dysfunctional families or survivors of the Holocaust; and/or (c) they have suffered trauma, such as children who were sexually or physically abused.

The very definition of resilience suggests that we must know something of the causes of success and failure. In the first place, the definition, by implication, distinguishes successful and unsuccessful adaptation and presumes to identify risk and asset factors that affect adaptations. This means we have made judgments about desirable and undesirable outcomes from some normative frame of reference. Further, employing some predictive framework, we have been able to assess the likelihood of successful and unsuccessful outcomes given some predictive contingencies. Masten discusses the work of a number of researchers who have delimited age-appropriate "developmental tasks" that are frequently employed as benchmarks against which adaptations of individuals are measured. For example, school-aged children should be adjusting to the demands of schooling, achieving at acceptable levels, relating in socially acceptable ways to peers, and so on. Inevitably, such expectations are contextually bound in time and place and culture. Such benchmarks frequently reflect values of, and assume access to resources characteristic of, White, middle-class families.

For each of the categories of life experiences where resilience has been applied, researchers have made judgments about desirable and undesirable outcomes, about risks and assets (both individual and social), and about assessments of the likelihood of successful adaptations, given the risks and assets. To make an analogy, researchers make value judgments about differences between expected and observed outcomes, where the expectation is based on a prediction equation combining risks and assets. "Resilient" individuals are those whose adaptations represent extreme positive residuals from a prediction equation where adaptations are predicted from a linear combination of risks and assets. In other words, determination of resilience depends on (a) judgments about outcomes and (b) assumptions about the causes of adaptations that may not have been explicitly described or consciously examined. An incomplete theory gives rise to the possibility of concluding that resilient adaptations have occurred because an incomplete theory explains less well (i.e., produces larger prediction errors).

There are other questions about resilience as well. How are we to understand its occurrence? What causes the adaptations we label *resilience*? Three possible explanations for resilience suggest themselves. First is that resilience is simply idiosyncratic or random. Arguments have been made recently by Cziko (1989) and Kontopoulos (1993) that many events and processes that we are interested in are simply inexplicable because they are random or systematic in ways that we cannot fathom. The second possibility is that resilience is an identifiable human characteristic or trait. If this is the case, we have invented a genetic explanation for resilience, the occurrence of which we can neither affect nor foster. However, Masten's chapter is particularly striking for its rich examples. Time and again the examples suggest that resilience grows out of the interaction of personality, social context, and opportunities for, or demands on, the person. Thus, the third possibility, and the one that I strongly prefer, is that resilience is the response to a complex set of interactions involving person, social context, and opportunities. We argue that resilience is useful for educational theorizing and policy only if it is conceived as developing in such a multilevel set of causal structures and processes.

The main problem I have had with the concept of resilience is that its users make it sound like the "spark theory of human development." This theory emerged in my work with a local school administrator a few years ago. This administrator remarked to me that children and families connected to his school "aren't like children and families used to be. They don't have that spark that allows them to overcome adversity. I look for that spark deep down inside them." Such a conception leaves open the likelihood that we will treat non-resilient girls and boys as failures who are beyond help or hope because they don't have that "inner spark." The multilevel alternative refocuses our attention to a wider field, opening the possibility that conditions for resilience can be created in the interactions of person, context, and structure of opportunities.

CAUTIONS FOR FUTURE RESEARCH AND POLICY

Researchers working on resilience must face two issues. First, we must be self-conscious about which values orchestrate delimitations of desirable and undesirable outcomes or adaptations. Social scientists, no less than other researchers, inevitably incorporate value judgments into research operations (no matter how much we are trained to deny it). We need to be conscious of these values and learn to distinguish between our values and interests and those of others who may very legitimately have different and opposing values. For example, if there had been developmental psychologists working in 16th-century Britain, the rebels in the American colonies might have been described as highly pathological and irresponsible in rejecting the colonial mandates of the British crown. From an American perspective, the colonists may be seen as resilient; the British perspective casts them as maladaptive.

More importantly, the "prediction model" with which we assess expected outcomes must be explicit and as complete as possible. A theory that does not take into account the multilevel causal structures[3] inevitably involved in complex human behavior carries the risk of leading us to classify behaviors as resilient that would be explicable and expected if we had a fuller theory.

Two hypothetical examples illustrate the point we wish to make. First, imagine a very simple model that only takes into account socioeconomic status (SES) in formulating expectations for adult economic success. This model structures our expectations so that we would be at risk of concluding that males and Whites in U.S. society were more likely to be resilient, and that females and minority group members were unusually nonresilient.

The second example is more complex and illustrates the importance of multilevel analysis. Again, let us consider the issue of economic success in U.S. society. Let us employ the most complete typical model of individual occupational success that exists, taking into account gender, race, education, family background, postsecondary educational and work experience, personality characteristics, age, migration status, family status, and so forth. Using this model to predict occupational success, despite its seeming comprehensiveness, would give very different results as we consider different phases of the business cycle over time. In fact, considering this nation's current economic situation, it would likely lead us to the conclusion that several hundred thousand people have just become pathological as they changed from being employed to being unemployed! In short, researchers studying resilience have to be very self-conscious and sensitive to space–time contingencies and multiple levels of causal structures in laying out the basis for their expectations about adaptations.

Our argument thus far has been that the very definition of resilience demands a model for formulating expectations and a normative basis for assessing the desirability of different outcomes. Further, one may observe that many of the uses of resilience are based on an implicit and unconscious "expectations" model and an unarticulated basis for judging outcomes. When value judgments and expectations remain implicit, arbitrary and ethnocentric values and expectations often predominate.

Why has this concept become so popular and powerful in recent years? We can only speculate on this for the moment. A definitive answer would entail a study of researchers and their social contexts of production. As Masten points out, resilience has its intellectual beginnings in psychopathology. The intellectual beginnings could just as easily have been said to be in the sociological counterpart to psychopathology—the sociology of criminality and deviance. Both of these disciplines have focused on understanding why people do not behave as they should. Theory and research in both disciplines have focused on failures

---

[3]Lerner (1991) made an important and compelling argument for the necessity of employing multilevel arguments in order to understand human development. Further, he argued that a research program centered primarily in a given discipline, and especially one that has historically been as individual-centered as developmental psychology, is particularly at risk of not looking at causal structures and processes beyond the level of the individual.

or maladaptations. Further, in both disciplines, marginal and resource-poor groups have been documented to be at higher risk of making adaptations that are judged to be poor or bad or unsuccessful. Social scientists are disturbed by these behaviors and want to diminish them, so their attention has been focused on psychopathology, criminality, and deviance.

Members of those groups whose failures have been studied have begun to object to the social science focus on the "failures and pathologies" of the group.[4] In the climate of political correctness that pervades intellectual discourse, researchers are, with justice, inclined to be sensitive to such objections. Talking about "resilience" is a way of avoiding talk about pathologies. Because the existence of the category "resilience" inevitably invokes its opposite, "nonresilience," it provides a way of focusing on many of the same problems and causal forces, but using a different language for talking about them.

Adopting the strategy of focusing our attention on the other end of the spectrum of adaptive success (on the successful end, rather than the unsuccessful end) may be both politically expedient and intellectually inexpedient. What we really want to understand are the processes of human development in different times and places, for individuals with varying risks and assets, and for individuals developing in a variety of social contexts. Further, we want to understand the causal structures and processes that occur in specific contexts. We need to study the details of the social contexts within which children are developing. We resort to concepts like resilience because there is a poverty of theory development in this area. Accumulating more correlates of resilience and failure will not be helpful if it is done outside the context of serious theory building in human development.[5]

THEORY DEVELOPMENT FOR FUTURE RESEARCH

The final point is a plea that goes beyond the topic of this chapter. Resilience research, like many areas of social science, needs serious attention given to theory building that focuses on understanding the causal structures and processes that give meaning and direction to social life. Further accumulation of new or redundant data that we do not know how to interpret will simply cause stagnation in the research tradition. The works of Bronfenbrenner (1989), Lerner (1991), and Kontopoulos (1993) seem promising in that they offer explicit, time-dependent, multilevel models of human affairs.

---

[4]Spokespersons for these groups have often made the point that "pathologies" may be seen to be created by larger social forces over which individual members of the identified group have no power. For example, they argue that homelessness is not a choice or adaptation, but rather is caused when jobs are moved from their city to a third world country with lower wages.

[5]A similar point is made regarding the general progress of psychology and of the social sciences generally by Manicas and Secord (1983).

One area to which we may turn for fruitful models of theorizing is that of gender research, especially the work growing out of feminist research on gender. Early ideas about gender, then called "sex" or "sex roles," emphasized "essentialist" or biological determination of "sex differences." As a consequence, all manner of social differences between men and women (access to valued kinds of work, remuneration for work, access to political office, value placed on artistic and literary contributions, division of labor in household tasks and child-rearing, etc.) have been interpreted to be natural and just. Differences between men and women in social and economic success have been interpreted to be a function of men's greater competitive drive or ambition, their assertiveness, their level of interest, the skills they have developed, and so on.

Of course, the major theme of feminist scholarship over the past 25 years has been to challenge these essentialist arguments. Modern gender research offers a more social and structural account of the development of gender that nevertheless acknowledges the practical relevance of biological characteristics of bodies to the social construction of gender (Connell, 1987). This research, and especially Connell's own contributions to it, offers a multilevel account of the construction of gender and how the construction has changed over time.

In some sense, the same kind of effort is needed for research on resilience. We need to problematize resilience in a manner analogous to the way gender has been problematized. We need to conceptualize how the values and motivations that may affect resilience are themselves affected by experience. We need to incorporate the structures that affect resilience into a theory of resilience. Pierre Bourdieu's (1977, 1984) concept of the "habitus" may be useful to accomplish this. Buchmann (1989) described the habitus as "an acquired system of dispositions, skills, knowledge, habits, worldviews, and representations" (p. 32). She stressed that the habitus is "the internalization and incorporation of one's position in the social structure and of the history of one's positions, that is, the social trajectory" (p. 32). Thus, habitus is the dynamically constituted, active self that behaves in interaction with a social context. This self reflects the cumulation of one's experience through time.

The implications we would draw for research on resilience from these recent developments in gender research, and in the work of Bourdieu, are that behaviors we label *resilient* represent the "practice" growing out of the habitus of individuals acting in contexts of opportunity. Bourdieu's concept of *habitus* makes explicit that the "dispositions, skills, knowledge, habits, worldviews, and representations" have formed over time and continue to be formed into the future. Research should then focus on how old experience and new experience shape the habitus through time.

A danger of employing the concept of *resilience* as it has heretofore been understood is that we may reinforce the negative consequences of the old Horatio Alger myth: an implicit belief that anyone can make it if he or she tries hard enough. An inevitable result is that we will again "blame the victim" of the complex processes that create and perpetuate poverty and stress in our society. Although we will be talking about resilience, we will be inferring "non-resilience" as well. If resilience is to be a truly useful concept in a progressive research tradition, it must be embedded in a rich theoretical framework that incorporates the complexity of multilevel causal structures and processes.

CONCLUSIONS

This chapter has problematized the concept of *resilience* both to uncover its origins in U.S. culture and to explore the likely consequences of uncritical uses of the concept in research and public policy. These uses often conceive of resilience as "unexplained" success. We argue that the term carries the potential, because of its origins in ideologies of individualism and mobility striving, of placing all blame or credit on individuals for their successes and failures. Placing blame or credit on individuals leaves aside many important structural influences on the behaviors we may otherwise call resilient. We end with a plea for the development of multilevel theory, to give us a richer understanding of human behaviors that relate to the relative successes of individuals and groups.

ACKNOWLEDGMENTS

The research reported herein was supported in part by the Temple University Center for Research in Human Development and Education (CRHDE) and in part by the Office of Educational Research and Improvement (OERI) of the U.S. Department of Education through a grant to the National Center on Education in the Inner Cities at Temple University. The opinions expressed do not necessarily reflect the position of the supporting agencies, and no official endorsement should be inferred.

Thanks are due to Mary Bortnyk Rigsby and Annette Lareau for critical comments on an earlier draft of this chapter. Both deserve great credit for improving its clarity and focus, and no blame for my neglecting their advice in some instances.

REFERENCES

Bourdieu, P. (1977). *An outline of a theory of practice*. Cambridge: Cambridge University Press.
Bourdieu, P. (1984). *Distinction: A social critique of the judgment of taste*. Cambridge: Harvard University Press.
Bronfenbrenner, U. (1989). Ecological systems theory. *Annals of Child Development, 6,* 187–249.

Buchmann, M. (1989). *The script of life in modern society: Entry into adulthood in a changing world.* Chicago: The University of Chicago Press.

Connell, R. W. (1987). *Gender and power.* Stanford, CA: Stanford University Press.

Cziko, G. A. (1989, April). Unpredictability and indeterminism in human behavior. *Educational Researcher,* pp. 17–25.

Downs, R. B. (1971). *Famous American books.* New York: McGraw-Hill.

Kontopoulos, K. (1993). *The logics of social structure.* New York: Cambridge University Press.

Laudan, L. (1977). *Progress and its problems: Towards a theory of scientific growth.* Berkeley: University of California Press.

Lerner, R. M. (1991). Changing organism-context relations as the basic process of development: A developmental contextual perspective. *Developmental Psychology, 27,* 27–32.

Manicas, P., & Secord, P. F. (1983). Implications for psychology of the new philosophy of science. *American Psychologist, 6,* 399–413.

Tocqueville, A. d. (1969). *Democracy in America.* Garden City, NY: Doubleday.

Turner, R. (1960). Sponsored and contest mobility and the school system. *American Sociological Review, 25,* 855–67.

Part II

Research on Resilience: Conceptual and Methodological Considerations

Chapter 6

On Resilience:
Questions of Validity

David W. Bartelt
Temple University

Resilience, either implicitly or explicitly, is a central concept in many approaches to maximizing inner-city educational attainment. More broadly, it is also central to many public policy and program issues connected to debates over the urban underclass, particularly toward programs aimed at identifying individuals who are likely candidates for transition from the underclass. This chapter concerns itself with several components of the external validity of this concept as it is employed at three levels: the individual, the family, and the city. Specifically, does the concept of *resilience* have a clear, unambiguous empirical referent in psychological states, behaviors, and/or forms of social organization, such that we can organize research and policy recommendations around it?

There are significant problems with the use of resilience even as a sensitizing concept. There is a clear ideological bias in the parallels between theories of resilience and the Horatio Alger myth (see Rigsby, chapter 5, this volume). Nathaniel West, better known for his novellas dealing with Hollywood and advice columnists (*The Day of the Locusts* and *Miss Lonelyhearts*), also addressed the Horatio Alger myth in his tale of Lemuel Pitkin, *A Cool Million* (1961). While Horatio Alger's characters triumph over adversity—thereby demonstrating resilience—Lemuel Pitkin perseveres as he loses a hand, a leg, an eye, and his good name, but is finally assassinated at the moment of his rise to power as the leader of a neo-fascist America-first movement.

Behind the black humor of West's cautionary tale is a striking critique of resilience. West's fictional question is one we will do well to consider as a research question: At what point does resilience approach irrationality on the part of individuals caught within an inexorably hostile social situation? Less normatively, what model of the social order, attainment, and opportunity is assumed if resilience is used as the basic intervention concept in inner-city education?

These are questions to which we return at the conclusion of this chapter. Resilience itself deserves closer attention. In particular, I would like to raise a series of issues that deal with the problem of making a direct connection between the concept as theoretically defined and its empirical referent(s). I have grave doubts that the concept can be extended easily beyond its psychological context, and I would raise a series of questions that need to be addressed even in that context.

To some extent, these questions are based on the fairly uncritical way in which the concept carries with it an everyday context. We commonly see resilience as a trait of individuals. As such, the variable level of resilience is seen as a predictor of success or failure, and is adduced from outcomes in the face of adversity. As Masten (chapter 1, this volume) reminds us, it is not necessary that we assume an individual trait. What she proposes is that we consider resilience to refer to a class of events: When successes persist in the face of substantial barriers, resilience is the appropriate label of that category of events.

I find this definition to be a distinct improvement over the everyday use of the term as a psychological trait. As the subsequent discussion of resilience indicates, if there is to be an appropriate use of the term, either as a predictor or as a mode of intervention, it will not be sufficient to rely on the everyday meaning of the term. Nonetheless, because it is just this everyday meaning that dominates discussions of the term, it is this sense of resilience that orients this chapter.

Frankly, I feel that we are imbuing resilience with the same overarching powers that early chemists attributed to phlogiston, the mystical substance that was ostensibly released during combustion and, being contained within the object being consumed, enabled it to successfully burn. Resilience, as a psychological trait, is seen as a component of the self that enables success in the face of adversity, and may either be consumed or, paradoxically, reinforced by adversity.

But just as chemists found that the combustion process involved the oxidation of known elements—and not the imputation of an invisible one—I argue that we need to pay closer attention to the social organization of success and failure within the schools, and the linkages between this organization and the social context of the schools, rather than impute the existence of a major causal variable that is not only difficult to observe, but contains logical dilemmas in its basic meanings. In short, I make the case that resilience as a concept is difficult, if not impossible, to empirically specify, and is too easily conflated with measures of situational success or failure. It suffers from its roots in subjective interpretations of biographical events, and it is too closely dependent on observer-imputed stresses and resources for dealing with stressors. Although it is an ideologically convenient concept in its reinforcement of ''bootstrapping'' approaches to achievement, it may not help us understand either the outcomes or the processes of inner-city education.

THE RESILIENCE MODEL:
EXPLICATION AND CRITIQUE

We are all too familiar with the contrasts between achieving and opting out strategies of students. Anthony (pseudonym), a 14-year-old ninth-grade student, has had only As in school. He lives in one of the poorest sections of Philadelphia in a female-headed household, with a supportive grandmother. His father has kept in contact with the family, and the mother has a steady paramour who acts as an ''old head'' for the boy. He has an outstanding attendance record, and has received special awards for perfect attendance. Anthony has begun ninth grade in the Scholar's Magnet Program.

Martin (also a pseudonym), on the other hand, shows a different face of life in a poor African-American family. Like Anthony, he is 14 and in the ninth grade, and comes from a female-headed household with the grandmother present. He has been absent 29 of 80 days this year (1992). He typically stays out on the street until 2 a.m., and exhibits strong hostility to the neighborhood, often acting out by breaking windows and stealing signs, harassing children, and confronting adults. He has been brought to juvenile court on charges of robbery and assault. He lives in the same neighborhood as Anthony.

It is the stark contrast of individuals with similar family and neighborhood backgrounds that makes us turn to a concept such as *resilience* to explain why some students succeed and some opt out. It is best, however, if we take this concept as a first approximation of either a psychological trait or a category of events until we can more carefully review its logical consistency and its essential validity.

I am concerned here with the relationship between a concept and the empirical reality it is said to represent. Kaplan (1964) argued that validity is a criterion of measurement, addressing the question of whether an indicator measures ''what it purports to measure'' (pp. 198–199). Technically, we are dealing here with a concept that has not yet been empirically specified. Nonetheless, it claims empirical standing by its reference either to an imputed individual characteristic or as a label of a category of events. It is thus appropriate to evaluate its validity, and particularly its ''face'' or ''content'' validity, as well as its ''construct'' validity.

According to Walizer and Wienir (1978), face validity addresses the following question: ''Do the indicators appear to be measuring what one has defined the concept to mean, and does the operational definition reflect what is intended by the conceptual definition?'' (p. 410). Content validity is equivalent to face validity when a construct is used, rather than a simple concept. More importantly, when a construct is used as an empirical measure (such as "authoritarian personality" or, perhaps, "resilience"), construct validity should also be discussed. Walizer and Wienir argued that there are three essential components of construct validity: (a) the construct can be seen to be a combination of identifiable concepts; (b) the construct will in fact offer a consistent relationship with other variables to which it is assumed to be related; and (c) the construct lacks a relationship to variables to which it is assumed to be unrelated (Walizer & Wienir, 1978).

This argument presses the discussion of validity because we are in the very process of evaluating the utility of the concept/construct of resilience. It will do us well to recall the difficulties that are found in research over the construct of intelligence (Gould, 1981). In an earlier statement, Kaplan (1964) made the following argument:

> If the meaning of "intelligence" . . . is specified by reference to certain tests, there can be no question that those tests do indeed measure what is called "intelligence." Unfortunately, it often happens that what is claimed to be a specification of meaning does not in fact perform that role. . . . The danger is that we succumb to . . . "operationism in reverse," that is, endowing the measures with all the meanings associated with the concept. . . . Validity involves both definitional and predictive considerations, particularly when the measure is of a magnitude which is conceptualized in descriptive generalizations, but in some theory as well. (pp. 198–199)

I take Kaplan's points to be important in two major respects regarding resilience. First, we run the danger of looking for an empirical indicator of resilience and then defining our theoretical construct in only operational terms— particularly if we have great difficulty clearly and unambiguously identifying the root of the construct. The parallel to "intelligence" is striking. We can easily detail a set of tests of resilience which "measure" greater or lesser degrees of success in the face of adversity. We run the risk, if we do not first consider the limits of the concept, of "operationism in reverse" (i.e., of letting our empirical success convince us that there exists a nonproblematic concept represented by these measures).

This forces a second issue upon us, that of the validity of the concept itself. Resilience as a psychological concept depends on a view of the actor as a goal-directed individual encountering barriers or stresses in day-to-day life, but overcoming them by a combination of skills and "persistence," to use a rough approximate. Resilience would seem to refer, at this level, to the individual trait of being able to confront unusual levels of stress (or numbers of stressors) and surmount them.

Masten (chapter 1, this volume) deals with the concept in much the same framework. Her discussions summarize the major thrust of the argument: Resilience refers to success in the face of adversity; it involves both a normative judgment of development of the person as well as the social situation; this process occurs over time; and the study of such an adaptation process will lead to successful intervention strategies.

This concept can also be extended to family and community contexts. Families, for instance, can be said to be "resilient" if they provide collective adaptation strategies for their members to confront risks or adverse circumstances. Similarly, communities may be observed to develop mechanisms that attenuate the worst effects of economic or other stresses. (Indeed, there is a strong literature within disaster research that looks at community indicators that predict adaptation to the sudden stress of floods, earthquakes, or other sudden disruptions of the physical environment.)

At the heart of resilience is its relational nature. Whether at the individual or social level, it cannot be identified without reference to: (a) the subjective experience of external "difficulties" (or stressors); (b) an inventory of resources (psychological as well as material); and (c) a "biography" of successes or failures. The concept itself is defined by triangulation and then imputed; in the presence of perceived stressors, with an absence of resources, and despite a track record of continual stress, a successful adaptation is regarded as evidence of resilience. Unsuccessful adaptation is regarded as an absence of resilience.

This is just the kind of "operationism in reverse" Kaplan noted. The imputation of a conceptual variable—a construct developed from a combination of empirical indicators—is a common means of conducting research. The discussion of resilience begins to run a risk when we conduct our discussions of learning outcomes and public policy as if we had directly observed it. Resilience is never directly observed—it is always imputed.

As an empirical concept, then, there is difficulty in identifying an unambiguous referent to this force/factor of resilience. What seems common to most discussions we have had is a "storage battery" model of resilience (i.e., each individual's charge level is different, and is used up by too many stresses without recharging). A contrary model, one that is the inverse of the resilience model, suggests that resilience is actually a systemic concept, determined by its place within a dynamic model of the self, the family, and the community, each part of a dynamic environment contextualizing the educational process. We return to this model later in this chapter.

Another major issue is the possible conflation of resilience with the relative degree of available resources. If an actor confronts stress, is not the presence of resources a major way of avoiding both the subjective perception of stress as well as of coping with it? Are not resources integral to the ability to persevere? In short, do we not run the danger of substituting a psychological construct with indefinite referents for a straightforward accounting of fairly traditional notions of human capital—skills, educational certification, income/wealth, job opportunities, segregation, and so forth?

But the concept of *resilience* obviously includes more. It has been developed within a specific educational framework: achievement that extends beyond what is expected, given the levels of stress factors present within an individual's biographical field (and by extension, the family's or community's as well). This specific meaning raises validity issues in two further ways. First, it makes resilience an artifact of the investigator's model of achievement, a statistical residual of a specific causal model. Second, it fails to distinguish between adaptation to socially approved goals and to those that may be personally meaningful. Consider a poorly skilled student facing a long series of personal stresses within school, who may "fail" according to that institution's measures of achievement. He or she may have exhibited a particular form of resilience by sacrificing their education, let us say, for parenthood, particularly if it is perceived that this status offers more than continued education would.

If this second instance is in fact the case, then resilience as a concept cannot be said to distinguish one class of psychological forces from another. Put differently, it is so dependent on the external evaluator's definitions of achievement that it cannot yet be said to refer to an unambiguous empirical instance of either behavior or a state of mind, or of a class of behaviors that are distinct from other classes of behavior.

This problem is reminiscent of Kaplan's (1964) injunction in *The Conduct of Inquiry* to not confuse *act* meaning with *action* meaning. Action meaning refers to the labels or categories that the observer attaches to behaviors, act meaning refers to those used by the actors themselves. Concepts used by the observer, even those that attempt to take subjective intention/experiences into account, must distinguish between them. *Resilience* is clearly a term that is externally applied (i.e., an action meaning) by observers of a series of actions and outcomes. But central to the concept is a set of subjectively defined goals, aspirations, and barriers—act meanings.

In fact, resilience takes the action meanings of third parties (e.g., schools, policymakers, etc.) and overlays them on both the observer and the actor. After all, successes in the face of stressors (i.e., resilience) may simply reflect our lack of understanding of either schools, families, communities, or individuals; further, they may simply be random events containing no special lessons for adaptation.

Clearly, this is an extreme statement of the methodological critique I am developing. It deserves reiteration that I am simply raising the issues of external validity here, in order that we try to define our concepts more clearly. At the heart of the problem, however, is a fear that we are extrapolating a normative version of the "Protestant ethic" and applying it to the educational context of very poor people. I am not sure that equating academic success with resilience is warranted in this instance. Put differently, if resilience is present in a person, simply getting to school, overcoming family, community, and personal stressors, may exhaust this resource for many students.

A specific example may serve to illustrate this point. Several representatives of Hispanic community organizations have put the following question to me: If family income is lower for Puerto Rican communities; if the day-to-day needs of the household for additional economic resources are strongly present; and if there is a strong pro-family ideology within the community that is threatened by continued poverty; why should we not expect that our teenagers will seek to leave school and obtain full-time employment as soon as possible? In turn I must ask myself, isn't this a form of resilience as we have come to define it? How then do we distinguish academic success as resilience from dropping out as resilience?

It is also possible to extend the concept of resilience to the social level, as a simple extrapolation of the psychological argument. That is, family or school resilience has been articulated as an unknown, to be ascertained by examining what is common to positive outliers in stressful environments. Poor families that remain intact, or that develop good students, are said to exhibit resilience; schools with few resources that regularly produce outstanding students are said to be resilient. Yet the issue is begged even more at the social level than at the psychological. Given the cross-cutting interests and differential resources present within most urban communities, to simply extend the basic concept is to ignore that which is vital to our understanding of the inner city: Many systems are established that essentially guarantee failure for many students.

At the social level, however, I do not feel that we have paid enough attention to the combination of resources, stresses, and histories that correspond to the individual-level meaning of resilience. Indeed, what we most often find is the overly simplistic identification of social institutions as either neutral, equally supportive, or penalizing to all individuals within them. Schools are regarded as providing training; families with providing social and material supports. Job markets are simply assumed to exist, regardless of economic conditions.

Nowhere in this version of social reality is the act meaning of schools and communities that emerges from ethnographies of urban life (Anderson, 1990; Jankowski, 1991; Moore, 1978, 1991). The image of the school as "lame," irrelevant to the needs of immediate survival, or as a "cooling out" institution, is absent from this story of urban life. But it is just this marginalized image of the school which is uppermost in many otherwise "resilient" students' minds.

To investigate resilience at the social level requires much the same concern for defining a systemic variable that exists at the psychological level. The question I wrestle with is this: What is the meaning of a resilient school in an environment that offers not support, but a systematic, long-term deprivation of educational resources; in which the learning that is ostensibly transmitted bears no relationship to the network of stresses confronting the families and residence communities of the students; and in which there is a multigenerational perception that whatever good happens in the rest of society, will be denied to the communities of the inner city?

Further, just as the concept of *individual resilience* involves the biography of the individual—the accumulation of stressful experiences and the learning curve that accompanies it, plus the depletion or development of a reserve "charge" of resilience—there is a history to both families and communities that must be taken into account. Cities that have developed complex economic bases, for instance, have an easier time adjusting to economic transitions. What then happens to their educational institutions? This is a question I am now investigating in greater detail.

This set of questions simply suggests the final critique that I would advance toward resilience. Resilience may well be born of our hopes, not necessarily our eyes and ears. It is born of our conviction that there will still be something left to draw upon in the continually stressful environments of our inner-city schools. It is a concept that is over-identified with a particular intervention strategy, and begs for a confirmatory, rather than hypothesis-testing mode of research. As a policy prescription, it is long on motivational techniques for overcoming barriers, has some value in helping us identify systematic arenas of stress for our children, and is thoroughly wedded to a model of educational/social class attainment that is dubiously applied to the inner-city neighborhoods we study. In short, I need far more explication before I am convinced that resilience is the appropriate concept on which to base our models of inner-city education and policy proposals.

If we begin our research into improving educational outcomes by using resilience as our core concept, we fail to grapple with the difficult question of nonresilience. Even if the psychological trait approach—the everyday knowledge concept of resilience—gives way to Masten's (this volume) "categories of events," a measure of outcomes needs to be tested that does, in fact, distinguish "resilient" versus "nonresilient" individuals, schools, or communities.

By beginning with a concept of *resilience*, we impute a prior property of the individual (school, community) by virtue of a set of outcomes (test scores vs. hardships). We certainly run the risk of committing the fallacy of affirming the consequent, where post hoc findings are assumed to demonstrate a logically prior state of affairs. In programmatic terms, this will limit our concern with educational reform to "creaming" the best students from poor schools, and ignore the remaining issues of resilience noted earlier.

TOWARD AN ALTERNATIVE MODEL

It makes sense to begin this discussion by recognizing the contextual nature of resilience. Whenever or wherever educators speak of resilience, it generally involves both a set of resources and a set of barriers. A significant literature has emerged in recent years that suggests that the urban neighborhood has been particularly reactive to the changing economic and political opportunity structures of the city. Some neighborhoods have been able to respond better to these changes than others; some worse. In particular, recent decades have seen the growth of what some have called the "underclass"—a group of neighborhoods that have been isolated from the forces of urban economic change, and that present a significant additional set of barriers to the educational process (Katz, 1993; Wilson, 1987).

A larger body of research on education and the "underclass" suggests that a significant paradox lies at the heart of educating our cities. Although opportunities have decreased in many inner cities, and although adolescent behavior across the country (particularly in inner cities) reflects, at best, an ennui regarding school, the educational certificate takes on greater and greater importance in allocating scarce jobs to a more-than-ample labor supply.

This paradox is, perhaps, most clearly stated in Wilson's (1987) arguments regarding the formation of an urban underclass. He argued that a profound educational retardation has impacted on underclass communities, in the face of increased educational expectations in the economy. This leads to his argument that the increasing isolation of the underclass creates significant disincentives for education within that community, whereas demands to the contrary continue to grow outside of the underclass.

Lest we pursue this argument in the sense in which many conservative policymakers have (e.g., ignoring the problems of the central city while prescribing better morals for its residents), we should note two important studies suggesting that: (a) small improvements in inner-city environments might be able to greatly reduce the rates of dropping out and teenage childbearing (Crane, 1991); and (b) that improved job access, and the holding of part-time jobs, increases the likelihood of school enrollment and completion (Ihlanfeldt, 1992).

In these models, the concept of resilience diminishes, and the social and spatial disjuncture between the inner city and the rest of the society increases as a causal factor. Put bluntly, strategies for resilience cause us to ignore the preconditions for valuing education: a perceived payoff for continued schooling. Because we, as external observers, can see the research findings, does not mean that the student in an inner-city school can see beyond surviving the next day.

A striking parallel exists in the disability literature. Goode (1979) wrote about the subjective worlds of children born deaf and blind. In particular, he forced the reader to acknowledge the extent to which he or she imposes his or her fully sighted, fully hearing understanding of social and personal dynamics onto individuals with radically different perceptual sets. The position of poor and minority children in inner-city schools, although closer to "mainstream" reality than the world of the congenitally deaf–blind, is still a world apart from that presumed by an academically oriented achievement model. To begin with resilience, as defined by success under that set of values, is to miss the important dynamics of the students' subjective world view.

Thus, the concept of resilience points to important elements of a model for dealing with educational attainment. It points to a central contradiction in the ways in which both social institutions and the self work. It is fairly clear that educational systems are, at least in part, mechanisms of social control within a class- and race-differentiated society. Yet performance, at least in achieving educational credentials, is generally regarded as a minimal prerequisite for participation in the job-based economic opportunity structure. Socioeconomic mobility, although much more restricted than commonly held within the U.S. value system, is also strongly dependent on the credentialing process.

I suspect that an important part of educational success (i.e., the rate at which students achieve these credentials, as well as the skills that the public expects to be attached to them; e.g., a high school degree indicates literacy, arithmetic skills, and behavioral adjustment) is itself stratified by the processes of social and spatial isolation (Bowles & Gintis, 1977). These forces maldistribute economic and human capital so that, over time, a communal expectation of educational failure emerges.

This expectation of educational failure is double-edged. Schools in poor communities are expected to fail, and students who fail to graduate from these same schools, or even succeed in graduating, are assumed to share in the expected failure of the school.

These processes do not work as perfectly predictable systems. Students succeed despite a model that distributes success in a limited fashion—and pre-"determines" failure for many. The question for debate, at once both theoretical and methodological, is this: Is resilience the appropriate conceptual anchor for the discussion and identification of these exceptions? Or should our attention be aimed at identifying patterns of "systemic failure" (e.g., those students, schools, and communities that defy systemically applied expectations of failure).

The task is daunting. Recall the cases noted previously, of Anthony and Martin. In fact, they are not different boys, but the same person: Andre McNatte, an Overbrook High School freshman, was shot while holding up a convenience store in his neighborhood. His funeral was January 28, 1992. How do we apply the concept of resilience, when resilience in dealing with the conflicting demands of a schizophrenic social existence make goal-seeking behavior, an integral part of the resilience construct, a set of profoundly difficult choices.

This argument implies that a prior issue to resilience exists (i.e., what are the changes that need to be made in community and school contexts to permit resilience strategies to be introduced?).

CONCLUSION

This chapter began with a consideration of the problems with external validity that are contained in the concept of resilience. The conclusion I present is that the concept has great difficulty not being confounded with subjective impressions of success and adversity, and that it cannot be disentangled from important issues of social and educational context. Further, the concept unnecessarily restricts policy options by focusing on the ''resilient'' student, school, or community. Instead of using this as the point of intervention, one option is to consider a slightly different approach to the concept.

The alternative model of resilience that we have discussed suggests a focus on resilient systems—ones that link school, community, and student performance in a functional relationship. The major barrier to such an approach is its fundamental assumption that students, schools, and communities are relatively consistent in their goals and values. Although this may hold true in some communities, it seems clear that this is not the case in the inner cities of urban areas that are feeling the worst effects of economic reorganization.

Given the difficulties in developing a useful conceptual meaning, let alone empirical referents, for resilience, it should be expected that my recommendation would be to discard the term altogether. But this is not entirely the case. Although I find its use as the central orienting concept for educational change problematic at best, there is a sense in which it should be considered within the debate over educational change. We should be asking a set of interrelated questions that are logically prior to those aimed at identifying ''resilient'' students, schools, and communities. Those questions are: What do we need to do to create communities within which resilient schools and students can function? What roles might schools play in establishing such communities? How do we marshal human and financial resources to break the mold for such communities?

It is in these questions that the issue of resilience is truly joined. Until we can guarantee some measure of coherence between everyday life, schools, and the transition from schools to community membership, we beg the issue of resilience, as we assume that our students attach value to schooling. Unless we can make that valuation real, resilient students will not perform in schools, but use their resilience for survival on the streets.

REFERENCES

Anderson, E. (1990). *Streetwise*. Chicago: University of Chicago Press.
Bowles, S., & Gintis, H. (1977). *Schooling in capitalist America*. New York: Basic Books.
Crane, J. (1991). Effects of neighborhoods on dropping out of school and teenage childbearing. In C. Jencks & P. Peterson (Eds.), *The urban underclass* (pp. 299–320). Washington, DC: Brookings Institution.

Goode, D. A. (1979). The world of the congenitally deaf-blind. In H. Schwartz & J. Jacobs (Eds.), *Qualitative sociology* (pp. 187–207). New York: The Free Press.

Gould, S. J. (1981). *The mismeasure of man.* New York: Norton.

Ihlanfeldt, K. R. (1992). *Job accessibility and the employment and school enrollment of teenagers.* Kalamazoo, MI: Upjohn Institute.

Jankowski, M. S. (1991). *Islands in the street.* Berkeley: University of California Press.

Kaplan, A. (1964). *The conduct of inquiry.* San Francisco: Chandler.

Katz, M. (1993). *The "underclass" debate: Lessons from history.* Princeton, NJ: Princeton University Press.

Moore, J. (1978). *Homeboys: Gangs, drugs and prison in the barrios of Los Angeles.* Philadelphia: Temple University Press.

Moore, J. (1991). *Going down to the barrio.* Philadelphia: Temple University Press.

Walizer, M. H., & Wienir, P. L. (1978). *Research methods and analysis: Searching for relationships.* New York: Harper & Row.

West, N. (1961). *A cool million.* New York: Berkley.

Wilson, W. J. (1987). *The truly disadvantaged: The inner city, the underclass, and public policy.* Chicago: University of Chicago Press.

Chapter 7

Resilience as a Dispositional Quality: Some Methodological Points

Joan McCord
Temple University

"Let no one think that it did not hurt baseball. That hurt will pass, however, as the great glory of the game asserts itself, and as a resilient institution goes forward." So claimed Bartlett Giamatti when he banished Pete Rose for life from baseball (Higgins, 1990, p. 200). Giamatti meant baseball would be little changed while its fans turned to Kirby Puckett and other new heroes.

A resilient institution is one that shows little change despite its losses. We speak of resilient people as well as institutions, but this does not mean that a resilient person shows little change as a result of adverse experiences. People do change. In fact, one could argue that a mark of personal resilience is the degree to which a person changes in response to altered circumstances. At a minimum, constancy seems an inadequate criterion for personal resilience. Resilience implies that a person thrives despite adversity, or perhaps because of it. For example, financial hardship seems to promote survival skills among some children (Elder, 1974). Being reared by schizophrenics has, according to Manfred Bleuler (1974), "a steeling—hardening effect—on some children, rendering them capable of mastering life with all its obstacles" (p. 106). Paternal loss, unemployment, and parental conflict apparently sometimes promote subsequent warmth within the family of procreation (McCord, 1984).

The search for conditions to protect people at risk from developing problems has an honored position in medicine. By looking for conditions that mark differences between healthy survivors and those who succumb to disease, scientists have discovered antibodies for a number of disorders. The discoveries have provided a foundation for vaccinations and rehabilitation techniques.

The concept of *resilience* has a considerable degree of appeal for a broader application to people. It suggests that there are qualities in individuals or their environments that enable them to face difficulties and overcome them. In addition, there might be forms of "vaccination" that could serve as protective factors, increasing the probability of favorable outcomes.

Studying resilience as a quality in people or their environments raises several difficulties, some of which are addressed in this chapter. The first occurs because opinions regarding what constitutes a "beneficial outcome" are diverse and sometimes contradictory.

In the study of physical disorders, a physician has reason to believe that consensus supports the view that health is the goal, and that health is defined in roughly the same terms by patients, their parents and children, and by doctors. In considering socially and psychologically defined disorders, there is no such consensus. What from some perspectives would be viewed as appropriate socialized behavior, from another might be seen as inappropriate docility. What from some perspectives seems to be using artistic imagination is condemned from others as inappropriate attacks on social norms. Drug abuse and alcoholism have long been perceived to be the companions, if not the cause, of such great artistic works as "The Raven," "Kubla Khan," and "A Long Day's Journey into Night." Some might judge that Poe, Coleridge, and O'Neill produced despite their addictions, but others assert that drugs provided the means by which these men withstood excruciating pressures to produce artistic syntheses. The first approach might be a basis for seeing addiction as disease, whereas the second would be marking drug use as a possible palliative.

The same sets of data can be interpreted to suggest opposite conclusions; whether the benefits of addiction outweigh the harms might depend on whether the judgment is made by the addicted, the family or friends, or the art-appreciating public. The world would surely be a poorer place if it lacked "Road with Cypresses" and "The Olive Orchard," although van Gogh doubtless suffered greatly from his mental disorder. Similarly, what counts as resilience often depends on the perspective. For example, consider Richard Rhodes. Rhodes' mother died during his infancy, and his stepmother was so cruel that the courts removed him from her care. Rhodes won a Pulitzer Prize for writing about the making of the atomic bomb. Because of this success, a reasonable claim could be made that he demonstrated resilience. Yet his autobiography reveals years of trouble and pain, psychotherapy, and alcoholism (Rhodes, 1990).

To return to the medical analogy, medical researchers have a finite set of conditions to consider when examining whether the elimination of one disorder generates an alternative problem. If replacing a valve in the heart creates immune reactions or infections, the procedure might be classified as undesirable. But the medical researcher need not consider whether heart replacement leads to unemployment, alcoholism, or high rates of divorce. On the other hand, if a social program were to reduce the rate of school dropout while increasing the amount of crime, it would be less clear whether the program should be judged successful.

The issue is not imaginary. For instance, in 1987 Gottfredson introduced a program of guided group interaction into several public elementary and high schools. Schools were randomly selected for inclusion in either the treatment or the control group. Positive leaders, negative leaders, troublesome children, and average children were included in the pool. Fifty-one percent of both the treatment and the control group were male, approximately the same proportions were Caucasian, and the groups were equivalent in terms of the prestige of parental occupations, prior police contacts, and age. The program was well received and apparently successful at the time of implementation. School tardiness, attachment to parents, self-reported delinquency, and "waywardness" were used to measure outcome. Gottfredson (1987) summarized the results of the posttreatment comparisons for high school students: "The magnitudes of these effects . . . are not large, but they imply adverse effects of the treatment program as implemented in this realization" (p. 705).

A second difficulty results from the overlapping nature of different disabilities. For example, both common and differential sets of conditions place children at high risk for dropping out of school, becoming delinquent, and developing drug problems. The differences tend to be minimized in studies that show a link between learning disabilities and conduct disorders (e.g., Coie & Krehbiel, 1984; Dodge, 1983; Farrington & Loeber, 1987; Green, Gustafson, & West, 1980; McGee & Share, 1988). Many studies indicate also that delinquents tend to lack interest in school (Bachman, Green, & Wirtanen, 1971; Elliott & Voss, 1974; Farrington, Gallagher, Morley, St. Ledger, & West, 1986; Reiss & Rhodes, 1959). Clearly, however, not all school dropouts become delinquents or use drugs. Nor are delinquents necessarily low in their desires for achievement (Gould, 1969).

Delinquents are, however, likely to have rejecting parents, and are likely to be reared in conflictful households (Farrington, 1986; Hirschi, 1969; Loeber & Stouthamer-Loeber, 1986; McCord, 1979; Werner, 1987). Conversely, children who do well in school tend to have warm, democratic, supportive parents (Amato & Ochiltree, 1986; Bachman et al., 1971; Barton, Dielman, & Cattell, 1974; Clark, 1983; McClelland, Atkinson, Clark, & Lowell, 1953; Rosen & D'Andrade, 1959; Strodtbeck, 1958). These facts could lead one to conclude that parental warmth and support in an egalitarian, tranquil environment serve as protective factors and tend to produce resilient individuals.

Unfortunately, this conclusion rests on insufficient evidence regarding resilience. A child brought up by loving, supportive parents who provide an egalitarian, tranquil environment might do well because such a child is unlikely to encounter difficulties that require resilience. If so, it would be a mistake to conclude that such families produce the kinds of people who could survive, for example, the hardships of war, disease, or social crises. As Rutter (1987) pointed out, psychosocial resilience involves successful engagement with risk, not the evasion of it.

A third difficulty rests on the easy confounding of absence of conditions that produce problems with presence of conditions that would mitigate or prevent them were such problems to arise. For example, evidence that crime rates increase with increasing "criminogenic" pressures, and decrease with fewer of these pressures, has tended to obscure the difference between protective conditions and prevention (Cass & Thomas, 1979; Farrington, 1988; Robins, 1966; Robins & Ratcliff, 1979). Prevention involves avoiding conditions that give rise to problems, whereas protective factors operate conditionally. Protective factors must be potent in the presence of risk. They need not be potent when risk factors are absent.

Many studies indicate that parental conflict is highly criminogenic, and may be responsible for most of the criminogenic effects attributed to broken homes (Emery, 1982; Farrington, 1978, 1986; Hirschi, 1969; Loeber & Stouthamer-Loeber, 1986; McCord, 1982, 1990; Power, Ash, Shoenberg, & Sirey, 1974; Werner & Smith, 1982). Low rates of crime among children reared in tranquil homes would suggest that removal from conflictful homes might provide protection against harmful effects. In fact, Rutter (1971) found such decreases in conduct disorder among children of psychiatric patients removed from conflictful homes and placed in tranquil environments. Whether removal from a conflictful home in the absence of psychiatric difficulties would reduce criminal behavior has not been tested.

A variety of methodological approaches have been used to identify conditions that appear to reduce risk, given exposure to adverse conditions (e.g., Garmezy, 1974; Kagan, 1976; Kobasa, 1979; McCord, 1986; Rutter, 1966). These approaches suggest that it might be fruitful to reconceptualize some variables in categorical terms so that they can be considered potent at only one pole. For example, strong affectional ties might serve to prevent delinquency in the presence of other risk factors, but absence of affection might not be criminogenic without those risk factors.

Among high-risk samples in London (Farrington & West, 1981), Kauai (Werner & Smith, 1982), Norway (Olweus, 1980), Finland (Pulkkinen, 1983), and Massachusetts (McCord, 1986), crime rates appeared to be reduced by the presence of an affectionate parent. Rutter and Giller (1983) suggested that a single good relationship might serve to insulate a child against potentially damaging childhood environments.

Social support has been found to be correlated with an ability to withstand a variety of stressful life events (Eaton, 1978; Holahan & Moos, 1981, 1985; Johnson & Sarason, 1979; Lindenthal & Myers, 1979). Soldiers in combat seem to survive better with comrades, and children in London apparently better handled the attacks over their homes when sheltered in groups (Bovard, 1959). Fewer birth complications appeared among pregnant army wives who reported having social support than among those who reported little social support (Cobb, 1976). Lower drug dosages were required to control asthmatic symptoms among people experiencing stressful changes (de Araujo, van Arsdel, Holmes, & Dudley, 1973). The beneficial effects of social support seem stronger for women than for men (Holahan & Moos, 1985), which might account for the failure to find a relation between having people with whom to talk and strain among lawyers (Kobasa, 1982).

Another candidate for unipolar prevention is shyness. Shy children who are not aggressive have been found unlikely to become criminals (Ensminger, Kellam, & Rubin, 1983; Farrington, Gallagher, Morley, St. Ledger, & West, 1988; McCord, 1987). Yet gregariousness is not seemingly criminogenic.

One apparently successful experimental study of protective factors used an approach based on moral reasoning. Huesmann, Eron, Klein, Brice, and Fischer (1983) asked a randomly selected group of children who watched violent television shows to produce a film indicating why watching television is bad and why imitating aggression is wrong. Compared with a control group, these children were considerably less aggressive at a follow-up 4 months later.

Education, intelligence, and legitimate opportunities to gain recognition might also be protective factors. Community variables also provide reasonable candidates for protective factors. Just as the availability of subcultures that support crime increase the probability of crime, the availability of prosocial influences can be expected to serve a protective role.

More work needs to be done to learn how protective factors should be identified. Experimental studies should be particularly useful in this regard. One way to avoid disease is to reduce exposure to infection. But vaccinations and prostheses may provide alternative models that are more fruitful as approaches to crime prevention. Children reared by cold, rejecting, aggressive parents may be helped without necessarily changing the parents or finding parental substitutes.

A fourth difficulty arises because signs of problems have different developmental triggers; what seems to be a protective factor during one period may not be at a later date. The invulnerable child may not be an invulnerable adult (Anthony, 1974). Werner (1986) found that resilient children of alcoholics, identified at age 18, had been good communicators whose temperaments promoted receiving affection and whose families lacked parental conflict. Yet children of alcoholics may appear to be adjusted, only later becoming alcoholic adults. Self-esteem has been found to be related to concurrent performance, although not to subsequent educational attainment or occupational status (Bachman & O'Malley, 1977).

What makes studying resilience particularly difficult—and interesting—is that resilience is dispositional. People, groups, neighborhoods, and organizations are resilient to the extent that they can withstand adversity. Of course, not every resilient person, group, neighborhood, or organization is "put to the test." That is, not all that could withstand adversity encounter it. Yet the qualities producing resilience are present even when, or perhaps only when, untested.

Like fragility, solubility, and combustibility, resilience is promissory. We can come to a better understanding of resilience by considering these parallel dispositional qualities.

A fragile friendship threatens to break, so one must be careful not to express too much displeasure, to yield handsomely, or to provide frequent support. Fragile relationships tend to be transformed by exposure to risk, either becoming stronger or disappearing. Were fragile relationships studied after such exposure, only the transformed characteristics would be evident. To study fragile relationships, one must identify them before they are tested.

A fragile object ought to be handled gently. If detection of fragility depended on exposure to risk, few fragile objects would be available for study. These might, in fact, have different characteristics from those that broke when they were exposed.

Studies of resilience only after exposure to risk may mistake the products of adversity for the qualities of resilience. For example, it is possible that the challenge of adversity serves to increase the ability of some people to think clearly. If so, high intelligence could be a product of successful encounters with adversity, rather than a description of one of the qualities of resilience. To avoid confusing transformed qualities with those that are essential to resilience, we must identify resilience prior to exposure to adversity.

A soluble chemical will dissolve in one of a number of possible liquids. Vitamin C is soluble in water, whereas vitamin A is soluble in fat. The property of solubility behaves in lawful ways. For example, a solution is homogeneous and the boiling point of the solvent is raised in proportion to the amount of dissolved substance. Discovering these laws required the study of processes involving interaction between soluble chemicals and solvents.

We know that there are strains of virus that are resilient to certain antibodies but not to all. It seems reasonable to suppose that some characteristics of individuals, groups, organizations, and neighborhoods are resilient to certain types of stress, but not to others. Children may be resilient to poverty in terms of mental health, if they have affection, but affection may be little protection from the stress of living with alcoholic parents. In order to understand processes that lead to resilience, studies should focus on the interactions between different forms of risks and different types of response.

A person has a combustible temperament if that person frequently gets angry. A combustible piece of property is one that will burn. But something that is combustible does not necessarily evidence anger or burn. Were one to depend on constancy of response, it might not be possible to identify the qualities that render a person or an object combustible.

Combustible clothing may not catch fire when exposed to flame, although sometimes the clothing will be weakened by the heat. We should not be surprised to find that people who seem resilient to a particular set of symptoms sometimes evidence alternatives. For example, females appear to be more resilient to the pressures leading to conduct disorders in males. Yet females are more likely to become depressed under similar circumstances.

Much of the work on resilience has confounded an emotionally or morally charged meaning with a descriptive meaning of resilience. That is, in using the term *resilient*, praise has been intended. This use, although perhaps politically wise, may be scientifically damaging.

We should be wary of premature closure on the qualities leading to resilience. For the same conditions that lead to resilience in one environment could be harmful in others. Such context effects can be found in biology. For example, sickle cells in homozygous form generate anemia; in heterozygous form, however, they provide protection against malaria (Rotter & Diamond, 1987). We might find, similarly, that strict regimens in tough areas of cities lead to resilient schools, whereas similar regimens in less chaotic areas produce boredom or resentment.

If we hope to increase such important characteristics as independence, desire for knowledge, or promotion of mutual respect, greater clarity is needed regarding the conditions leading from various types of difficult experiences to these outcomes. The judgment that independence, desire for knowledge, and mutual respect are worth promoting is, of course, evaluative. Yet the study of how to promote such outcomes ought not confound approval with scientific method.

Techniques that may themselves appear undesirable may acquire positive overtones if it is discovered that they promote resilience. Consider the case of vaccination. Sticking needles into babies is not ordinarily thought of as an activity worthy of approval. Through discovering how the body works in relation to invading bacteria, however, the sticking of certain types of needles into babies acquired a different description—one that showed that sticking needles into babies could be an act of kindness.

We may eventually discover that schools of a certain type, perhaps of a type not seemingly worthy of praise, promote characteristics in children that help them develop into productive adults. We need to look for outcomes in order to evaluate processes. Without such examination, we are likely to promote processes which lead to undesired outcomes.

Cross-sectional observational studies are tempting because they can be done quickly and relatively inexpensively. They cannot, however, identify protective conditions, and they are inappropriate for the study of resilience. Only through carefully designed longitudinal studies, incorporating conditions of risk and adequate measures of environments as well as personality, can we expect progress in the development of adequate social programs.

ACKNOWLEDGMENTS

The research reported herein is supported in part by the Temple University Center for Research in Human Development and Education (CRHDE) and in part by the Office of Educational Research and Improvement (OERI) of the U.S. Department of Education through a grant to the National Center on Education in the Inner Cities (CEIC) at Temple University. The opinions expressed do not necessarily reflect the position of the supporting agencies and no official endorsement should be inferred.

REFERENCES

Amato, P. R., & Ochiltree, G. (1986). Family resources and the development of child competence. *Journal of Marriage and the Family, 48,* 47–56.

Anthony, E. J. (1974). The syndrome of the psychologically invulnerable child. In E. J. Anthony & C. Koupernik (Eds.), *The child in his family: Children at psychiatric risk* (pp. 529–544). New York: Wiley.

Bachman, J. G., Green, S., & Wirtanen, I. D. (1971). *Youth in transition: Dropping out: Problem or symptom?* (Vol. 3). Ann Arbor, MI: Institute for Social Research.

Bachman, J. G., & O'Malley, P. M. (1977). Self-esteem in young men: A longitudinal analysis of the impact of educational and occupational attainment. *Journal of Personality and Social Psychology, 35*(6), 365–380.

Barton, K., Dielman, T. E., & Cattell, R. B. (1974). Child rearing practices and achievement in school. *The Journal of Genetic Psychology, 124,* 155–165.

Bleuler, M. (1974). The offspring of schizophrenics. *Schizophrenia Bulletin, 8,* 93–107.

Bovard, E. W. (1959). The effects of social stimuli on the response to stress. *Psychological Bulletin, 66,* 267–277.

Cass, L. K., & Thomas, C. B. (1979). *Childhood pathology and later adjustment.* New York: Wiley.

Clark, R. (1983). *Family life and school achievement: Why poor black children succeed or fail.* Chicago: University of Chicago Press.

Cobb, S. (1976). Social support as a moderator of life stress. *Psychomatic Medicine, 38,* 300–314.

Coie, J. D., & Krehbiel, G. (1984). Effects of academic tutoring on the social status of low-achieving, socially rejected children. *Child Development, 55,* 1465–1478.

de Araujo, G., van Arsdel, P., Holmes, T., & Dudley, D. (1973). Life change, coping ability and chronic intrinsic asthma. *Journal of Psychomatic Research, 17,* 359–363.

Dodge, K. A. (1983). Behavioral antecedents of peer social status. *Child Development, 54,* 1386–1399.

Eaton, W. W. (1978). Life events, social supports, and psychiatric symptoms: A reanalysis of the New Haven data. *Journal of Health and Social Behavior, 19,* 230–234.

Elder, G. H., Jr. (1974). *Children of the Great Depression.* Chicago: University of Chicago Press.

Elliott, D. S., & Voss, H. L. (1974). *Delinquency and dropout.* Lexington, MA: Heath.

Emery, R. E. (1982). Interparental conflict and the children of discord and divorce. *Psychological Bulletin, 92,* 310–330.

Ensminger, M. E., Kellam, S. G., & Rubin, B. R. (1983). School and family origins of delinquency: Comparisons by sex. In K. T. Van Dusen & S. A. Mednick (Eds.), *Prospective studies of crime and delinquency* (pp. 73–97). Boston: Kluwer-Nijhoff.

Farrington, D. P. (1978). The family backgrounds of aggressive youths. In L. A. Hersov & M. Berger (Eds.), *Aggression and anti-social behaviour in childhood and adolescence* (pp. 73–93). Oxford: Pergamon.

Farrington, D. P. (1986). Stepping stones to adult criminal careers. In D. Olweus, J. Block, & M. Radke-Yarrow (Eds.), *Development of antisocial and prosocial behavior* (pp. 359–384). New York: Academic Press.

Farrington, D. P. (1988). Advancing knowledge about delinquency and crime: The need for a coordinated program of longitudinal research. *Behavioral Sciences & the Law, 6*(3), 307–331.

Farrington, D. P., Gallagher, B., Morley, L., St. Ledger, R. J., & West, D. J. (1986). Unemployment, school leaving, and crime. *British Journal of Criminology, 26*(4), 335–356.

Farrington, D. P., Gallagher, B., Morley, L., St. Ledger, R. J., & West, D. J. (1988). Are there any successful men from criminogenic backgrounds? *Psychiatry, 51*(2), 116–130.

Farrington, D. P., & Loeber, R. (1987, October). *Long-term criminality of conduct disorder boys with or without impulsive-inattentive behavior.* Paper presented at the Life History Research Society, St. Louis, MO.

Farrington, D. P., & West, D. J. (1981). The Cambridge study in delinquent development (United Kingdom). In S. A. Mednick & A. E. Baert (Eds.), *Prospective longitudinal research: An empirical basis for primary prevention* (pp. 137–145). Oxford: Oxford University Press.

Garmezy, N. (1974). The study of competence in children at risk for severe psychopathology. In E. Anthony & C. Koupernik (Eds.), *The child in his family: Children at psychiatric risk* (pp. 77–97). New York: Wiley.

Gottfredson, G. D. (1987). Peer group interventions to reduce the risk of delinquent behavior: A selective review and a new evaluation. *Criminology, 25*(3), 671–714.

Gould, L. C. (1969). Juvenile entrepreneurs. *American Journal of Sociology, 74*(6), 710–719.

Green, J. A., Gustafson, G. E., & West, M. J. (1980). Effects of infant development on mother-infant interactions. *Child Development, 51*(1), 199–207.

Higgins, G. V. (1990). Fields of broken dreams. *The American Scholar, 59*(2), 199–210.

Hirschi, T. (1969). *Causes of delinquency.* Berkeley: University of California Press.

Holahan, C. J., & Moos, R. H. (1981). Social support and psychological distress: A longitudinal analysis. *Journal of Abnormal Psychology, 90*(4), 365–370.

Holahan, C. J., & Moos, R. H. (1985). Life stress and health: Personality, coping, and family support in stress resistance. *Journal of Personality and Social Psychology, 49*(3), 739–747.

Huesmann, L. R., Eron, L. D., Klein, R., Brice, P., & Fischer, P. (1983). Mitigating the imitation of aggressive behaviors by changing children's attitudes about media violence. *Journal of Personality and Social Psychology, 44*(5), 899–910.

Johnson, J. H., & Sarason, I. G. (1979). Moderator variables in life stress research. In I. G. Sarason & C. D. Spielberger (Eds.), *Stress and anxiety* (pp. 151–167). New York: Halstead.

Kagan, J. (1976). Resilience and continuity in psychological development. In A. Clarke & A. Clarke (Eds.), *Early experience: Myth and evidence* (pp. 97–121). New York: The Free Press.

Kobasa, S. C. (1979). Stressful life events, personality, and health: An inquiry into hardiness. *Journal of Personality and Social Psychology, 37*(1), 1–11.

Kobasa, S. C. (1982). Commitment and coping in stress resistance among lawyers. *Journal of Personality and Social Psychology, 42*(4), 707–717.

Lindenthal, J. J., & Myers, J. (1979). The New Haven Longitudinal Survey. In I. G. Sarason & C. D. Spielberger (Eds.), *Stress and anxiety* (Vol. 6, pp. 269–288). New York: Wiley.

Loeber, R., & Stouthamer-Loeber, M. (1986). Family factors as correlates and predictors of juvenile conduct problems and delinquency. In M. Tonry & N. Morris (Eds.), *Crime and justice* (Vol. 7, pp. 29–149). Chicago: University of Chicago Press.

McClelland, D. C., Atkinson, J.W., Clark, R. A., & Lowell, E. (1953). *The achievement motive.* New York: Appleton-Century-Crofts.

McCord, J. (1979). Some child-rearing antecedents of criminal behavior in adult men. *Journal of Personality and Social Psychology, 37*, 1477–1486.

McCord, J. (1982). A longitudinal view of the relationship between paternal absence and crime. In J. Gunn & D. P. Farrington (Eds.), *Abnormal offenders, delinquency, and the criminal justice system* (pp. 113–128). Chichester: Wiley.

McCord, J. (1984). Early stress and future personality. In N. R. Butler & B. D. Corner (Eds.), *Stress and disability in childhood* (pp. 105–112). Bristol: Wright.

McCord, J. (1986). Instigation and insulation: How families affect antisocial aggression. In J. Block, D. Olweus, & M. Radke-Yarrow (Eds.), *Development of antisocial and prosocial behavior* (pp. 343–357). New York: Academic Press.

McCord, J. (1987). *Aggression and shyness as predictors of problems: Another view.* Paper presented at biennial meeting of the Society for Research in Child Development, Baltimore, MD.

McCord, J. (1990). Long-term perspectives on parental absence. In L. N. Robins & M. Rutter (Eds.), *Straight and devious pathways from childhood to adulthood* (pp. 116–134). Cambridge: Cambridge University Press.

McGee, R., & Share, D. L. (1988). Attention deficit disorder—hyperactivity and academic failure: Which comes first and what should be treated? *Journal of the American Academy of Child and Adolescent Psychiatry, 27*(3), 318–325.

Olweus, D. (1980). Familial and temperamental determinants of aggressive behavior in adolescent boys: A causal analysis. *Developmental Psychology, 16,* 644–660.

Power, M. J., Ash, P. M., Shoenberg, E., & Sirey, E. C. (1974). Delinquency and the family. *British Journal of Social Work, 4,* 13–38.

Pulkkinen, L. (1983). Search for alternatives to aggression in Finland. In A. P. Goldstein & M. H. Segall (Eds.), *Aggression in global perspective* (pp. 104–144). Elmsford, NY: Pergamon Press.

Reiss, A. J., Jr., & Rhodes, A. L. (1959). Are educational norms and goals of conforming, truant and delinquent adolescents influenced by group position in American society? *Journal of Negro Education, 28,* 252–267.

Rhodes, R. (1990). *A hole in the world.* New York: Simon & Schuster.

Robins, L. N. (1966). *Deviant children grown up.* Baltimore: Williams & Wilkins.

Robins, L. N., & Ratcliff, K. S. (1979). Risk factors in the continuation of childhood antisocial behavior into adulthood. *International Journal of Mental Health, 7,* 96–116.

Rosen, B. C., & D'Andrade, R. G. (1959). The psychosocial origins of achievement motivation. *Sociometry, 22,* 185–218.

Rotter, J. I., & Diamond, J. M. (1987). What maintains the frequencies of human genetic diseases? *Nature, 329,* 289–290.

Rutter, M. (1966). *Children of sick parents: An environmental and psychiatric study.* London: Oxford University Press.

Rutter, M. (1971). Parent–child separation: Psychological effects on the children. *Journal of Child Psychology and Psychiatry, 12,* 233–260.

Rutter, M. (1987). Psychosocial resilience and protective mechanisms. *American Journal of Orthopsychiatry, 57*(3), 316–331.

Rutter, M., & Giller, H. (1983). *Juvenile delinquency: Trends and perspectives.* Middlesex, England: Penguin.

Strodtbeck, F. L. (1958). Family interaction and achievement. In D. C. McClelland, A. L. Baldwin, U. Bronfenbrenner, & F. L. Strodtbeck (Eds.), *Talent and society* (pp. 135–194). Princeton: D. Van Nostrand.

Werner, E. E. (1986). Resilient offspring of alcoholics: A longitudinal study from birth to age 18. *Journal of Studies on Alcohol, 47,* 34–40.

Werner, E. E. (1987). Vulnerability and resiliency in children at risk for delinquency: A longitudinal study from birth to young adulthood. In J. D. Burchard & S. N. Burchard (Eds.), *Prevention of delinquent behavior* (pp. 16–43). Newbury Park, CA: Sage.

Werner, E. E., & Smith, R. S. (1982). *Vulnerable but invincible.* New York: McGraw-Hill.

Chapter 8

Risk and Resilience: Contextual Influences on the Development of African-American Adolescents

Ronald D. Taylor
Temple University

Masten (chapter 1, this volume) states that resilience in individuals refers to successful adaptation despite risk and adversity. When individuals are judged to be resilient, the implication is that they have displayed adaptive behavior despite facing risks and adversities. Risk factors or adversities may come in a variety of forms, and those discussed by Masten include parental mental illness, economic disadvantage, teenage motherhood, chronic illness, criminal behavior, and delinquency. Indeed, it is possible for individuals to fall into groups having more than one risk factor (e.g., economically disadvantaged teenage mothers).

Understanding resilience requires that obstacles to adaptation be understood, and that the standard for or definition of adaptive behavior be delineated. *Adaptation* in the study of resilience, as in the study of developmental psychopathology, is defined in terms of the attainment of psychosocial milestones called *developmental tasks* (Masten & Braswell, 1991). Developmental tasks represent broadly defined standards or expectations for behavior at various points in the life span.

The focus of this chapter is a discussion of the developmental tasks of adolescents, the major environmental risks that confront African-American adolescents, evidence of resilience in light of the risks faced and explanations for the observed adaptation, and implications for the education of African-American adolescents.

DEVELOPMENTAL TASKS DURING ADOLESCENCE

The developmental tasks facing adolescents prepare them to assume adult roles and responsibilities. According to Steinberg (1990), developmental tasks facing adolescents are in three areas: (a) intimacy and interpersonal responsibility, (b) identity and personal responsibility, and (c) achievement and social responsibility. Intimacy and interpersonal responsibility are important because adolescents, in order to grow into mature adults, must develop the capacity for forming satisfying interpersonal attachments to others. Adolescents' capacity to competently manage their interpersonal relations will have implications for how well they function in multiple domains, including family, work, and leisure.

The developmental task concerning identity and personal responsibility involves the need for adolescents to develop a clear sense of their attitudes, values, and beliefs, and the "ability to make informed decisions, exercise judgement, and regulate one's own behavior appropriately" (Steinberg, 1990, p. 25). During adolescence, individuals are required to make choices based on a consideration of both their own values and opinions and the optimal alternatives in a given situation. Those adolescents who are uncertain about their views, and unwilling or unable to make informed choices, are at a decided disadvantage in managing this developmental task.

For African-American youngsters, the issue of identity formation has added complexity due to the status of African Americans in U.S. society. As Spencer and Dornbusch (1990) noted, minority adolescents face the task of developing an identity in the context of a mainstream culture that views the attributes and values of minority groups as unfavorable. The decision making of African-American adolescents is further complicated because mainstream cultural values and African-American cultural traditions sometimes conflict (see Boykin & Toms, 1985, for a discussion).

The developmental task of achievement and social responsibility involves the need for adolescents to develop the skills and knowledge necessary to participate as active members of society, as well as a personal belief system that will be a foundation for moral and ethical behavior. The changing nature of the labor market with respect to high-skill jobs makes it essential that adolescents develop higher order competencies. In order to function as adequate members of their communities, they must also develop the values and beliefs from which decisions about moral and ethical issues or dilemmas can be made.

RISKS AND THE DEVELOPMENT
OF AFRICAN-AMERICAN ADOLESCENTS

Mastery of these developmental tasks is defined as resilience if there is evidence of significant odds that would block or impede their attainment. Genetic liabilities or assets may constrain or facilitate adaptation, but the focus of this chapter is on environmental liabilities or assets, on understanding the nature of resilience as a function of environmental conditions that pose a challenge to development. The conditions associated with poverty and economic disadvantage are, perhaps, the environmental factors most challenging to the adaptation of African American families and adolescents.

Obviously, not all African-American families are poor, but African Americans and other minorities shoulder a disproportionate share of the burden of poverty and unemployment in the United States. In 1985, the poverty rate for African-American children under 18 years old was 41% compared to 13% for White children (Duncan, 1988). The unemployment rate of African Americans is typically twice that of White workers. Approximately 45% of all African-American children live in female-headed households, and the majority of these children (70%) are poor (Center for the Study of Social Policy, 1986).

A host of problems linked to poverty and economic hardship currently plague inner-city life, including high rates of joblessness, crime, drug addiction, teenage pregnancy, and a general social isolation from mainstream society (Wilson, 1987). For parents, negative psychological outcomes associated with poverty include depression (Dressler, 1985; Pearlin & Johnson, 1977) and other forms of psychiatric impairment (see Liem & Liem, 1978, for a review). Economic hardship has also been linked to marital conflict (Bishop, 1977; Furstenberg, 1976). In children, economic hardship has been associated with depression (Gibbs, 1986; Lempers, Clark-Lempers, & Simons, 1989), somatic complaints (McLoyd, cited in McLoyd, 1990), and conduct disorders (Myers & King, 1983).

The processes through which conditions associated with economic hardship act as risk factors, impeding adolescents' adjustment, are not well known. Research has shown that economic disadvantage can have a negative impact on parents' childrearing practices (Conger, McCarty, Yang, Lahey, & Kropp, 1984; Lempers et al., 1989; Longfellow, Zelkowitz, & Saunders, 1982; McLoyd & Wilson, 1991). For example, McLoyd and Wilson (1991) found that economically disadvantaged mothers experiencing psychological distress perceived parenting as more difficult, and were less nurturing of their children, than less distressed mothers. Several researchers (e.g., McLoyd, 1990; Taylor & Roberts, 1992) noted that economic hardship has a negative influence on parents' behavior, which in turn has deleterious effects on adolescents' behavior.

Economic hardship, as it influences family functioning and the nature of families' living conditions, may also affect adolescents' capacity to master developmental tasks. The ability to form satisfying interpersonal attachments may be at risk, given the nature of parent–child relations in homes where economic resources are insufficient. For example, economic hardship has been linked to problems in children's peer relations (Elder, 1974; Langner, Herson, Greene, Jameson, & Goff, 1970). McLoyd (1990) noted that children and adolescents of parents experiencing economic hardship are more likely to be exposed to power-assertive and punitive discipline practices. These practices may be transferred to the child or adolescent, affecting how she or he interacts with peers. Thus, adolescents may learn coercive methods of negotiating interpersonal conflicts from the form of parental discipline or control displayed in the home. Such forms of behavior may not, however, be popular among the adolescents' peers.

Exposure to crime, drug abuse, or teenage pregnancy may influence the process of identity formation and adolescent decision making in important areas. For instance, as Scott-Jones and White (1990) suggested, to the extent that adolescents perceive economic hardship looming in their futures, they may see little advantage in delaying sexual activity and childbearing. Also, to the extent that economically disadvantaged African-American adolescents are at a greater risk for such problems as depression, somatic complaints, or conduct disorders, their capacity for engaging in behaviors aimed at promoting the development of skills and abilities necessary for active citizenship may be endangered.

Minority status is also a factor that may impede efforts by African-American youngsters to attain expected developmental outcomes. Clearly, minority status and social class are linked; indeed, untangling the effects of minority status versus social class status represents a challenge to those studying the functioning of African-American families. Although working-class and middle-class African Americans may not face many of the environmental stresses that imperil poor adolescents and their families, all African-American adolescents must confront the effects of racial bias and discrimination in U.S. society. This bias takes a variety of forms, including (a) daily experiences of discriminatory behavior from individuals or institutions (or both); and (b) adolescents' recognition of the political, occupational, and residential restrictions facing African Americans.

A number of researchers have recently examined adolescents' reactions to their experiences and awareness of racial bias. For example, Anderson (1990) discussed the social experiences and behavior of African-American males as they cross into and out of two inner-city communities, one an economically disadvantaged African-American community, the other an integrated community experiencing gentrification. Anderson's analysis clearly reveals that adolescents' behavior is shaped by the nature of the environment they inhabit, and by their perceptions of how they are viewed (e.g., with fear, suspicion, or apprehension) by those with whom they interact. For instance, to ward off victimization by others, adolescents may adopt styles of speech or physical posture that are defensive in nature and designed to preempt exploitation by others. Conversely, individuals may, because they are aware of the suspicion with which others view them, engage in acts of kindness and helpfulness aimed at disproving stereotypical characterizations of them as uncivil and inclined toward criminal behavior. Anderson suggested that the net effect of the social environment, and the strategies of negotiation the adolescents use, is to clearly indicate to youth the fragile status they hold in their communities.

Ogbu (1986) discussed African-American adolescents' perceptions of their subordination and exploitation, and its impact on their educational performance. Ogbu suggested that as a consequence of their perception that racial discrimination limits their social mobility, African-American adolescents are more likely to reject White middle-class values and attitudes in the area of education. School learning is viewed as a subtractive process with few identifiable benefits, in which individuals must sacrifice something of their collective sense of identity in adopting the behaviors and values favored in school.

Ogbu (1988) also argued that as a consequence of their awareness of and experiences with racial barriers to conventional means of achieving social mobility, African Americans in inner cities have responded by developing alternative theories and strategies for achieving social and economic success. According to this view, although inner-city African-American parents stress the importance of formal education and conventional jobs, they also consciously or unconsciously teach their children the value of "instrumental competencies of clientship, hustling or other survival strategies" (p. 57).

These theories and strategies for achieving success have implications for the characteristic behaviors that adolescents may develop, and are reflected in the groups into which they allegedly fall (e.g., "Squares," "Ivy Leaguers," "Regulars," "Cool Cats," "Jesters," and "Gowsters/Antagonists"). Squares, Ivy Leaguers, Regulars, and to some extent Jesters, are adolescents who are more likely to accept and pursue conventional means of achieving success. Adolescents classified as Cool Cats and Gowsters/Antagonists are more likely to be members of the "street culture," and to reject conventional means of achieving success. It should be noted that the evidence that parents, in their child-rearing practices, encourage the development of unconventional strategies for achieving success (and thus, indirectly, the adolescent categories) is not clearly established (Ogbu, 1988).

All three adolescent developmental tasks are implicated in Ogbu's discussion. The development of skills and social responsibility, identity and personal responsibility, and intimacy and interpersonal responsibility is clearly relevant. The experiences and perceptions of adolescents and their family members regarding racial discrimination and racial barriers may directly influence the conscious and unconscious commitment of parents and adolescents to the adolescents' schooling and to the assumption of mainstream values and behaviors. Further, the adolescent categories discussed by Ogbu represent ways in which adolescents may rationalize their identity and self-concept. They represent sets of values, attitudes, and behaviors that African-American adolescents may adopt to help guide them in decision making in critical areas such as schooling and peer relations.

Experiences and perceptions of racial discrimination have also been implicated in African-American children's peers relations. Lareau (1991), using participant observations to assess parents' views of interactions with schools, found that African-American parents across social class lines were distrustful and suspicious of the school regarding race relations. To the extent that these feelings are transferred to children and adolescents, and that adolescents actually experience racial discrimination, their engagement in school may be diminished. These factors may partially explain why peers and interpersonal relations, particularly among African-American males, appear more important than school as a source of self-esteem (Hare & Castenell, 1988).

EVIDENCE OF RESILIENCE
IN AFRICAN-AMERICAN ADOLESCENTS

As Masten notes (chapter 1, this volume), evidence abounds of individuals who, despite coming from high-risk groups, overcome obstacles to their development. Indeed, the preoccupation of both researchers and the media with the negative outcomes seen in the African-American population has often obscured that despite multiple risks, evidence of adaptation in African-American families and their children is plentiful.

A number of investigations (Clark, 1983; Greenberg & Davidson, 1972) have examined high- and low-achieving economically disadvantaged African-American preadolescents and adolescents. The high-achieving subsamples in this work consisted of individuals who, despite living in poor, inner-city neighborhoods, managed to do well in school. Several factors appeared to separate high-achieving from low-achieving students, including the organization of their homes and the nature of their parenting experiences.

Interpreting these findings, Clark (1983) suggested that the parents of high-achieving adolescents appear more likely to employ authoritative parenting practices in the home than the parents of low-achieving adolescents. Authoritative parenting involves a constellation of behaviors, including warmth, firm control and monitoring, and the encouragement of mature behavior. Similarly, in a sample of younger children, Scheinfeld (1983) found that parents of high achievers encouraged self-motivation, autonomy, and engagement of the environment, whereas parents of low achievers discouraged autonomy and engagement of the environment. The processes underlying these differences in parental behavior, such as parent personality differences or differences attributable to the social environment experienced by the family, deserve further attention.

Fordham and Ogbu (1986) reported on strategies that high achievers may employ to facilitate their schooling. They found evidence that for some African-American adolescents attending school in poor inner-city neighborhoods, achievement in school is accomplished by "cloaking" or disguising their efforts, by forming protective alliances, or by diverting attention away from their efforts. Fordham and Ogbu (1986) suggested that African-American adolescents attending school in integrated settings may seek to diminish their self-identification as African Americans in order to sustain their academic strivings.

In other related research on the adjustment of African-American males, a number of writers (Gordon, personal communication, 1992; Majors & Billson, 1991) suggested that adolescents commonly adopt and ritualize codes of behavior, speech, and dress, which serve the function of maintaining and protecting individuals' psychological well-being. In this work it is argued that in the face of racial hostility and discrimination, and lack of access to mainstream avenues to success and fulfillment, adolescents may create a system of actions and symbols permitting self-validation.

Further evidence of adaptation has been observed in research focusing on the psychosocial adjustment of African-American adolescents (e.g., Taylor, Casten, & Flickinger, in press; Taylor & Roberts, 1992). Poor inner-city adolescents displayed levels of adjustment (self-reliance, few problem or delinquent behaviors, and few signs of psychological distress) similar to that of adolescents in other published reports focusing on working- and middle-class families. The factors apparently responsible for the adolescents' adjustment were their parenting experiences and kinship social support. Kinship support enhanced the well-being and parenting practices of the adolescents' parents, and better parenting experiences enhanced the adolescents' psychological well-being.

Peters (1988) asserted that African-American parents may actively socialize their children to prepare for encounters with racial discrimination. Peters suggested that African-American parents often seek to inoculate their children against discriminatory mistreatment by promoting the self-esteem and self-confidence of their children and by stressing the importance of school achievement. Bowman and Howard (1985) obtained data showing that to the extent that African-American parents discuss with their adolescents the nature of race-related barriers to social mobility, the youngsters perform better in school.

The research discussed here demonstrates that resilience and adaptation are common, and that despite economic disadvantage and the awareness of racial discrimination, adolescents often display behaviors relevant to the mastery of developmental tasks. The findings offer evidence of adolescents who, despite their risk circumstances, perform adequately in school, perceive themselves as self-reliant, avoid problem or delinquent behavior, and adequately manage their peer relations. These results also offer insight into the factors and processes that promote resilience in African-American adolescents. These factors are what Masten (this volume) describes as protective factors, and they appear to moderate the effects of risk factors on adolescent development.

Several protective factors that may play a significant role in the resilience of children and adolescents (effective parenting, connections to competent adults, good intellectual skills, self-efficacy, self-worth, hopefulness, etc.) are apparent in the research just discussed. African-American parents who are involved in their children's and adolescents' schooling, stress its importance, and who inform their children about the occurrence and meaning of racial discrimination, tend to have more competent children and adolescents. In poor African-American families in which social support from extended kin is available, parents experience less psychological distress and are more effective in their parenting, which benefits adolescent competence and adjustment. For the high achievers in Fordham and Ogbu's (1986) research, good intellectual skills are the protective factors that are probably responsible for their ability to devise strategies for sustaining academic performance.

IMPLICATIONS FOR EDUCATING
AFRICAN-AMERICAN ADOLESCENTS

We recognize that schools in inner cities are being called upon to play an increasing role in the lives of their students, and that there are real limits to what can reasonably be expected of schools. It is also clear that the problems and life stresses facing inner-city families and communities are unprecedented. Wilson (1987) amply described the problems of poverty, crime, and social isolation that beset our inner cities. These problems occur at a time when federal funding to cities and political leadership on domestic issues are in short supply; thus, the problems fall squarely on the shoulders of children and adolescents, those who are least able to cope with them. Schools in inner cities are situated where they can play an active role in fostering the development of inner-city children and youth. In fact, some of the practices and procedures that might benefit youngsters currently either already exist or should be easy to implement.

Masten (this volume) describes several strategies used by schools to facilitate students' learning. For instance, homeless and economically disadvantaged families move frequently, forcing children to cope with the disruption of changing schools. Mobility magnet schools would allow families to cross boundaries into new school zones while the children remain in their original schools. This practice, although avoiding the potential impediments to youngsters' school performance and engagement, also allows them the opportunity to maintain relationships with peers. Some inner-city school districts, recognizing the potential negative effects on teenage mothers of a severe disruption in schooling, have established on-site day-care centers, enabling the adolescents to continue their schooling while receiving instruction on effective parenting.

Efforts aimed at improving the quality of inner-city schools by, among other things, increasing parent–school connections (see Comer, 1988) have the potential to benefit youngsters' development and adjustment. The success of some of these ventures is evidenced by the academic gains that children have made, and the improved social climate for learning seen at the target schools.

There are also other possible benefits of parent–school involvement and greater school involvement in community affairs. Cochran and Henderson (1990) showed that interventions aimed at promoting the social networks of African-American families, particularly single-parent families, is associated with better school performance by children. Parental involvement in schools, such as that depicted in the work of Comer (1988), would present a unique opportunity to promote parental social networks that benefit communities, schools, and most importantly, youngsters. For some families these social networks may help buffer the negative effects of economic hardship, and enhance parents' ability to engage in better parenting practices. Expanded social networks may also make children's social and physical environments safer by placing them in greater contact with other competent adults.

Another implication of the research reviewed here is that frank and honest discussion is needed on the issues of race and racism in U.S. society. Taylor, Casten, and Flickinger (1992) found that African-American adolescents perceive themselves and their families as targets of discrimination. The adolescents' perceptions have a negative impact on their view of the value of schooling for social mobility. These findings are consistent with Fordham and Ogbu's (1986) work suggesting that adolescents question the value of schooling because they perceive the racial inequalities in U.S. society. Taylor et al. also found that in some African-American students awareness of discrimination is associated with increased symptoms of psychological distress.

Schools, given the amount of time they have with youngsters, have an opportunity to address students' concerns about race and racial discrimination. In fact, given the prominent part played by race in U.S. social relations, schools have a responsibility to attempt to address the issue of race in society. Instructional units should be included in school curricula focusing on the history of race relations in the United States and the manner in which race has shaped schooling, housing, and political issues. It is also important to discuss the legal and economic means of addressing and redressing some forms of discrimination. A critical underlying theme should be (the effects of discrimination notwithstanding), that the long-term consequences for anyone lacking schooling and skills are severe. If many African-American adolescents are to become hopeful about their futures, and look beyond the issue of race as the single determining factor for the poor status of many inner-city communities (as, e.g., in Wilson, 1987), the significant adults and institutions in youngsters' lives must provide them with the necessary tools and knowledge.

CONCLUSIONS

Normative research on the development of African-American children and adolescents is sorely needed. The manner in which African-American adolescents address developmental tasks has not been a focus in the literature on adolescent development. Social and educational policymaking is presently handicapped by a lack of basic information on the social and emotional development of African-American youngsters. For example, as African-American adolescents address the task of rationalizing their identity, they must do so in the context of constant negative portrayals of African Americans. It is not known how most adolescents reconcile these negative depictions with their own self-conceptions and maintain high self-esteem (Spencer & Dornbusch, 1990). The means by which adolescents address these tasks have clear implications for their schooling. Adolescents who are unable to develop clear personal decisions, lack the skills to successfully manage relations with peers, and who fail to perceive the relationship between basic academic skills and social well-being, are educationally at risk.

Far too little is currently known about the obstacles to the development of African-American adolescents. Specifically, African-American families must often confront economic hardship for extended periods, but we know little about the correlates of poverty and the impact on youngsters. There is a relationship between poverty, parental distress, and less adequate parenting. There are a variety of factors linked to economic hardship that could produce distress in parents, including poor health and services, crime in the neighborhood, and environmental wastes and hazards. A clear understanding is needed of the factor(s) linked to parental distress that lead individuals to function less well as parents.

Research on resilience must be open to the possibility that adaptive behaviors come in a variety of forms. Because adaptive behavior is largely defined by its environmental context, behaviors that meet the criterion for resilience may be behaviors that concerned adults would prefer that adolescents avoid. But unless all children and adolescents are exposed to social environments and behaviors associated with the middle-class attributes valued in schools, it is folly to expect that all children and adolescents will display similar behaviors.

Finally, there must be only careful application of resilience research to intervention efforts. There may be a danger, implicit in research on resilience, of coming to expect extraordinary outcomes from all individuals facing obstacles to development. Not all individuals or families are equally equipped to overcome impediments to development. Indeed, there are obstacles to children's and adolescents' development, such as poverty, for which intervention at the individual or family level may be counterproductive, and intervention at the societal level holds the greatest promise for lasting positive change.

REFERENCES

Anderson, E. (1990). *Streetwise: Race, class, and change in an urban community*. Chicago: University of Chicago Press.

Bishop, J. (1977). *Jobs, cash transfers, and marital instability: A review of the evidence*. Madison: University of Wisconsin Institute for Research on Poverty.

Bowman, P. J., & Howard, C. (1985). Race related socialization, motivation, and academic achievement: A study of black youth in three generation families. *Journal of the American Academy of Child Psychiatry, 24*, 134-141.

Boykin, A. W., & Toms, F. D. (1985). Black child socialization: Conceptual framework. In H. McAdoo & J. McAdoo (Eds.), *Black children: Social, educational, and parental environments* (pp. 33-51). Newbury Park, CA: Sage.

Center for the Study of Social Policy. (1986). The flip-side of Black families headed by women: The economic status of Black men. In R. Staples (Ed.), *The Black family: Essays and studies* (pp. 232-238). Belmont, CA: Wadsworth.

Clark, R. (1983). *Family life and school achievement: Why poor black children succeed or fail.* Chicago: University of Chicago Press.

Cochran, M., & Henderson, C. R. (1990). Formal supports and informal social ties: A case study. In M. Cochran, M. Larner, D. Riley, L. Gunnarsson, & C. R. Henderson (Eds.), *Extending families: The social networks of parents and their children* (pp. 230-261). New York: Cambridge University Press.

Comer, J. P. (1988). *Maggie's American dream: The life and times of a black family.* New York: New American Library.

Conger, R., McCarty, J., Yang, R., Lahey, B., & Kropp, J. (1984). Perception of child, child-rearing values, and emotional distress as mediating links between environmental stressors and observed maternal behavior. *Child Development, 54*, 2234-2247.

Dressler, W. (1985). Extended family relationships, social support, and mental health in a southern black community. *Journal of Health and Social Behavior, 26*, 39-48.

Duncan, G. (1988). *The economic environment of childhood.* Paper presented at a study group meeting on poverty and children, University of Kansas, Lawrence, KS.

Elder, G. (1974). *Children of the Great Depression.* Chicago: University of Chicago Press.

Fordham, S., & Ogbu, J. U. (1986). Black students' school success: Coping with the "burden of 'acting white'." *Urban Review, 18*, 176-206.

Furstenberg, F. F. (1976). *Unplanned parenthood: The social consequences of teenage childbearing.* New York: The Free Press.

Gibbs, J. (1986). Assessment of depression in urban adolescent females: Implications for early intervention strategies. *American Journal of Social Psychiatry, 6*, 50-56.

Greenberg, J. W., & Davidson, H. H. (1972). Home background and school achievement of black urban ghetto children. *American Journal of Orthopsychiatry, 42*, 803-810.

Hare, B. R., & Castenell, L. A. (1988). No place to run, no place to hide: Comparative status and future prospects of black boys. In M. Spencer, G. Brookins, & W. Allen (Eds.), *Beginnings: The social and affective development of black children* (pp. 201-214). Hillsdale, NJ: Lawrence Erlbaum Associates.

Langner, R., Herson, J., Greene, E., Jameson, J., & Goff, J. (1970). Children of the city: Affluence, poverty, and mental health. In V. Allen (Ed.), *Psychological factors in poverty* (pp. 185-209). Chicago: Markham.

Lareau, A. (1991, November). *"It's more covert today": The importance of race in shaping parents' view of the school.* Paper presented at the American Anthropological Association annual meetings, Chicago, IL.

Lempers, J., Clark-Lempers, D., & Simons, R. (1989). Economic hardship, parenting, and distress in adolescence. *Child Development, 60*, 25-49.

Liem, R., & Liem, J. (1978). Social class and mental illness reconsidered: The role of economic stress and social support. *Journal of Health and Social Behavior, 19*, 139-156.

Longfellow, C., Zelkowitz, P., & Saunders, E. (1982). The quality of mother–child relationships. In D. Belle (Ed.), *Lives in stress: Women and depression* (pp. 163-176). Beverly Hills, CA: Sage.

Majors, R. G., & Billson, J. M. (1991). *Cool pose: The dilemmas of Black manhood in America.* Lexington, MA: D. C. Heath.

Masten, A. S., & Braswell, L. (1991). Developmental psychopathology: An integrative framework. In P. R. Martin (Ed.), *Handbook of behavior therapy and psychological science: An integrative approach* (pp. 35–56). New York: Pergamon Press.

McLoyd, V. C. (1990). The impact of economic hardship on black families and children: Psychological distress, parenting, and socioemotional development. *Child Development, 61,* 311–346.

McLoyd, V. C., & Wilson, L. (1991). Maternal behavior, social support, and economic predictors of psychological distress in children. In V. C. McLoyd & C. Flanagan (Eds.), *New direction for child development. Economic stress: effects on family life and child development* (pp. 49–69). San Francisco: Jossey-Bass.

Myers, H. F., & King, L. (1983). Mental health issues in the development of the Black American child. In G. Powell, J. Yamamoto, A. Romero, & A. Morales (Eds.), *The psychosocial development of minority group children* (pp. 275–306). New York: Brunner/Mazel.

Ogbu, J. U. (1986). The consequences of the American caste system. In U. Neisser (Ed.), *The school achievement of minority children: New perspectives* (pp. 19–56). Hillsdale, NJ: Lawrence Erlbaum Associates.

Ogbu, J. U. (1988). A cultural ecology of competence among inner-city blacks. In M. Spencer, G. Brookins, & W. Allen (Eds.), *Beginnings: The social and affective development of black children* (pp. 45–66). Hillsdale, NJ: Lawrence Erlbaum Associates.

Pearlin, L., & Johnson, J. (1977). Marital status, life-strains and depression. *American Sociological Review, 42,* 704–715.

Peters, M. F. (1988). Parenting in families with young children: A historical perspective. In H. McAdoo (Ed.), *Black families* (pp. 228–241). Newbury Park, CA: Sage.

Scheinfeld, D. R. (1983). Family relationships and school achievement among boys of lower-income urban black families *American Journal of Orthopsychiatry, 53,* 127–143.

Scott-Jones, D., & White, A. B. (1990). Correlates of sexual activity in early adolescence. *Journal of Early Adolescence, 10,* 221–238.

Spencer, M. B., & Dornbusch, S. M. (1990). Challenges in studying minority youth. In S. Feldman & G. Elliott (Eds.), *At the threshold: The developing adolescent* (pp. 123–146). Cambridge, MA: Harvard University Press.

Steinberg, L. (1990). The logic of adolescence. In P. Edelman & J. Ladener (Eds.), *Adolescence and poverty: Challenge for the 1990s* (pp. 19–36). Washington, DC: Center for National Policy Press.

Taylor, R. D., Casten, R., & Flickinger, S. (1992). *Explaining the school achievement of African-American adolescents.* Manuscript submitted for publication.

Taylor, R. D., Casten, R., & Flickinger, S. (in press). The influence of kinship social support on the parenting experiences and psychosocial adjustment of African-American adolescents. *Developmental Psychology.*

Taylor, R. D., & Roberts, D. (1992). *Kinship support and parental and adolescent well-being in economically disadvantaged African-American families.* Manuscript submitted for publication.

Wilson, W. J. (1987). *The truly disadvantaged: The inner city, the underclass, and public policy.* Chicago: University of Chicago Press.

Chapter 9

Special Education as a Resilience-Related Venture

Maynard C. Reynolds
University of Minnesota

David Vail[1] once said of the professions that they do "the dirty work of society." Lawyers struggle daily through problems of crime and broken contracts; physicians excise tumors or treat infections; nurses stay up all night with the sick; teachers are closeted in egg-crate classrooms with 30 active juveniles; and social workers sort out family disorders. All professionals cry out for opportunities to work more positively and at earlier stages of life, to reduce the rates at which disease and disorder come into their various work chambers. So it is with educators, particularly special educators.

The work on resilience (cf. Masten, chapter 1, this volume) emphasizes the positives. It starts with recognition of the tough realities faced by some children. It then proceeds to analyze not only what is stressful, defective, or threatening, but what enhances the development of children, even when they live in perilous circumstances. The focus is on those who succeed, rather than those who fail, and on assets, not deficiencies. By inventing techniques to magnify the "positives" in the lives of children who face risk and adversity, perhaps we can help more children develop successfully.

---

[1] Dr. David Vail served as head of mental health programs in Minnesota for a period in the 1960s.

SCHOOLS AND PATTERNS
OF NORMATIVE DEVELOPMENT

Both resilience and psychopathology are judged on the basis of normative patterns of development in normative environmental contexts (Masten, this
volume). The school gives us one frame of reference for making such judgments. Schools look much like the society that supports them in curriculum,
prevailing concepts of aptitudes, patterns of evaluation and rewards, and so
on. Thus, what one sees in schools may help us to judge more generally what
is adaptive and nonadaptive in a culture at a given time. Indeed, if we look
at the kinds of "special" programs created in our schools at this time, we may
be able to identify the domains of adaptation considered most critical in our
community—what Stoddard (1961) labeled the *cultural imperatives*.

Children are referred to special programs in the schools for three general
reasons:

1. failure to learn in ordinary school programs in the basic literacy domains
   of language, reading, writing, and arithmetic;
2. unacceptable social behavior, including disruption, noncooperation, and
   assault; and
3. extreme lack of self-dependence (i.e., not possessing the self-help skills
   for feeding, toileting, mobility, etc.).

Correctives in these areas are not electives; they are imperatives in the school
curriculum and for successful life in our society. An elaborate and expensive
set of categorical "back-up" or "second system" educational programs has
been created in our society to teach children who have difficulties in these areas
(Wang, Reynolds, & Walberg, 1988).

Failure to develop in these areas is itself stressful. The history of children
who are identified for special help in these areas shows high rates of adversity
and risk of the kinds that Masten (this volume) describes. But some children
manage to achieve very well in all of these essential domains, despite adversity. These students are termed *resilient*.

Sometimes children are referred to "special" programs because they have
a manifest problem, such as unacceptable social behavior or failure to learn
to read. In many other cases, children are specially placed in school because
they fall into high-risk groups. They are predicted to have achievement problems
on the basis of group rates. For example, children from migratory families,
from economically poor families, or from non-English-speaking families qualify
for special school programs. Whether the special programs are helpful or harmful is another question.

Binet's work in Paris at the turn of the century provides an example of trying to predict academic problems at an individual level. He developed the well-

known Binet test that has since been adapted for use around the world. Millions of children who scored low on the Binet tests were thus predicted to be laggards in academic learning, and from there it was but a small step to set them aside in special school programs. Unfortunately, there were no indications that the referred students would learn better in special places. That lesson has only been learned in recent decades, after millions of children were "set aside" in special places in undemanding classes.

Many types of categorical programs have been developed, and new ones seem to be emerging constantly. Currently, attention is shifting rapidly to cover such morbidities as "crack babies," the homeless, children with attention deficit disorders (ADD), and abused children. The group or base rates for developmental problems in all of these groups are relatively high.

SPECIAL EDUCATION
AS RESILIENCE-RELATED PROGRAMS

Categorical school programs can be interpreted within the resilience framework. They start with students showing serious developmental problems, or with groups known to have high rates of risk for developing such problems. The history and present life situation of many of these students show high rates of adversity. Some show resilience; others show deepening problems and pathology.

There may be merit in joining resilience research and theory with the field of special education. Special education, at its best, is a flexible and experimental field. It provides research and developmental capital (Deno, 1970) for much of education; perhaps it can do so for resilience researchers as well.

LACK OF PROGRAM EVALUATION

One serious problem is that educators often do not engage deeply in research, or even in evaluation of the programs they conduct. Frequently, they are overwhelmed by large numbers of children with problems in their programs, and find it difficult enough just to cope with day-to-day practical problems. Research and evaluation tend to be neglected. So it is today in many categorical programs, including special education.

Educators today face growing numbers of children living in adversity and at risk, and whose school performance is perplexing. They need much help as they try to understand the children and the conditions of their lives, and to design helpful instructional programs. Many special programs have been launched, but usually with only a thin knowledge base for guidance and little attention to evaluation and research.

Another explanation for the dearth of research may be that the special fields of education do not sufficiently provide their own researchers. Instead, they tend to borrow from other fields, mainly psychology and sociology. But this is an off-and-on affair. There is a great lack of consistent and systematic research, which results in programs that persist and grow without useful tests of outcome and validity.

An example of a serious shortcoming is provided in the case of school programs for "mildly retarded" children. Binet gave us a way of predicting academic casualties with some degree of success, through the use of a test. This frequently involved labeling low-scoring children as *mentally retarded* and giving them special placements. The negative labels assigned to the children are frequently resented by parents, especially parents in minority groups that show disproportionately high rates of categorical labels and placements. There is still little, if any, evidence that the special programs enhance the lives of the mildly retarded children and no data that systematically address the reasons why these interventions do not work.

Today, many children showing behavior problems are displaced from regular classes and schools into special programs. Unfortunately, the special programs may serve only a relief or arresting function. That is, they make regular classes more orderly because disturbing children have been removed. But too many of the students given the special placements show little improvement in the abilities required to reenter the ordinary classes of the schools or to thrive in other institutions of the community.

Some special programs are successful, of course, especially in cases where teachers and parents combine efforts to serve their children. Nevertheless, in far too many cases, special school programs result in negative labeling and stigma, segregation, lowered expectations, watered-down curricula, and superficial and untested treatments. There is extraordinary need to bring creative ideas into special education programs and to test them with care. Bringing researchers in the field of resilience together with educators may be one way of developing programs creatively, and of testing them thoroughly.

ALTERABLE VARIABLES

Each profession tends to analyze problems in terms of variables it can manipulate. Astronomers may be the exception, because they are often content with mere prediction of planetary movements and events in space. But teachers are employed to influence pupils, not just make predictions about them. Thus, educators will look first at the resilience research for variables they have some chance of manipulating.

From a teacher's perspective, one might rate each of the factors Masten's review (this volume) shows to be significant in resilience according to its manipulability.

TABLE 9.1
Teachers' Influence on Resilience Factors

Factor	Direct	Indirect	
		Collaboration with Others	Next Generation Influence
Effective parenting	—	x	x
Connections to other competent adults (e.g., mentoring programs)	x	x	x
Appealingness to other people, particularly adults	—	—	—
Good intellectual skills	x	—	—
Areas of accomplishment or talent valued by self and others	x	x	—
Self-efficacy, self-worth, and hopefulness	x	x	—
Religious faith or affiliation	—	—	—
Socioeconomic advantages	—	—	x
Good schools and other community assets	x	x	—

Teachers can work directly on intellectual skills, self-evaluation, enhanced internal controls by students, skills in interpersonal relations, and activity levels. (See Table 9.1 for the variables that teachers influence.) Each involves complex and challenging work.

Teachers may be able to help improve the effectiveness of parenting by working with parents of students in their classes. Still further progress can be made indirectly through collaboration with others. For example, if social agencies provide counseling and training to parents, the teacher may be able to help by making referrals and by joining in "teaming" activities. Teachers can help in long-range ways, of course, by teaching and modeling desirable adult behavior to students who will themselves move to adult roles over time.

The newly developing collaborative arrangements among schools, social and health agencies, and parents, create opportunities for teachers to be helpful in the broad life situation of their students. Through broad consortium arrangements, it is likely that more aspects of the resilience research will become relevant and fruitful. Teachers can be helpful by scanning for what they know about children and changes they see taking place as various social and health agencies proceed in their work. Similarly, the social agency may be able to help arrange a home situation in a way that will be helpful in achieving goals set by a teacher. If a church group is seeking to improve home and school collaboration in a situation involving much initial distrust, for example, educators can and should join in such trust-building activities.

At the school level, a number of things can be done. One important possibility is a schoolwide program to provide adult mentors for at-risk children.

Perhaps no single fact emerging from resilience research is more important than the finding that having contact with a genuinely caring adult (beyond the family) is important to every child. Another possibility is arranging the assignment of teachers in ways to maximize instructional outcomes for children. Some teachers are resilient in the sense that they consistently produce rapid learners, even in the face of adversity. A specific possibility for a school is to assign the teachers who are strongest in reading instruction to kindergarten and low primary classes. Even before we know how to explain their success, we can identify such resilient teachers and assign them where most needed. Then we can do research in the classroom situation, to try to identify what it is that results in a high success rate. Special education, at its best, involves highly successful or resilient teachers assigned to students whose base rates for success are low.

Increasing numbers of studies suggest characteristics of successful or resilient schools. These schools are identified as those: (a) in which there is every expectation of good progress in learning by students; (b) where teaching is aggressive, uncompromising in curriculum, and high in density of instruction; and (c) that are clear about their mission and led by strong principals. We, at the National Center on Education in the Inner Cities (CEIC), have begun a series of studies to help further specify the characteristics of resilient schools. It is urgent that findings of these studies be applied in inner-city schools.

Many of today's children and adolescents find their lives in disorder, perhaps more so in inner cities than elsewhere. Clearly, schools cannot and will not solve these problems on their own, but there are increasing opportunities to address the problems in cooperation with parents and other agencies of the community. Work on resilience suggests a positive orientation in these broad ventures: a search for what each person and agency can contribute in helpful and hopeful ways. A partnership between resilience researchers and special education teachers is potentially very productive.

CONCLUSION

Some years ago, Campbell (1969) wrote about "reforms as experiments." There is much need to reform education at this time, especially in the cases of children whose life situations are adverse and perilous. But it will be important to see the reforms as experiments, and to evaluate them with much care. A number of special school programs have been launched, most of them narrowly categorical and involving labels for children. This is the way schools have traditionally tried to meet the needs of students whose lives show adversity and whose school progress is troubled. But most of the programs are like unfinished, heavily laden hulls of ships at sea—in troubled waters. There is great need to bring researchers into collaborative efforts with others to steady the craft.

Resilience research and theory provide a promising starting point for such collaboration. Perhaps it will be of interest to the researcher, both as scientist and as good citizen, to join in this large undertaking—not by taking vessels to dry dock for repairs, but by experimenting in the troubled seas of inner-city life and education. Well-informed teachers will also be able to undertake research within their own classrooms, testing whether ideas from the resilience research can be applied with favorable results to particular students in the particular context of their own classrooms.

What I have offered only restates an important theme of the work included in this book: to conjoin the research and theory on resilience with the work of the schools. Sometimes even researchers work in narrow channels, doing parallel rather than cooperative work. I suggest that, particularly as the resilience researchers move toward an emphasis on intervention, some of the developmental capital and sites for this work can be provided by the categorical school programs and by the emerging coalitions of schools, parents, and community agencies.

REFERENCES

Campbell, D. T. (1969). Reforms as experiments. *American Psychologist, 29,* 409–429.
Deno, E. (1970). Special education as developmental capital. *Exceptional Children, 37,* 229–237.
Stoddard, G. D. (1961). *The dual progress plan.* New York: Harper & Brothers.
Wang, M. C., Reynolds, M. C., & Walberg, H. J. (1988). Integrating the children of the second system. *Phi Delta Kappan, 70,* 248–251.

Part III

Fostering Educational Resilience

Effectiveness and Efficiency in Inner-City Public Schools: Charting School Resilience

Lascelles Anderson
University of Illinois at Chicago

Organizational resilience is a much broader concept than organizational effectiveness. In fact, it includes organizational effectiveness as part of its predicate. This chapter is an attempt to develop and apply a concept of organizational resilience to the specific organizational type known as the school. The discussion focuses particularly on inner-city elementary schools.

CONDITIONS OF RESILIENCE

Organizational resilience requires the clear demonstration of successful performance, so that no organization that persistently underperforms can be regarded as resilient. On the other hand, it does not appear sufficient merely to observe the demonstration of good performance at discrete moments in time, and to assert resilience on the basis of such observations. Resilience seems to require the following conditions: (a) demonstrable evidence of consistently good performance; (b) that such evidence be linked to processes internal to the organization, and that can be shown to be clearly linked to such perceived performance; and (c) that the organization's internal processes that lead to the observed performance are the result of conscious and deliberate design and redesign efforts, that is, efforts made by the organization to secure a measure of dynamic (over-time) sustainability in performance.

A FRAMEWORK FOR RESILIENCE

The resilience construct can best be understood in a dynamic framework. In such a framework, only over-time behavior can be expected to throw up elements of data that are sufficiently robust and powerful to support inferences of the presence or absence of resilience. It is being asserted also that resilience can profitably be understood at the organizational level. In other words, it is simply being assumed here that application of the concept at that level is not inappropriate. Furthermore, it suggests that a systems viewpoint of organizational behavior, with a control theory perspective at its center, may prove more useful than the stimulus–response (S–R) theory typically exhibited in the literature. With the systems viewpoint, the behavior of the system can be postulated as coming from its internal structure and goal-seeking behavior, rather than being only a function of the external influences acting on the organization and the organization's response to them.

Successful application of the resilience framework requires bringing together three interrelated perspectives. The first is the dynamic (over-time) nature of the organization's behavior. Resilience evokes notions of overcoming, of persistence, and of "living to fight another day," all of which require observing the organism at several points in its life passage.

The second relates to a set of underlying qualities of organizations which predispose them to success (survival) or failure (death). The work of Peters and Waterman (1982) is influential in this regard but is preceded by the exceedingly rich work in organizational psychology, particularly that of Argyris and Schön (1978). More recently, work done in applying systems dynamics to corporate establishments has concentrated on identifying and representing the deep structural dimensions of these highly complex entities, in an attempt at uncovering those generic properties that can be associated with sustainability and survival across a variety of environmental domains (Lyneis, 1980; Senge, 1990).

The third criterion is that the organization is thought of as an intelligent system. At the most basic level, the organization is seen as a collectivity in which the parts interact with each other in order to function as a unit. A more important emphasis is on uncovering the internal intelligence-gathering and governance mechanisms of the organization that predispose it to surviving or not surviving. Such mechanisms include information feedback loops that lie wholly within the organization and that are structured to bring the organization's behavior, over time, ever closer to predetermined norm or reference points (Hanneman, 1988; Powers, 1973, 1978, 1990; Wolstenholme, 1990). Work in this tradition employs terms such as *visioning, goals, capacity of the organization to learn, reflection in practice, internal alignment, commitment,* and *organizational integrity*, all of which are critical in ensuring organizational success defined in terms of sustainability or resilience.

Effective information flow processes are considered critical constituent elements when organizations are viewed as systems with intelligence-gathering and smart guidance mechanisms. These processes often dictate major shifts in structure, away from highly bureaucratic organizational types and toward more decentralized ones; they underscore the importance of feedback in the structuring of successful organizations (Hall, 1984).

Organizations may exhibit several types of feedback processes having differing implications for their dynamic behavior. In addition to the typical S–R pattern of behavior, theorists in the system dynamics tradition have identified self-referencing feedback, in which the organization references its own current status, as well as exogenous disturbances, in deciding how to respond to stimuli. At the other extreme from the S–R pattern there is a very complex feedback pattern, in which the organization is conceived of as having a goal or set of goals that define its expected performance levels and its dynamic behavior is conditioned not only by how it responds to external influences but, more importantly, how it responds to disturbances in reference to its goal or structure of goals (Powers, 1990).

Although the goal-referencing feedback structures are not the most complex identifiable types, the assertion of a goal or set of goals, to which the system continually refers in charting its over-time behavior, is critical in the understanding of resilience from an organizational point of view. Resilience implies, in this context, that organizations will exhibit stable sustainable behavior if they possess (a) a clear vision of what they are about, and (b) the information-gathering capability needed to compare performance data against some norm so as to afford continuous adjustment of internal processes deemed critical in bringing received information in line with the norms established for guiding performance. It is being asserted that organizations exhibiting these characteristics will be eminently more successful in responding to the variety of environmental intrusions normally impacting them. Resilience in this view implies a kind of intentionality that must eventually be realized (Hall, 1984; Hanneman, 1988; Senge, 1990).

In summary, organizations can be understood as (social) systems having an organizational structure with interacting individuals who perform a variety of roles. Organizations can also be seen to have a purpose or purposes that provide a framework for consistent patterns of interaction (organizational behavior) over time (Morgan, 1990). What emerges clearly from much of the recent literature is that successful organizations are those that (a) recognize and actively structure and restructure themselves to support proper and consistent articulations of a mission, (b) support the optimal development of shared decision making, (c) build trust, (d) encourage openness, and (e) are tireless in their efforts to support the growth of individual and collective competence (Bolman & Deal, 1991; Senge, 1990). Organizations exhibiting these characteristics are considered healthy, and are the ones most likely to survive typical external intrusions and to avoid persistent incompetence.

Although key researchers in the effective school tradition of the early 1980s did not define the issues in these dimensions, they were clearly moving in that direction. Much of the work and much of the literature on effective schools, for example, that which grew out of the work on organizations' internal processes, resonates with the same emphases on the organizations' (a) academic press (focus), (b) consistent patterns of expectations across the school (organizational integrity and internal alignment), (c) quality of school leadership (transformational leadership), and so on.

Thus, one may argue, schools as organizations must exhibit characteristics of organizational health if they are to sustain success over time (Hoy & Feldman, 1987; Miles, 1965, 1969). Health is an apt metaphor, in which schools are seen as either healthy or not. Healthy organisms are those that survive; they often grow stronger in their problem-solving mechanisms when they use these mechanisms. In other words, resilient schools are healthy schools.

SCHOOL EFFECTIVENESS AND EFFICIENCY:
GOAL ACHIEVEMENT AND SUCCESS

School resilience, when viewed as an evaluational characteristic of organizations, may be seen to require at least the following two sets of criteria: effectiveness and efficiency. In other words, goal achievement and success in resource allocation. In this section, school effectiveness and efficiency are discussed as analytic tools for charting resilience. This way of using effectiveness and efficiency to characterize schools as organizations seeks to bring these two dimensions of school performance together in a manner not typically attempted.

Effectiveness analysis, the more common type, seeks to evaluate schooling outcomes, in the form of test score data, by relating such outcomes to a range of variables that can be reasonably regarded as having some independent effect on these test scores. These variables include the usual independent factors, such as teacher input variables (quality and quantity), class size, measures of student socioeconomic status (SES), and so on; they may also include program variables, such as whether a school has any of a variety of categorical programs for student enrichment.

The usual methodology for investigating the effectiveness with which these resources are utilized in producing test score results is regression analysis, or some other variant of the general linear model. Test score results for any particular year may alternatively be related to test score results from a previous year, as a way of measuring how accurately prior results predict future ones. Some schools will show substantial gains while others may show no gains, or even demonstrate declines, in year-to-year performance. Such year-to-year changes may be normalized to identify positive and negative outliers, in year-to-year performance, among the population of schools.

Efficiency analysis, on the other hand, seeks to answer questions relating to the internal allocative skill exhibited by each school in turning schooling inputs into schooling outcomes. The theoretical underpinnings of efficiency analysis derive from microeconomic theory; the methodology for the empirical investigation of such questions is a variant of mathematical programming called data envelopment analysis.

Thus, in bringing together two analytic approaches in representing each school in two dimensions, an effectiveness one and an efficiency one, school performance is characterized simultaneously along dimensions of effectiveness and efficiency. This joining of effectiveness and efficiency analysis is a first step in charting school resilience. The classification of schools in this manner could provide some interesting and insightful understanding of schools as organizations. For example, the analysis may show which school variables are powerful predictors of school performance, which schools substantially outperform the rest given their readings on these variables; alternatively, the efficiency and effectiveness indicators may provide a database for ranking schools by how well they use resources in combination in generating any stated range of schooling outcomes and, in turn, how this impacts the achievement of school goals.

Although the independent variables for analysis of school performance may include those that are thought to constitute serious inhibitors to outstanding school performance (e.g., low SES), the leap to assert resilience for those schools that "beat the odds," so to speak, at any one point in time, appears unwarranted. Consistent with the foregoing discussion, resilience resonates with understandings of capacity over time, of a broad-ranging capability to deal effectively with one's environment; in the typical conditions of urban existence, this means demonstrating survival capability and displaying an organizational strength that insures success no matter what the environmental stressors happen to be.

One difficulty in applying the resilience concept to organizations such as schools resides in the research base on the concept of resilience. That research base is characterized, on the one hand, by a focus on pathological aspects of behavior and, on the other, a focus on observations about and inferences from individual behavior. Recent reviews of the extant literature amply demonstrate this tendency (see chapters by Masten, and Gordon & Song, this volume). Despite the obvious richness of the insights generated at the individual level of the literature, a haunting sense remains that the varieties of experiences are so great that it may be unrealistic to hope for any more reasonably stable empirical regularities, beyond the ones that are already known and can be specified with some degree of confidence. The alternative viewpoint proposed in this chapter, namely, to look at resilience defined at the organizational level, avoids this difficulty. The following section includes a discussion of a way of viewing effectiveness and efficiency in inner-city public schools, as a first step in charting school resilience.

CHARTING RESILIENCE:
A PROPOSED ANALYSIS DESIGN

The research design discussed in this section involves several stages of discrete kinds of research activities that, when brought together and done in a longitudinal manner, can be expected to shed light on the factors affecting school organizational resilience.

In the first stages of the work, all the schools in the system are evaluated according to effectiveness and efficiency. Recall that effectiveness refers to a school's performance from year to year in a specified set of outcomes. Clearly, a school may be differentially effective across a range of outcomes. Averaging the outcomes is one way of dealing with this issue. Efficiency, on the other hand, refers to the degree to which resources are used well in "producing" the outcomes in question; the methodology used to measure efficiency permits evaluating the use of several resources in the production of more than one outcome at the same time, a consistent limitation of the more typical the case. Although regression analysis is used to evaluate effectiveness, mathematical programming is used to study efficiency.

Each school is identified along an effectiveness dimension and an efficiency one. The entire set of schools can be represented as a set of points in two-dimensional space, and the space can be divided so as to isolate four groupings of schools: Group A, effective and efficient schools; Group B, ineffective and inefficient schools; Group C, effective but inefficient schools; Group D, efficient but ineffective schools.

Based on the results of the analyses, the schools can be characterized more grossly as healthy schools (Group A), or less than healthy schools (Group B). Recall that school/organizational resilience is defined by a set of outcome characteristics—effectiveness and efficiency—but also, importantly, by a degree of organizational health and by a capacity of the organization to learn, an active, powerfully enabling capacity. In order to test the validity of the groupings based on the effectiveness and efficiency analyses, a school health survey would be administered. The Organizational Health Inventory for Elementary Schools (Hoy, Tarter, & Kottkamp, 1991) is used in this aspect of analysis in this part of our work at the CEIC. Schools regarded as healthy "effectively meet the instrumental needs of adaptation and goal achievement as well as the expressive needs of social and normative integration" (Hoy et al., p. 68). The hypothesis is that schools in Group A will score significantly higher along all measures of school health than those in Group B.

We chose to use the Organizational Health Inventory for Elementary Schools because the 37-item instrument is soundly anchored theoretically, and although it has not (to our knowledge) been applied to urban schools, it appears appropriate for the tasks we wish to accomplish. Five subtests, representing the dimensions necessary for school health, comprise this inventory. They are: (a) institutional integrity, (b) collegial leadership, (c) resource influence, (d) academic emphasis, and (e) teacher affiliation. These dimensions are associated with the organizational functions stated in the work of Parsons (1961) and Parsons, Bales, and Shils (1953). Parsons and his colleagues postulated that survival of a social system was a function of the successful completion of four critical functions: (a) adaptation, the system's ability to respond to its environment; (b) goal attainment, the ability to set and achieve goals; (c) integration, the ability to maintain cohesiveness among system elements; and (d) latency, the ability to foster and sustain appropriate motivational driving value systems within the organization.

One might well ask whether, from among these efficient or effective organizations, all those organizations exhibiting characteristics of organizational health are resilient, or if there is some other dimension to resilience that must be accounted for. As one would expect from the foregoing discussion, the answer is yes. The other such ingredient is the capacity for learning exhibited by the organization over time. An organization must exhibit a clear sense of what its objectives are, and demonstrate the capacity to continually monitor its present position compared to internal norms. Over time, such exercises will afford the organization the creation and accumulation of certain mental regularities, mental maps that become part of its collective memory, to be called upon in later problem-solving situations (Argyris & Schön, 1978).

Given appropriate management sophistication, organizations will differentiate between those responses sufficient for low-level intrusions and those requiring changes in the organization's mental models. Hedberg's (1981) work is rich in comparisons and contrasts between individual learning and organizational learning. In particular, he points out the difference between imitative learning and generative learning, and underscores the interactive nature of learning. Learners and their environments change in the process of learning; stability can often be a hindrance to learning. Organizational learning is some function of individual learning, but not simply the sum total of such learning. In other words, organizations have memories that preserve the recollections of behavioral norms over time. Organizations learn.

Argyris and Schön (1978) carried the analysis of organizational learning forward by showing that organizations are capable of repeating behavior that might look like real learning, but in fact are not. Real learning takes place only when the assumptions framing the organization's responses are constantly reexamined to see how they fit with current reality. This is the distinction between learning and "learning to learn" drawn by Morgan (1990) and by Argyris and Schön (1978) in their later work on single-loop and double-loop learning modalities. According to Argyris and Schön:

> Single-loop learning is sufficient where error correction can proceed by changing organizational strategies and assumptions within a constant framework of norms of performance. It is concerned only with effectiveness. . . . [In] double-loop

learning, there is [a] double feedback loop which connects the detection of error not only to strategies and assumptions for effective performance but to the very norms which define effective performance. (pp. 22–23)

The especially important dimension of resilience postulated enters, namely an organization's capacity to learn, may now be addressed in the context of school health. Its inclusion as a critical dimension of school resilience is a clear challenge in this part of our work.

Thus, an important next step in analyzing school resilience, or more importantly in determining ways to foster organizational resilience, is to engage the school staff in the reflective interpretation of the analytical findings coming out of effectiveness and efficiency analyses and readings on school health. Findings for the effectiveness and efficiency analysis and the organizational health survey results, when shared between the principals and their school staffs, on a continuous basis, are likely to result in insights that are central to determining what aspects of the schools' organizations appear to work or not work, and the possible reasons for the results if organizational learning is present. It is anticipated that, using the dimensions of health and organizational learning as foci for dialogue, a broadened understanding of the conditions of organizational health would surface as would creative opportunities for improving school health, and thereby school resilience.

CONCLUSION

Organizations such as schools clearly exist and function within larger networks, which may be supportive or not, capable or otherwise, resourceful or resource poor; these networks constitute important sources of the stressors that impact the school. The stress and coping model, used so effectively by Masten to review the literature on individual resilience, suggests strongly that due emphasis must be placed on the broader structure of relationships in which the school exists, in order to understand school organizational resilience. Such a perspective immediately highlights the critical role of the policy framework that defines the policy environment of urban public education. Well-known demographic factors linked with economic conditions in the inner city, and their relationship to conditions of health and general well-being of the reference populations suggest that a broader framework, framed in terms of state and national policy on youth, may well be among the most critical research areas relating to school resilience. It is being argued that very substantial benefits can be reaped if we begin to see the importance of the permeability of the school's organizational boundary to the attainability of school resilience, and begin to focus our research efforts in that direction also.

REFERENCES

Argyris, C., & Schön, D. (1978). *Organizational learning*. Reading, MA: Addison-Wesley.

Bolman, L., & Deal, T. (1991). *Reframing organizations: Artistry, choice and leadership*. San Francisco: Jossey-Bass.

Hall, R. I. (1984). The natural logic of management policy making: Its implications for the survival of an organization. *Management Science, 30*(8), 905–927.

Hanneman, R. A. (1988). *Computer-assisted theory building: Modeling dynamic social systems*. Beverly Hills, CA: Sage.

Hedberg, B. (1981). How organizations learn and unlearn. In W. Starbuck & P. Nystrum (Eds.), *Handbook of organizational design* (Vol. 1, pp. 3–27). New York: Oxford University Press.

Hoy, W. K., & Feldman, J. A. (1987). Organizational health: The concept and its measure. *Journal of Research and Development in Education, 20*(1), 30–38.

Hoy, W. K., Tarter, C. J., & Kottkamp, R. B. (1991). *Open schools/healthy schools: Measuring organizational climate*. Newbury Park, CA: Sage.

Lyneis, J. M. (1980). *Corporate planning and policy design: A system dynamics approach*. Cambridge, MA: MIT Press.

Miles, M. B. (1965). Education and innovation: The organization in context. In M. Abbott & J. Lovell (Eds.), *Changing perspectives in educational administration* (pp. 54–72). Auburn, AL: Auburn University.

Miles, M. B. (1969). Planned change and organizational health: Figure and ground. In F. D. Carver & T. J. Sergiovanni (Eds.), *Organizations and human behavior* (pp. 375–391). New York: McGraw-Hill.

Morgan, G. (1990). *Images of organization*. Newbury Park, CA: Sage.

Parsons, T. (1961). An outline of the social system. In T. Parsons, E. Shils, K. D. Naegele, & J. R. Pitts (Eds.), *Theories of society: Foundations of modern sociological theory* (Vol. 1, pp. 30–79). New York: The Free Press.

Parsons, T., Bales, R. F., & Shils, E. A. (1953). *Working papers in the theory of action*. Glencoe, IL: The Free Press.

Peters, T. J., & Waterman, R. H. (1982). *In search of excellence*. New York: Harper & Row.

Powers, W. T. (1973). *Behavior: The control of perception*. Chicago: Aldine.

Powers, W. T. (1978). Quantitative analysis of purposive systems: Some spadework at the foundations of scientific psychology. *Psychology Review, 85*(5), 417–435.

Powers, W. T. (1990). Control theory: A model of organisms. *Systems Dynamics Review, 6*(1), 1–20.

Senge, P. M. (1990). *The fifth discipline: The art and practice of the learning organization*. New York: Doubleday.

Wolstenholme, E. F. (1990). *System inquiry: A systems dynamics approach*. New York: Wiley.

Chapter 11

Understanding Resilience: Implications for Inner-City Schools and Their Near and Far Communities

H. Jerome Freiberg
University of Houston

Why do some children survive, in fact flourish, in the most adverse conditions? This question reflects an area of research and discussion that has been missing from recent literature on the inner cities. The preoccupation with the failings of the urban environment and its inner-city schools has masked an opportunity to examine the successes. The study of resilience provides an important environment for discussing attributes of families, students, peers, schools, and communities that foster resilience in the inner cities. This chapter provides direction for future research that examines alterable variables for creating constructs of resilience, building on proactive and additive models, rather than on individual or collective deficits.

DEFINING RESILIENCE

The examination of resilience must draw from across the literature (Carta, 1991; Garmezy, 1974, 1991; Kagan, 1990; Werner, 1989; Winfield, 1991) of the helping professions (counseling, education, psychology, and sociology) to define and construct working definitions for resilience that are transferable to educational settings in the inner cities. The definitions by Masten, Best, and Garmezy (1991) and Rutter (1990) reflect the nature of positive individual responses to adverse conditions. The literature (Eisenberg, 1982; Hogman, 1983; Kestenberg, 1982) supports additional views that resilience in children is the ability to learn from and seek out the positive, and not replicate the disabling, elements of their environment. Studies of children who survived Nazi concentration camps and separation from their parents during World War II found that children had a definable set of resilient characteristics.

STUDIES OF RESILIENCE

Studies of resilience draw from the literature on children, youth, and adults who move beyond the pathology of their current lives to become healthy and productive individuals. Examples of resilience can be gleaned from Holocaust survivors to dysfunctional families to decaying inner-city schools and communities. The following is a selective review of the research literature from the helping professions. The studies build a case for establishing protective strategies that lead to greater resilience, as opposed to focusing on risk factors alone. Additionally, this chapter explores the role of schools and communities as partners in accelerating the protective factors of youth who live in at-risk environments.

Holocaust Survivors

Using a series of interviews, Hogman (1983) developed case histories of 11 adults who as children (aged 2 weeks to 11 years old) survived the Holocaust. Her study indicated that children who either saw their parents killed or became permanently separated from them, built their lives on a set of family values, cultural identities, and religious beliefs that sustained and protected them in desperate times. She found that ''the existence of memories, especially happy ones, seemed to help survivors fill the vacuum created by the war'' (p. 64).

Very young children, the author concluded, suffered the greatest problems as adults because they lacked memories and constructive role models. The successful survivors also had a strong sense of defiance that propelled them into adulthood. For many of the children, detailed fantasies about parents helped create an inner emotional climate to minimize the trauma of their environment.

Resilience may be viewed as the ability to become proactive rather than reactive. The sense of responsibility for siblings as well as nonfamily in the concentration camps helped the survivors as adults. Hogan concluded that ''from trauma can emerge a new identity; trauma does not only create psychopathology'' (Greer, 1980, p. 65). The affective qualities evident in studies of survivors of the Holocaust are also reflected as important factors in healthy children, adolescents, and adults.

Caring Parents

Franz, McClelland, and Weinberger (1991) conducted a follow-up study initiated in 1951 by Sears, Maccoby, and Levin (1957) of the childrearing practices of 379 mothers and their 5-year-old children in the Boston area. The
36-year (1951–1987) prospective study examined "the long-term influence of
parental warmth on adult social skills" (p. 587). The study provides important insights into the roles mothers and fathers can play in the well-being and
resilience of their children, which last through adulthood.

Franz et al. (1991) conducted a follow-up study, including 94 subjects of
the original sample of 379 five-year-olds, now 41 years old. The researchers
found that children had higher self-esteem at age 12 (Sears, 1970), cooperative interpersonal style at age 23 (Edwards, 1973), and higher adult social accomplishment at age 41 (Franz et al., 1991) when either parent showed warmth
(as opposed to strictness) through hugs, kisses, holding, and cuddling, as measured when the children were 5 years old (Sears et al., 1957). In midlife, children who came from either a warm mother or father "were able to sustain
long and relatively happy marriages, raise children, and be involved with friends
outside their marriage at midlife" (p. 592). Antithetically, coldness by parents in the study was associated with the 5-year-olds having "feeding problems,
bed-wetting, greater aggression, and slower conscience development" (p. 586).
Contrary to what was predicted by some researchers, parental harmony was
not associated with adult social accomplishment in this study.

Supportive Schools

The results of the Franz et al. (1991) research provide support for a study conducted by Rogers and Freiberg (in press). In spring 1991, secondary students
in six inner-city schools in Chicago, Houston, New Orleans, and Philadelphia
were interviewed regarding their attitudes toward school. Each school was pre-
selected for its reputation as a successful inner-city school. In each of the interviews, students indicated they liked (and, in many cases, loved) school because
teachers treated them with respect. In all but one high school, students also
indicated that teachers gave them hugs. The following is a representative sample of student comments:

- "They teach you by relating to you" (Chicago 7th grader)
- "They don't push you, they help you" (Chicago 8th grader)
- "They give good greetings . . . Some even give hugs" (Philadelphia 9th
  grader)
- "They don't just teach you math, but they'll find out how you are do-
  ing" (Houston 12th grader)

The communities in which many of these students lived were appalling. In Chicago, for example, the school was located directly across from a high-rise public housing project. The evening before the interview, a 5-year-old child was being dressed by his mother when he suddenly slumped to the floor. On the 20th floor of a public housing project, the child had been hit by a bullet that pierced the walls of the apartment, striking the child. The killing was a result of a drug-related gang fight at street level. The students in this school had to negotiate their way through abandoned vehicles, roving gangs, homeless people, and an environment that resembled a war zone. The school had an armed guard at the door, and researchers were asked to present identification before entering the building. Once inside, the environment was cheerful, bright, safe, and joyful, in stark contrast to the gray and dangerous external world in which the students lived the other 16 hours a day. One constant intrusion to this oasis of color and tranquility was the noise and physical shaking that occurred on a regular basis from the elevated trains that passed within 100 feet of the school.

The students were randomly selected for the interview, which was conducted in the cafeteria during lunch. Located on the top floor of the school, the cafeteria had both students and teachers eating lunch together. The mingling of faculty and students during lunch is becoming a rare sight in many elementary schools, but even more unusual at the middle school level. The students talked about a caring faculty and individual teachers who went beyond the three Rs to provide them with information about their options for high school. The seven students interviewed all indicated they would not stay in their neighborhoods to attend high school, but would take Chicago's extensive public transportation system to attend school across town. They expressed a strong sense of direction in their lives, and were constantly supporting each other's comments throughout the interview. Their information about which high school to attend came from other students who had left the neighborhood and reported back their successes at the school across town. They indicated that support, encouragement, and information came from teachers (not only the guidance counselor), who related examples of students who have gone to college from their school.

When asked why they would not stay and try to change their neighborhood high school, the students smiled at the naive question. One student said, ''We want to live.'' Another added, ''We want to do more than survive.'' The students all expressed appreciation for their teachers making them aware of options and providing support to them as persons as well as students.

The interviews highlight the importance of multiple sources of support for children and youth, support that emanates from outside the family to create ''positive memories'' that will last into adulthood. When a strong basis of value and cultural support is present, children have shown remarkable resilience in overcoming the most devastating conditions without having lasting negative

effects into adulthood. The concept of resilience needs to be broadened beyond the nuclear family to others who foster and nurture resilience within the
child, including teachers, extended families, peers, schools, and communities.

Protective Factors

A study recently reported by the Northwest Regional Educational Laboratory
(Benard, 1991) entitled *Fostering Resiliency in Kids: Protective Factors in the Family,
School and Community* found that children who overcome adversity in their surroundings have four basic protective traits: social competence, strong problem-
solving skills, autonomy, and a sense of purpose for the future. The researcher
concluded that family, school, and community can foster these protective traits
in children. Benard stated that individuals who have succeeded despite adverse
environmental conditions in their families, school, and/or communities have
''often done so because of the presence of environmental support in the form
of one family member, one teacher, one school, one community person that
encouraged their success and welcomed their participation'' (pp. 18–19). She
indicated in her study that communities that establish literacy programs, day-
care facilities where teens provide for younger children and elders, and other
support programs, can assist children in achieving a foundation for resilience.

Hull-House

The concept of community support programs is not new to the urban environment. In *Twenty Years at Hull-House*, Adams (1910) provided similar experiences
for urban youth at the turn of the century in Chicago. Hull-House was an oasis for youth and adults who were impoverished, lost, and disengaged from
their immigrant roots. The Hull-House charter stated its mission: ''To provide a center for higher civic and social life; to institute and maintain educational and philanthropic enterprises; and to investigate and improve the
conditions in the industrial districts of Chicago'' (p. 88). To these ends, Hull-
House provided tutoring sessions for youths and adults, trips to the country
for youngsters during the summer, lectures from the city's educational leadership (e.g., John Dewey), medicine for the sick, food for the hungry, housing
for the homeless, and a caring hand for the dying.

Adams also focused her efforts on ''protective legislation'' for children's
rights to an education and safe working conditions for adults. She researched
community needs. Studies were conducted on tuberculosis, typhoid fever, infant mortality, and the timing of garbage collection and causes of disease in
the tenements, to list only a few. A study entitled ''An Intensive Study of Tru-
ancy'' was also conducted, including 300 families.

Adams marshaled the forces of the city to improve the quality of life of its poorer residents. Many poor children who benefited from Hull-House were able to leave the squalor of the sweatshops and tenements to form a growing middle class. However, Adams warned about the dangers and futility "of the individual conscience which would isolate a family from the rest of the community" (p. 211). She described a widow who lived in her own comfortable little house and worked to put her two girls through college to give them a better life. Both girls were stricken with typhoid fever when they came home to visit during summer vacation; one daughter died. The mother had isolated herself from the community around her that was trying to improve housing and sanitation conditions, a key source of typhoid.

Cohort Support

Resilience may be broadened further to include resilient cohorts (i.e., groups that are able to protect themselves, as well as the individual). In a study entitled "Indochinese Refugee Families and Academic Achievement," Caplan, Choy, and Whitmore (1992) described the success of 536 school-aged children from 200 nuclear families in inner-city schools in Boston, Chicago, Houston, Seattle, and Orange County, California. The children who did not speak English, and had little or no contact with Western culture prior to immigrating to the United States, succeeded exceptionally well in terms of grades and standardized achievement in inner-city schools, which are not typically associated with high success with people of color.

The authors credited this success to a value system of "interdependence and family-based orientation to achievement" (p. 41). They concluded that the value system fostering academic rigor and excellence is not culturally unique. Caplan et al. cited studies by Reingold Clark of Claremont Graduate School, who showed parental support for the schools and teachers resulted in "outstanding achievement of low-income African-American students in Chicago" (p. 42). Caplan et al. also cited the work of Caudill and DeVos, who in 1948 found Japanese children were able to overcome racial and other prejudices after World War II to thrive academically in U.S. schools. Their third example of group success was a 1961 study by Kramer and Leventman that reported that 90% of third-generation Jewish children attended college, even though first-generation Jewish immigrants had no education when they arrived in the United States (see Caplan et al., 1992, p. 42).

Caplan et al. also cited an analysis of cultural support for schooling by Hess and Azuma (1991) in which cultural or group support are also identified as important variables in the success of Japanese students in Japan, and in their ability to adapt and be highly successful when they immigrate to the United States and attend U.S. schools. The literature on children who survived war and separation from their families, or who grew up in the civil wars of Ireland

and Angola, shows that protective intervention factors sustained the individual or group. In some cases, there was a strong sense of faith or belonging (i.e., a sense of identity and connectedness, of being part of a total community in which people supported and sustained each other). The potential for learned helplessness as a defensive measure is balanced by adaptive distancing and learned responsibility.

HOME, SCHOOL, AND COMMUNITY VALUES

The problems of the inner cities are complex, and the solutions must be multidimensional (Freiberg, 1989). Schools alone cannot make lasting social changes without a focused effort from all aspects of society.

During the last three decades, the public, media, and educational community have focused primarily on the deficits of our schools. The failure of our schools to prepare students for the workplace, the high dollar expenditures for declining achievement gains (when compared to other economic peers in the international community), and the rising levels of social pathology (violence, suicide, teen pregnancy, gangs, and drugs) have taken center stage in our nation's assessment of the future (National Commission on the Role of the Schools and the Community in Improving Adolescent Health, 1990).

When family, community, and values are strong, schools are strong—and the nation is strong. This becomes evident by comparing the resources that various nations spend for education. Of all industrialized countries, Japan spends the least for education of its youth. The United States is second highest in per-student expenditure (Barro, 1990). Japan spends far less because families, communities, and religious and cultural groups expend something more valuable than money on the education of their youth: time and the social resources needed to support successful learning environments.

Pillars of Support

In the 1950s, the education of students was sustained by five pillars of support: the family and home, the school, religion, community, and culture. The high rate of divorce, combined with the economic need for both parents to work outside the home, has shattered the ability of families to focus on and support the education of their children. Divorce, job changes, and housing mobility resulting from poverty have also destabilized the community. According to Pallas, Natriella, and McDill (1989), if current trends remain the same, nearly 50% of all students will be educationally disadvantaged by the year 2020. This is due in part to a mismatch between the values, experiences, and resources of the home and community and those of the school.

Approaches to community involvement by educators have focused, with limited success, primarily on parents in the community. Adults without children in public school make up a larger segment of any urban community. Unidimensional approaches to parental involvement, although successful in the past, work for only a small segment of today's parents. A multidimensional approach to parent and community involvement is necessary if communities are to regain their involvement in the education of youth, and if schools are to gain their balance of meeting the needs of students.

When family and home, religion, community, and culture are not supporting the child, then the school is expected to increase its share, requiring not more time from the other sectors but more money. Money alone becomes a poor substitute for parental involvement, community support and awareness, and religious and cultural values. Additionally, as Caplan et al. (1992) gleaned from their study of Indochinese immigrants, ''As the social needs of our students have moved into the classroom, they have consumed the scarce resources allocated to education and have compromised the schools' academic function'' (p. 42). Countries that have a good balance between the five supporting pillars create an environment for strong leadership, quality of life, and economic success. The state of schools and educational support systems today will predict the well-being of a country in the future, as well as the nation's ability to be resilient in difficult economic and political times.

It becomes increasingly evident that coordinated efforts of multiple services and support systems are needed to provide noninvasive programs for children, families, and adults living in the inner cities. In designing and implementing programs, a new definition of community may emerge.

Defining Community

There are many definitions of *community*. Some elicit a sense of sharing and caring, others emphasize the power of working together, and some simply define a geographic boundary. The research on resilience may redirect our focus of community as moving beyond the geographic to: (a) the joining together of people with common values, beliefs, and interests; (b) people working together for the good of the child as well as the group; and (c) a process in which the efforts of individuals are multiplied through cooperative efforts to achieve common goals.

Community and Schools

Community takes on a special meaning when we talk about schools. Communities may be geographically near or far from a school, but the collective need for all youth to be effective learners and productive citizens transcends geographic boundaries. Within the context of resilience, the community may be seen from a multidimensional rather than a unidimensional perspective. Adults, youths, students, parents, residents, employers, and employees live, work, and learn in their communities.

Each community has unique needs and aspirations and different realities. Meeting the needs of community must begin by meeting immediate needs. For example, if literacy is a major problem in a community, then literacy programs are needed. But if people are afraid to walk alone in their community, transportation must be provided before any impact can be made on literacy rates. Meeting community needs requires a much broader definition of community, and a rethinking of "school."

Current research on resilience and school–community relations could result in schools moving beyond brick and concrete walls into unique "learning communities." These learning communities would provide educational opportunities for children, their parents, senior citizens, and other adults who have a stake in the future. The new learning communities would be healthy, caring, and productive environments building protective factors where children and youth can learn from all members of the community. Isolation and detachment of schools from the community, commonplace in recent years, must be broken in order to provide new opportunities and experiences for both children and adults. The learning communities, which would foster alterable risk and protective factors, would need to incorporate a tapestry of features to enhance intergenerational growth and well-being. The following represents a conceptual framework for the integration of home, school, and community into a learning environment that will build protective factors and lead to greater resilience in meeting the ever-increasing demands of a stressful society.

Tapestry of Programs

In the past, an open house or a school play would attract a majority of parents to the school. At Sherman School in Chicago, where 1,000 students are enrolled, 5 mothers and fathers attended an open house. As the demographics indicate, parents are working during the day and have little time or energy to support school programs during evenings or on weekends. The concept of a tapestry (Freiberg, 1990) builds from small patchwork quilts of programs. Each program (see Fig. 11.1) may account for a relatively small number (5%–10%) of parent or community participants but, when linked together over time, can account for 80% to 90% parent participation, and inclusion of a significant number of other adults.

The tapestry represents several years of piloting parent and community programs to provide multiple sources of entry for parents. Many parents have negative memories of school, and encouraging them to actively participate in

FIELD TRIPS	MENTOR PROGRAM	EXTENDED LEARNING PROJECTS	SHOWS & PLAYS	PTA/PTO CLASSES	PARENT BOOK REPORTS	PARENT HELP
PARENTS TAKE PLACE OF STUDENT	PARENT CONVENTION	CLUBS	ADOPT A ROOM/SCHOOL	CERTIFICATES	CLEAN UP	CREATIVE BOOKBINDING
POSTCARDS	PARTNERS IN EDUCATION	TEACH FOR A DAY	PARENTS MAKE CENTER ACTIVITIES	BEAUTIFY THE SCHOOL	FATHERS DAY	PARENTS FIX FURNITURE
BIG BROTHERS AND SISTERS	REPORT CARD NIGHT	CALL HOME "ET"	PARENT PACKETS FOR HOME (HOLIDAYS AND SUMMER)	SATURDAY SCHOLARS PROGRAM	PARENTS GRADE DAY	GRANDPARENT DAY
SEAT TIME: READING PARENT	PARENT HOBBIES IN CLASS: MASONRY AND CARPENTRY	PARENTS DONATE BOOKS ON CHILD'S BIRTHDAY	LUNCH THEATER FOR PARENTS AND BUSINESS	PARENTS DONATE BOOKS AND WORK IN LIBRARY	HOMEROOM PARENTS	PARENT BREAKFAST
BOOK COVER ON CLASS DOOR	MOTHERS DAY	SHELL II				

FIG. 11.1.   Tapestry of parent–community involvement (© 1990 H. Jerome Freiberg).

school and support their children is a challenging task. The level of effort needed to involve parents increases for each succeeding generation as the dropout rates increase. Parents' "failing memories" of school inhibit creating a successful and resilient generation of children in the future.

Each program taps a different source of need and interest for parents and students. For example, creating a positive and protective school culture is a stated mission for many inner-city schools. There are several ways schools can achieve this goal. In working with librarians, a plan was devised to allow parents, grandparents, or other friends and relatives to purchase a book from a prescribed list (cost range from $1.50 to $15) to be placed in the library on a child's birthday. The book would have a dedication in the flap, identifying the donor and the child the book is honoring. The child has the first opportunity to read the book. Librarians and teachers of schools who have used this strategy report students returning to their school years later to see how their book is doing.

Other programs focus on intergenerational opportunities for parent, community, and child involvement. These include special days and events dedicated to parents, grandparents, guardians, and community members. Several schools have conducted conferences on Saturdays for the community, with topics ranging from "How to Start a Business" to "How to Help Your Child Succeed in School." The latter meeting attracted over 60 parents and grandparents to an inner-city elementary school at 9:30 a.m.

A tapestry of programs allows people with a stake in the school to become directly involved, while giving other adults the opportunity to share in educating the next generation of leaders.

Stakeholders (Near Community)

Each school has both a near and a far geographic community (Freiberg, 1990). The neighborhood surrounding a school, or its near community, includes parents with children going to the school and adults who are in some way influenced by the school. Schools have historically served as locations for night classes for new immigrants, and have thus been kept open in the evenings and on the weekends (Perry, 1908) without the need for an elaborate bureaucracy. It is important to emphasize that the near community is more than parents and their children; it is all adults who have a stake in the education of the young living in the neighborhood.

In the age of megacorporations, leveraged buyouts, and consolidations, corner stores or gas stations are rarely owned by a member of the near community, which causes a detachment from the neighborhood. The concept of *stakeholder* can be expanded to include all members of the near community, including those businesses controlled by corporate headquarters thousands of miles away. Working with corporate leaders, school–business partnership programs can provide for decentralized support and decision making for local community efforts. The corporate store can thus respond as if it were owned by a neighbor, enabling businesses that are geographically removed to become shareholders with schools and communities. These new business and corporate shareholders become another supporting pillar for student success, adding to protective resilience.

Shareholders (Far Community)

The near geographic community has a direct and immediate interest in the success of the learning community and its students. Shareholders comprise the far geographic community (Freiberg, 1991). Although shareholders have a less immediate interest in a particular learning community, they see the cumulative effect on the well-being of a city, county, state, or nation as significant. Shareholders include elected officials at all four levels, as well as business and residential communities. Participation by business reflects far community concerns that skilled and well-educated (rather than simply trained) workers remain available in the future.

Recent Gallup polls (Elam, Lowell, & Gallup, 1992) indicate that Americans see their local schools as effective, but schools in general as ineffective. Case studies have shown that when members of the far community see a general community danger, they can respond to the problem. One example is an area of Houston known as "Crack City," a group of nearly 4,000 apartments located across the street from an elementary school. Several murders had occurred in the area. The police, city council, school district, Drug Enforcement Agency (DEA), and other agencies joined together to cordon off the area and only allow residents into the apartments. Landlords were ordered to tear down unsafe buildings. In just 2 years, the area has been transformed. Many apartments have been renovated, and others destroyed. When political pressure from the near community (in this case, a middle-class neighborhood near "Crack City") was placed on city leadership, the community outlook changed from fear to hope.

School as Learning Community

The word "school" derives from a Greek word meaning leisure. There was a time when only a small proportion of society needed to be educated for the society to prosper. That time has long passed. Along with food, clothing, and shelter, education has become a basic necessity. Without education, a democracy cannot survive. Woodrow Wilson, speaking in Boston in 1904, concluded: "Without popular education . . . no government which rests upon popular action can long endure: the people must be schooled in the knowledge, and if possible in the virtues, upon which the maintenance and success of free institutions depend" (Perry, 1908, p. 8).

Economics plays an important role in the overall success of the community and the school, and the opportunities for parents and their children. Although some individuals may be resilient and successful in oppressive economic environments, lack of resources diminishes educational and future economic opportunities for all members of the community. To meet the growing challenges, we must redefine not only community, but the way schools function within a community in their new role as academies for learning.

The Academy

The terms *academy* and *learning communities*, may more accurately than school, reflect the educational requirements of the future. A learning community would bring together all learners from childhood through adulthood. The academy within the learning community would provide excellent neighborhood schools, as called for by the leadership in inner-city communities. The academy would be a hub for adults and senior citizens as well as youth. As part of the learning community, students would learn from each other, from teachers, and from other adults in the near and far communities.

Highly successful schools, such as Houston's High School for the Performing and Visual Arts, have drawn their teachers from the community at large since the 1970s. Within the visual arts community, masters work with and learn from their apprentices.

Integenerational Centers

The need for intergenerational learning centers is critical for a modern society. Literacy centers, for example, should be a part of every school. Programs to teach adults who lack basic skills in reading and mathematics are a national priority. The best of these programs have shown gains of 2 years in mathematics and reading for every 120 hours of instruction (Freiberg, Stein, & Gauthier, 1990).

In Houston, there are an estimated 500,000 illiterate and semi-literate adults. Since 1992, the Houston Read Commission has provided literacy education for more than 1,000 adults. Although the Read Commission has a program that works, it will take decades for a fraction of the adults to receive literacy support. With more than 200 learning centers (school buildings) in Houston, nearly 200,000 adults could receive literacy support if the concept of the school is expanded into the academy and the learning community.

Neighborhood Meeting Center

The academy would also be the meeting place for community activities. Community events such as civic club meetings, voting, and stakeholder and shareholder meetings would take place in learning community centers.

Governance Through Community Councils

Knowledge is power, and budgets validate that power. The learning community should be governed by a community council modeled after the Teacher Corps Community Councils (Freiberg, Townsend, & Buckley, 1982) and in accordance with the legal parameters of each state (e.g., Texas House Bill 2885 and the implications of Site-Based Management legislation provided in section 21.931).

Members would be elected to the community council from the near and far communities. The council would provide advice to the administrative support group, teachers of the academy, and other elements of the learning community. In addition to the council's advisory role to the academy, the council would be allocated a budget each year to establish, in collaboration with the academy, programs that enhance the education of all members of the learning community. The community council would become part of the tapestry, which would enhance past, current, and future generational learning. The community council would help recapture the community as the centerpiece of the academy, and the academy as the centerpiece of the community.

CONCLUSION

If our nation is to be resilient, extraordinary collaborative efforts are needed. We face serious issues relating to education, the economy, and politics. No one system will meet all the challenges of preparing the next generation of youth for local, state, and national leadership, or to become members of a world-class work force. We must begin to rethink the nature and structure of education, and build from positive models that foster resilience and protective systems for students, their families, and communities. Resources must be refocused to support intergenerational efforts to achieve the goal of a healthy, caring, and productive society.

REFERENCES

Adams, J. (1910). *Twenty years at Hull-House*. New York: The New American Library.

Barro, S. M. (1990). *International comparisons of educational spending*. Washington, DC: SMB Economic Research.

Benard, B. (1991). *Fostering resiliency in kids: Protective factors in the family, school and community*. Portland, OR: Western Regional Center for Drug-free Schools and Communities Far West Laboratory.

Caplan, N., Choy, H. C., & Whitmore, J. K. (1992). Indochinese refugee families and academic achievement. *Scientific American, 266*(2), 36–42.

Carta, J. J. (1991). Education for children in inner-city classrooms. *American Behavioral Scientist, 34*(3), 440–453.

Edwards, C. N. (1973). Interactive styles and social interaction. *Genetic Psychology Monographs, 87*, 123–174.

Eisenberg, A. (1982). *The lost generation: Children in the Holocaust*. New York: Pilgrim.

Elam, S., Lowell, R., & Gallop, A. (1992). 24th annual Gallop/PDK poll of the public's attitude towards public schools. *Phi Delta Kappan, 74*(1), 41–55.

Franz, C., McClelland, D., & Weinberger, J. (1991). Childhood antecedents of conventional social accomplishment in midlife adults: A 36 year prospective study. *Journal of Personality and Social Psychology, 60*(4), 586–593.

Freiberg, H. J. (1989). A multi-dimensional view of school effectiveness. *Educational Research Quarterly, 13*(2), 35–46.

Freiberg, H. J. (1990). Tapestry of parent/community involvement. In H. J. Freiberg (Ed.), *Consistency Management handbook of instructional materials*. Houston: University of Houston.

Freiberg, H. J. (1991). *Freedom to learn: Technology as a source of freedom*. Paper presented at the meeting of the International Electron Device, Washington, DC.

Freiberg, H. J., Stein, T., & Gauthier, L. (1990). *Read Commission learning center evaluation report*. Houston: University of Houston.

Freiberg, H. J., Townsend, K., & Buckley, P. (1982). Does in-service make a difference? *British Journal of In-service Education, 8*(3), 189–200.

Garmezy, N. (1974). The study of competence in children at risk for severe psychopathy. In E. J. Anthony (Ed.), *The child in his family. Vol. 3: Children at psychiatric risk* (pp. 77–98). New York: Wiley.

Garmezy, N. (1991). Resiliency and vulnerability to adverse development outcomes associated with poverty. *American Behavioral Scientist, 34*(4), 416–430.

Greer, F. (1980). Toward a developmental view of adult crises: A re-examination of crisis theory. *Journal of Humanistic Psychology, 20*(4), 17–27.

Hess, R. D., & Azuma, H. (1991). Cultural support for schooling: Contracts between Japan and United States. *Educational Researcher, 20*(9), 2–8.

Hogman, F. (1983). Displaced Jewish children during World War II: How they coped. *Journal of Humanistic Psychology, 23*(1), 51–66.

Kagan, D. M. (1990). How schools alienate students at risk: A model for examining proximal classroom variables. *Educational Psychologists, 25*(2), 105–120.

Kestenberg, J. (1982). Survivor—Parents and their children. In M. Bergmann & M. Jucovy (Eds.), *Generations of the Holocaust* (pp. 83–102). New York: Basic Books.

Masten, A. S., Best, K. M., & Garmezy, N. (1991). Resilience and development: Contributions from the study of children who overcome adversity. *Development and Psychopathology, 2*, 425–444.

National Commission on the Role of the Schools and the Community in Improving Adolescent Health. (1990). *Code blue: Uniting for healthier youth.* Atlanta, GA: Centers for Disease Control.

Pallas, A., Natriella, G., & McDill, E. (1989). The changing nature of the disadvantaged population: Current dimensions and future trends. *Educational Researcher, 8*(5), 16–22.

Perry, A. C. (1908). *Management of a big city school.* New York: Macmillan.

Rogers, C. R., & Freiberg, H. J. (in press). *Freedom to learn.* Columbus, OH: Merrill.

Rutter, M. (1990). Psychosocial resilience and protective mechanisms. In J. Rolf, A. S. Masten, D. Cicchetti, K. H. Nuechterlein, & S. Weintraub (Eds.), *Risk and protective factors in the development of psychopathy* (pp. 181–214). New York: Cambridge University Press.

Sears, R. R. (1970). Relation of early socialization experiences to self-concepts and gender role in middle childhood. *Child Development, 41*, 267–289.

Sears, R. R., Maccoby, E. E., & Levin, H. (1957). *Patterns of child-rearing.* Evanston, IL: Row, Peterson.

Werner, E. E. (1989). High-risk children in young adulthood: A longitudinal study from birth to 32 years. *American Journal of Orthopsychiatric, 59*(1), 72–81.

Winfield, L. (1991). Resilience, schooling, and development in African-American youth. *Education and Urban Society, 24*(1), 5–14.

Chapter 12

Contextualizing Resiliency

Howard A. Liddle
Temple University

Concepts have a life all their own. Sometimes they appear and then suddenly depart, like fashion trends. These early exits are not necessarily premature, at least when the ideas were insubstantial to begin with. With this in mind, consider our current fascination with the notion of resilience. Does resilience qualify as an organizing concept with sufficient logical and emotional resonance to yield systematic theoretical and research inquiry that will make it a lasting contribution? Clearly, it is too early to form a conclusive opinion on this question. This chapter examines the potential ''resiliency of resilience'' with the basic premise that the continued revision or extension of resilience as a concept is in order. This chapter offers areas in which this can be accomplished.

THE CONTEXTUAL PERSPECTIVE: RESILIENCY AS A MULTIDIMENSIONAL CONCEPT

Resiliency represents more than a single concept or idea. Gordon and Song (chapter 2, this volume) suggest that it should be considered a companion concept vis-à-vis other related ideas—that it should, in short, be considered in the natural ecology of ideas and sensibilities in which it is embedded. This conceptualization is syntonic with modern-day theorizing. In my own area of work, the development and testing of family-based interventions for adolescent drug abuse, we understand the need to conceptualize the targeted clinical problem along systemic lines. Researchers sometimes refer to ''co-morbidity'' (contemporary work in this area appreciates the importance of what has come to be called a "problem behavior syndrome"), seeking to understand how problem behaviors co-occur, as well as the interpersonal, familial, social, and societally embedded nature of the behaviors. The intellectual spirit of the times rejects reductionism and favors multivariate, multidimensional conceptualizations of behavior. Although this perspective is helpful in some ways, it poses a difficult challenge. Thinking multidimensionally is a worthwhile goal, but in practice how are we to define complex concepts of this nature?

Definition Difficulties

There is considerable variance in our definitions of resiliency (Gordon & Song, this volume). With this in mind, and considering our objective of constructing resilience in relation to other related notions (risk-factor research, stress and coping research developmental psychopathology), the danger exists of producing a mushy and ill-defined set of concepts.

Developing connections between propositions can be a very abstract affair. In our intervention model, the clinical world of interventions has been joined with the developmental world of understanding people as they progress through the life course (Liddle, Dakof, & Diamond, 1991). Our interventions are based on and deeply rooted in the developmental knowledge base a therapist brings to his or her work (Liddle, Schmidt, & Ettinger, in press). For example, attachment theory, reformulated to fit the adolescent years, is not a remote set of interesting ideas but a set of findings that practically informs a clinician's work (Liddle & Diamond, 1991). This work may have relevance for the task ahead with resilience. There are many implications for the resilience complex, such as how it might shape the way we think of problems, coping, and interventions. These ideas have great potential for shaping how we think about the targets of our interventions and the mechanisms by which people change their lives. Interventionists must be as aware of pathways to successful coping and adaptation, as they are of those that have seemingly led to destructive or maladaptive outcomes.

Specifying the Process Links Between Related Concepts

We have moved from intrapersonal conceptions of resilience to interpersonally located ones; we now speak of the resilient community versus the superkid. This movement represents progress, but the next step in theorizing will be to specify the processes of interconnection between these levels of analysis. Resiliency is not simply a characteristic or trait. It can also be seen, given our expanded vision, as a series of coping mechanisms and responses by the organism plus the environment. The concept of *isomorphism*, the tendency for a similar process to appear at different levels of a systems functioning (while being manifested by different content), may be relevant for resiliency. That is, can we think of resilience as something that can manifest itself across levels of systems (even though it might be different in appearance at these various levels)?

Linking Context and Phenomenology

Along these same lines, the move to the phenomenological or meaning level is a must (Gordon & Song, this volume). Similar life circumstances and events can be perceived as either disabling or enhancing. This is the systems principle of equifinality—that the same outcomes can come from different starting places and from different processes. The phenomenological level is critical, but alone it is as insufficient as any other intrapersonal viewpoint that tends to omit interactions across levels.

If we add behavioral and contextual dimensions to this formula, the picture becomes more complex, and many questions emerge. If I perceive something as a threat, or as an annoyance, how does my context react to this perception? Will my significant others support or challenge this perspective? If they support it, does this shared social cognition help my individual coping processes? If my environment challenges my perception, what are my options; do I go underground with these viewpoints, and simply not discuss my observations or feelings with a disagreeing other? Or, does this interpretation discrepancy of the stimulus events create stress and tension in this primary relationship? When this occurs, where does this leave me, considering the importance of primary relationships in coping with life's stressors? Further, from this perspective (i.e., broadening theorizing beyond the phenomenological level), how does development fit in (i.e., what if we inform our discussion of this matter by the different expectations and capabilities associated with different life-cycle stages?). And finally, contextually speaking, how do supportive or challenging aspects of other environments fit in, such as extended family relations, or extrafamilial environments such as schools?

In the psychotherapy research field, we were at one time challenged about the uniformity myth that had infiltrated our thinking (Kiesler, 1966), reminded to discuss the results of our interventions in a differentiated way and not as if the clients and families were uniform. This is another challenge to the resiliency concept. We must understand the varieties of contexts in which resiliency occurs and describe some of the many characteristics of these contexts, as well as, at a process level, chart the interactions between the various system levels. Basic and applied researchers and scholars would do well to follow the Gordon and Song method of work. The methods and philosophy of their chapter remind us of some important ideas: Concepts can have a human face, and the resiliency concept, although sounding abstract, can be clearly found in the narratives of the subjects interviewed.

These respondents, with their powerful life stories, are indispensable contributors to the evolution of the resiliency notion.

RESILIENCE CONSIDERED DEVELOPMENTALLY

The developmental aspects of resiliency remain in need of further elaboration. There are traditions still evolving in the social sciences, and in psychology in particular, arguing for the potentiating effects when various areas are linked, such as research and practice (Forsyth & Strong, 1986; Liddle, 1991), and clinical and developmental psychology (Furman, 1980; Kendall, Lerner, & Craighead, 1984; Liddle et al., in press). The specialty of developmental psychopathology offers evidence of the conceptual and intervention benefits from this integrative perspective (Achenbach, 1986; Cicchetti, 1990; Kazdin, 1989). A major challenge, as this chapter asserts, is the possibility of resiliency becoming a more contextually sensitive, and thus more usable, concept. Both development and psychopathology were enriched as separate specialties when their perspectives were considered simultaneously. Like psychopathology, resiliency must be understood developmentally. What are the different definitions or manifestations of resiliency when considered in this way? How does an adolescent's resiliency differ from a child's, or an adult's? The uniformity myth, applied to this area, challenges an assumption about developmentally uniform resiliency characteristics or processes.

Some contemporary research utilizes the integration of developmental and resiliency perspectives. Radke-Yarrow and Sherman (1990) examined children who appeared to be surviving (i.e., without psychiatric diagnoses; school performance at grade level; relating well to others; and with a positive self-concept) despite "multirisk conditions of genetic and environmental origins." *Coping* was understood from three vantage points: biological, societal and psychological. Although each child studied developed an individual coping style, some process commonalities emerged. Perhaps most importantly, no children were identified as "invulnerable," but rather as "survivors," because each child who managed to grow and develop in the face of extreme stress also suffered from such adverse conditions. Moreover, although intelligence, curiosity, pleasing physical appearance, and "socially winning ways" were established as general protective factors, each child was also found to fulfill a need of one or both parents, and thus received many of the limited social and emotional resources available to the family. Radke-Yarrow and Sherman (1990) cautioned that:

> underlying these children's relatively successful adaptations . . . also harbor the
> seeds of possible future serious problems. We have speculated that with further
> development, especially with adolescence, these children will be able to satisfy

their parents' needs and their own needs only at increasing costs to the children themselves. . . . The straightjackets they have been forced to adopt will become increasingly difficult to wear as they continue to develop. (p. 118)

In this work, developmental sensibilities have informed conceptions of the concept of and processes related to resilience.

OTHER CONTEMPORARY FRAMEWORKS
TO MAKE RESILIENCY MORE CONTEXTUAL

There are other contemporary sensibilities, in addition to the developmental lens, that may prove helpful in deepening the resiliency concept. A framework that offers an opportunity to intersect individual differences such as temperament with a systemic perspective, would be one of these lenses (Bugental & Shennum, 1984). When the contextual perspective was taken to an extreme, as it was during a particular stage of its history, the family systems viewpoint minimized individual differences, preferring to focus on system-level variables (Nichols, 1987). There is currently an appreciation of the reductionist excesses that occurred in the name of systems thinking, and an understanding of how individual and family level phenomena, among others, can co-exist and be understood for additional benefit. Resiliency will also struggle to form complex "both–and," rather than "either–or," kinds of theorizing.

The cross-cultural perspective is another tradition that would help resiliency develop. In intervention research, we now know that treatment can be specified to previously impossible degrees. One way in which this occurs is through particularizing the client population, including, of course, cultural and ethnic characteristics. Interventions are thus tailored to the population that the interventions hope to affect. This tailoring includes a deep understanding of the cultural and ethnic characteristics of those we are trying to help (e.g., Malgady, Rogler, & Costantino, 1990).

Gender sensitivity is another contemporary sensibility that has transformed the way we think about designing and delivering interventions. Gender sensitivity is a viewpoint, embedded in modern-day society, intended to fight the gender-role stereotyping predominant in earlier periods of our society. As a political force and intellectual tradition, this movement has revolutionized the way we think about interventions (Johnson & Kaplan, 1988). It has the same potential in our contextualization of resiliency. Resiliency processes, to an as-yet-unspecified degree, may be suitably informed through the lens of gender.

Another contextual informer of the resiliency notion is the dimension of time (as distinguished from development, which also has a temporal dimension). Resiliency occurs over time and within certain time frames. People can be expected to be more resilient at certain times than at others, rather than uni-

formly (on all occasions over time) resilient. Adding the temporal frame focuses us in the direction of resilient processes, and, again, informs the construct contextually.

BEYOND RESILIENCY
AS AN INTRAPERSONAL TRAIT

An additional challenge concerns the degree to which resiliency can move beyond its consideration as an intrapersonal trait, while at the same time avoiding a reductionistic mistake at the other extreme—only considering resiliency
as a context characteristic. Some contemporary work offers an example of how
this middle position might look. Although Garmezy (1983, 1984, 1985) stimu-
lated considerable interest in the study of "stress-resistant children," Baldwin, Baldwin, and Cole (1990) focus on what they call the stress-resistant
family—the high-risk family that is able to protect its children from surrounding dangers. Although it might be said that a stress-resistant child may succeed in resisting the dangers of a high-risk environment, children from
stress-resistant families may or may not have resistant internal mechanisms,
but be "shielded" from environmental risks by a protective family. A protective family creates a low-risk proximal environment that shields the adolescent
from noxious elements in a high-risk distal environment.

CONCEPT POLITICS:
ARE WE "ROMANCING RESILIENCY"?

There is another critical aspect of resiliency considered from a contextual vantage point, an aspect that may go unnoticed. It pertains to something that lies
outside intellectual or conceptual boundaries. Sometimes, a new concept or,
more broadly, a new paradigm, gets discovered, and we hang onto it for all
it is worth. Surely resiliency has been an important addition to our thinking
about human problems and, potentially, also to their resolution. But many
of us have for some time known about and used certain forms of the resiliency
notion. In 1975, as an avid young protege of Salvador Minuchin, I learned
that the resiliency concept and the clinical methods attached to it had the power to transform one's clinical conceptualization. Minuchin would chastise us
for focusing too heavily on dysfunction; he called us "sleuths for psychopathology." We were challenged to look beyond problems and into areas of strength
that were underdeveloped or hidden from immediate view. These areas of human functioning had to do with resilience—the ways in which people over-

came formidable environmental and personal odds to raise competent, happy children, and to succeed in work. Minuchin would often say that these processes were key to access in treatment. Overemphasizing pathology leads to more pathology. From this position, solutions are less likely to materialize.

This perceptual reorientation, although clinically powerful and philosophically syntonic with many a clinician, began over time to lose its power. I began to think of it as a concept in need of assistance; standing alone it was too limited, too prone to Pollyannalike, anything-is-possible perspectives. Clearly, not all things are possible for all kids in trouble or, for families struggling, mostly in vain, to cope. Our fascination with activating a family's resources or strengths, perhaps like all interventions, has political and ideological implications. A focus on the resilient aspects of a child's or family's experience and behavior is functional, emotionally and practically; it gives the clinician something to hang onto in the face of probabilities against success. As a frame or perspective, it helps to defy the predictions of negative outcomes. Of course, the contribution and power of this frame exists not solely in its benefit to clinicians. When interventionists maintain an outlook that includes resources, strengths, and alternatives, the family is more likely to develop one as well. At least this is the assumptive logic.

However, what has been missing is the possible co-existence of the two perspectives that I am describing. Accessing strengths and focusing on resiliency does not mean we forget how to assess problems, any more than defining problem domains means we become blind to present but less obvious resources. We need a process notion of the dialectic between these perspectives. Is it possible to avoid unidimensional or overly narrow interpretations of resiliency? A new conceptualization might be called *the resiliency complex*. It would reject not only a politically correct but a naive and, in terms of the clients we serve and the people to whom the notion is usually applied, cruel promise that all things are possible, and reject the nihilistic conclusion that the odds facing the truly disadvantaged are impossible to overcome. Neither of these views leads to constructive action; worse yet, they offer a lie to those we seek to serve. Life is complex, and the concepts we use to try and understand it must match this multivariate reality.

Therefore, it is necessary to include the political perspective in defining resiliency contextually. These are difficult times for those who want to take social problems seriously. Too often, there is a shortage of models of thoughtful, appropriately complex, realistic solutions. For example, many in government urge us to treat drug abuse among our youth primarily as a national security problem. Proven strategies of treatment, and framing such problems within the social sphere, are avoided in favor of simplistic, control-oriented strategies. Complex concepts and solutions are too often ignored in favor of emotionally appealing but narrow realities.

With the decay of our urban landscapes and the institutions that reside within them, solution-potentiating resources are scarce. Especially in these times, we are more likely to embrace frameworks that provide a "resource" that is in short supply in the tough times in which we live. The resiliency concept exudes hope and hopefulness. The stories that accompany the resilient child, family, or community are not those that appear on the nightly news. Resiliency narratives warm our heart, fight cynicism, and remind many of us why we got into the field in the first place. The challenge for resiliency lies not only in conceptual rigor, empirical connectedness, and practical utility, but also in understanding its connection to the critical context of the politics of ideas. To say that something has political overtones or dimensions is not to demean it, make it lose its magical quality, or align it with a cynical world. It is simply to remind us that if we really want to consider something contextually, then the ideological and political aspects of it must be included.

EXPECTATIONS FOR RESILIENCY: WHAT ARE THE IMPLICATIONS OF NONRESILIENT BEHAVIOR?

Although the study of resilient behavior is aimed at producing a robust and reproducible set of ideas for researchers and practitioners, Sameroff and Seifer (1990) underscore that "children exposed to continuous family and cultural disruption become increasingly unable to develop in a healthy, competent direction and become more vulnerable to developing severe psychopathology" (p. 61). They argued that what emerges as key from this research is neither the individual type or specific combination of risk factors, nor the categorization of risk versus protective factors, but the multiplicity of factors and their impact on the formation of strong family relationships and, in turn, competency in children. A summary of the risk and protective factor research as it pertains to adolescent drug abuse has yielded a comparable conclusion. Hawkins, Catalano, and Miller (1992) recommended designing coherent multiple-component or comprehensive strategies that target a number of risk factors while attempting to enhance protective factors.

Although the hope-inducing functions of the resiliency concept are important, it is at the same time important not to use this framing to minimize certain empirically related realities. As the risk-factor literature reminds us, there are predictive realities associated with certain clusters of risk factors, the most powerful aspects of which lie in their cumulative power, rather than individual determinative potentialities (Hawkins et al., 1992; i.e., the more risk factors that are present, the greater the prediction of negative effects).

INTERVENTION IMPLICATIONS
OF A CONTEXTUAL VERSION OF RESILIENCY

If we can develop a contextual understanding of resiliency, the intervention possibilities of the concept will be multiplied. Consider how one's view of interventions changes with the following two statements:

> Drug use among teenagers is one component of an integrated lifestyle involving attitudes and other behaviors. Thus a strict focus on teenage drug use will be too limited for effective prevention or treatment. At an individual level, the surrounding and correlated aspects of drug use must also be carefully considered and integrated in programs. (Newcomb & Bentler, 1988, p. 27)

> A major implication of this view is that efforts toward prevention and rehabilitation aimed at changing adolescent alcohol and drug use may not be maximally effective if they are limited in focus to the use behavior itself or on an isolated domain of the adolescent's life. Instead, interventions should focus simultaneously on multiple domains. (Pandina & Schuele, 1983, p. 967)

If we have narrow concepts and targets of intervention, considering the ecological embedded nature of social problems, our intervention approaches may become too narrow as well. The psychotherapy field has been challenged on the scope or narrowness of its interventions (Kazdin, 1982). Resiliency holds the potential to enrich not only our conceptualization of intervention targets but their hoped-for outcomes. By detailing pathways to success and processes by which individuals, in the context of a supportive environment (or aspects of environment, such as a friendship outside of a problematical family situation) beat the odds, we gain emotionally (hope is restored) while simultaneously gaining a clearer vision of success routes. These pathways, although idiosyncratic to the individuals, their contexts, and the times, may still hold principles that can be generalized. Returning to the isomorphism principle, perhaps an answer lies in the ways in which the content of these resilience tales may differ, whereas the underlying structure, form, or basic (reproducible) principles remain the same.

The "big bang" of the discovery of resilience may be over, but the most fruitful and productive rewards from this notion lie ahead. Critical examination and reexamination of resilience can help realize this possibility.

REFERENCES

Achenbach, T. M. (1986). The developmental study of psychopathology: Implications for psychotherapy and behavior change. In S. L. Garfield & A. E. Bergin (Eds.), *Handbook of psychotherapy and behavior change* (pp. 117–154). New York: Wiley.

Baldwin, A. L., Baldwin, C., & Cole, R. E. (1990). Stress-resistant families and stress-resistant children. In J. Rolf, A. S. Masten, D. Cicchetti, K. Nuechterlein, & S. Weintraub (Eds.), *Risk and protective factors in the development of psychopathology* (pp. 257–280). Cambridge: Cambridge University Press.

Bugental, D. B., & Shennum, W. A. (1984). "Difficult" children as elicitors and targets of adult communication patterns: An attributional-behavioral transactional analysis. *Monographs of the Society for Research in Child Development, 49*(1), Serial No. 205.

Cicchetti, D. (1990). A historical perspective on the discipline of developmental psychopathology. In J. Rolf, A. S. Masten, D. Cicchetti, K. Nuechterlein, & S. Weintraub (Eds.), *Risk and protective factors in the development of psychopathology* (pp. 2–28). Cambridge: Cambridge University Press.

Forsyth, D. R., & Strong, S. R. (1986). The scientific study of counseling and psychotherapy: A unificationist view. *American Psychologist, 41*, 113–119.

Furman, W. (1980). Promoting social development: Developmental implications for treatment. In B. Lahey & A. Kazdin (Eds.), *Advances in clinical child psychology* (Vol. 3, pp. 1–40). New York: Plenum.

Garmezy, N. (1983). Stressors of childhood. In N. Garmezy & M. Rutter (Eds.), *Stress, coping and development in children* (pp. 43–84). New York: McGraw-Hill.

Garmezy, N. (1984). Children vulnerable to major mental disorders: Risk and protective factors. In L. Grinspoon (Ed.), *Psychiatry update: The American Psychiatric Association annual review* (Vol. 3, pp. 91–104). Washington, DC: American Psychiatric Press.

Garmezy, N. (1985). Stress-resistant children: The search for protective factors. In J. E. Stevenson (Ed.), *Recent research in development psychopathology* (pp. 213–233). Oxford: Pergamon Press.

Hawkins, J. D., Catalano, R. F., & Miller, J. (1992). Risk and protective factors for alcohol and other drug problems in adolescence and early adulthood: Implications for substance abuse prevention. *Psychological Bulletin, 112*, 64–105.

Johnson, R. J., & Kaplan, H. B. (1988). Gender, aggression, and mental health intervention during early adolescence. *Journal of Health and Social Behavior, 29*, 53–64.

Kazdin, A. E. (1982). Symptom substitution, generalization, and response covariation: Implications for psychotherapy outcome. *Psychotherapy Bulletin, 91*, 349–365.

Kazdin, A. E. (1989). Developmental psychopathology: Current research, issues and directions. *American Psychologist, 44*, 180–187.

Kendall, P. C., Lerner, R. M., & Craighead, W. E. (1984). Human development and intervention in childhood psychopathology. *Child Development, 55*, 71–82.

Kiesler, D. J. (1966). Some myths of psychotherapy research and the search for a paradigm. *Psychological Bulletin, 65*, 110–136.

Liddle, H. A. (1991). Empirical values and the culture of family therapy. *Journal of Marital and Family Therapy, 17*, 327–348.

Liddle, H. A., Dakof, G. A., & Diamond, G. (1991). Adolescent substance abuse: Multidimensional family therapy in action. In E. Kaufman & P. Kaufman (Eds.), *Family therapy approaches with drug and alcohol problems* (2nd ed., pp. 120–171). Needham Heights, MA: Allyn & Bacon.

Liddle, H. A., & Diamond, G. (1991). Special problems in working with adolescent substance abuse: Engaging reluctant teenagers in family therapy. *Family Dynamics of Addictions Quarterly, 1*, 55–69.

Liddle, H. A., Schmidt, S., & Ettinger, D. (in press). Adolescent development research: Guidelines for clinicians. *Journal of Marital and Family Therapy*.

Malgady, R. G., Rogler, L. H., & Costantino, G. (1990). Culturally sensitive psychotherapy for Puerto Rican children and adolescents: A program of treatment outcome research. *Journal of Consulting and Clinical Psychology, 58*, 704–712.

Newcomb, M. D., & Bentler, P. M. (1988). *Consequences of adolescent drug abuse: Impact on the lives of young adults.* Newbury Park, CA: Sage.

Nichols, M. P. (1987). *The self in the system.* New York: Brunner/Mazel.

Pandina, R. J., & Schuele, J. A. (1983). Psychosocial correlates of alcohol and drug use of adolescent students and adolescents in treatment. *Journal of Studies on Alcohol, 44,* 950–973.

Radke-Yarrow, M., & Sherman, T. (1990). Hard growing: Children who survive. In J. Rolf, A. S. Masten, D. Cicchetti, K. Nuechterlein, & S. Weintraub (Eds.), *Risk and protective factors in the development of psychopathology* (pp. 97–119). Cambridge: Cambridge University Press.

Sameroff, A. J., & Seifer, R. (1990). Early contributors to developmental risk. In J. Rolf, A. S. Masten, D. Cicchetti, K. Nuechterlein, & S. Weintraub (Eds.), *Risk and protective factors in the development of psychopathology* (pp. 52–66). Cambridge: Cambridge University Press.

Chapter 13

Organizing for Responsiveness:
The Heterogeneous School Community

Diana Oxley
Temple University

The educational critiques of the 1980s portrayed public schools, especially secondary schools, as dysfunctional, calcified institutions that are unresponsive to dramatic changes in family structure, demography, and the economy. Despite decades of classroom-based reform efforts, basic instructional practices and school structures remain in place (Cuban, 1986). Given the enormous differences in the needs of local communities, the organization of schools in New York City and Philadelphia is fundamentally the same as it is in suburbia (Goodlad, 1984). There seems to be no exit from traditional school practices that include large size, academic departmentalization, homogeneous grouping, 50-minute periods, and whole class instruction.

Some educational analysts have argued that the best way to effect school improvement is to create stronger community pressure for change through the enactment of school choice policies (Chubb & Moe, 1988). Others have made the case that the present system of education is fundamentally flawed and requires reorganization at all levels. Some of these advocates for restructuring have identified the structural rigidities of traditional school organization as a central problem; they see a need for restructured school formulae that include the capacity to adapt to local needs on a continuing basis (Louis & Miles, 1990; Schlechty, 1990).

School restructuring emerged in the 1980s as a vehicle for dismantling the existing school structure to make way for new, more flexible arrangements of people, space, and time. The school restructuring movement overtook dropout prevention programs geared toward "fixing" at-risk students. It quickly eclipsed effective schools reforms designed to strengthen the traditional school organization.

A primary concern of school restructuring advocates is enabling and empowering school professionals. That concern stems from the observation that professionals closest to the work of teaching and learning lack sufficient authority to deploy resources in a manner dictated by real and present needs. Consequently, much of the school restructuring agenda consists of efforts to shift a certain degree of power and authority from district to school and from school administrator to teacher. School-based management, shared decision making, and teacher career ladders are all viewed as a means to make more effective use of schools' human resources.

Critics of school restructuring charge that reforming authority structures is only loosely tied to student achievement (Finn, 1990). They point out that the empowerment of professionals does not guarantee their responsiveness to changing educational needs. Some may not know how or be motivated to take the next step toward instituting more effective instructional practices; traditional school organization tends to be taken for granted.

The concept of school community, on the other hand, offers an organizational arrangement that links increased teacher authority to other educational structures and processes more closely related to teaching and learning. Increasingly, educators and researchers describe effective schools as learning communities (Bryk & Driscoll, 1988; Fine, in press; Gregory & Smith, 1987). They refer to an organizational context of intimate, flexible, and sustained working relationships among students and school staff, both of whom are allowed to assume active roles in the teaching–learning process. It is argued that a socially and psychologically meaningful context is required for effective teaching. They point out that small, intimate schools give teachers greater access to students and their families and vice versa. In this sense, school community addresses a wider range of concerns of the ''enabling and empowering'' perspectives than the other concepts cited here.

However, the concept of *school community*, like that of school restructuring, lacks a coherent conceptual framework. Its structural features have not been delineated, and the specific pathways by which a new organizational context can influence educational goals have not been identified. A theory of how redeployed human resources can be used to enhance students' educational attainment has not been articulated. Equally important, the capacity of the school community to respond effectively to the changed and changing conditions of inner cities (i.e., its adaptability) has not been appraised.

Although the term *resilience* is used in this volume to refer to the ability to overcome adverse, highly threatening circumstances, I refer to the school's capacity to meet educational challenges posed by ever-changing but not necessarily negative environmental conditions. Therefore, I apply the terms *adaptability* and *responsiveness* to school community, in order to preserve the conceptual distinctiveness of resilience. Appropriately, these descriptors shift the focus away from the survival and persistence of the school organization to its relationship with the environment of changing social and economic needs.

This chapter presents a conceptual framework and theoretical underpinnings for a school community that is responsive to the needs of inner-city children. I first provide a general definition of a school community, and then specifications for it on three key, interdependent dimensions of schooling: structures, processes, and goals. I then briefly describe current school organization in each of these dimensions to highlight the differences between the two approaches, especially with respect to their responsiveness to student needs.

IDENTIFICATION OF A SCHOOL COMMUNITY

The concept of *school community* rests on the sociological notion of community as a social group that is bound by personal as well as utilitarian ties (Weber, 1947). Members of a community care about one another on the basis of shared values and experiences and, in addition, perform practical functions for each other. Communities bestow feelings of belonging and identity. In the context of a school community, teachers' roles are not limited to instruction and professional interchange; they also function as friend, supporter, and advisor to students and colleagues alike. In other words, teachers and students have personal meaning for one another. Recent research helps to make two important additional points about schools as communities. Small school size has a significant, positive effect on communal relations. Staff and students of small schools are much more likely to report feelings of belonging, involvement in school activities, and collegiality (Bryk & Driscoll, 1988; Gregory & Smith, 1987; Oxley, 1990; Pittman & Haughwout, 1987). Second, whereas shared learning experiences appear to be a requirement of communal schools, racial and socioeconomic similarity are not (Bryk & Driscoll, 1988).

A CONCEPTUAL FRAMEWORK
FOR A SCHOOL COMMUNITY

Recent approaches to school improvement are instructive inasmuch as they address a complementary set of issues that serve to describe a multidimensional framework for a theory of school community. Schoolwide reform efforts, such as the effective schools movement (Edmonds, 1979, 1981; Purkey & Smith, 1983, 1985), provided a rationale for school-level reform and identified key school features related to successful student performance. At the same time, the effective schools literature based conclusions about effective practices on a narrow set of academic outcomes, and left many effective schools features, especially sociocultural aspects of schooling, poorly defined (Purkey & Smith, 1983). School improvement programs (Purkey, Rutter, & Newmann, 1985) addressed some of these problematic aspects of school culture inasmuch as they attempted to specify school management processes (e.g., shared decision making) related to the successful implementation of reforms.

Sociopsychological interventions in schools have also helped to close gaps in effective schools programs. School–community collaborations (Comer, 1976, 1985, 1987) further specified management practices needed to enlist parental support for school objectives and to handle student behavior problems sensitively. House systems (Newmann, 1981; Oxley, 1989, 1990) defined school structures that are needed to create a social context conducive to learning, as well as to support the effective school management processes described here.

A sound theory of school restructuring depends on the specification of a mutually reinforcing group of processes, structures, and goals, because of the ecological interdependence of such key dimensions of schooling (Eisner, 1988). Some have argued that one or another of these is primary, for example, that performance goals should be used to dictate the rest (Finn, 1990; Wiggins, 1991). However, the simultaneous focus on process, structure, and goal helps compensate for the limitations associated with each. A concentration on goals or process seldom leads to the kind of deep structural changes needed to support them (Purkey et al., 1985). Purely structural formulae inhibit creativity and adaptation.

The framework for a school community must also apply to different levels of the educational system. A several-decade-long history of failed educational reforms, mostly classroom based, points to the need to simultaneously address aspects of the classroom and school (Cuban, 1986), as well as higher levels of the system (e.g., district; Elmore, 1988).

In the following sections, I specify the structural, processual, and goal parameters of a school community.

Current School Structure

Schools appear to be a combination of bureaucratic and loosely coupled structures (Boyd, 1990; Purkey & Smith, 1983). They conform to a bureaucratic model of organization, in that management is centralized and staff roles are highly differentiated. School policy is formulated by a few individuals at the top of the administrative hierarchy, and communicated to line staff who are expected to act in accordance with the policy. School functioning is organized into narrowly defined activities performed by individuals who specialize in these activities. Thus, administration, student support, and instruction are sharply bound functions, each of which is further divided into discrete tasks carried out by different people. Schools, like bureaucracies in general, tend to be organized on a large scale. Large size is required to support specialized person nel and, in theory, affords an economy of scale because a centralized management system does not need to grow as fast as the organization as a whole (e.g., both small and large schools have only one principal).

Schools diverge from the bureaucratic model in that administrative and instructional functions are much less tightly coupled than one would expect to find in a bureaucracy. The independence of teachers, afforded to a large extent by the isolation of the classroom, appears to diffuse the effect of school directives. Moreover, the qualitative nature of measures of teacher performance, as well as the difficulty in interpreting measures of student performance, limit administrators' ability to use such feedback directly in managing the organization. Efforts to change or improve school functioning in the inner city are often thwarted because these school systems' unusually large size, numbers of programs, and specialized operations, exacerbate the weak links between policymaking and practice and between related student services.

Structural Features of a School Community

Current critiques of schooling and school improvement models converge to a great extent on the kinds of generic attributes of organizational structure that are needed to create a productive context for learning. These features are consistent with, and indeed define, the structural dimension of a school community. They include, but are not limited to, the following interdependent features:

- smaller organizational scale (Boyer, 1983; Carnegie Foundation for the Advancement of Teaching, 1988; Children's Defense Fund, 1988; Committee for Economic Development, 1987; Goodlad, 1984; National Coalition of Advocates for Students, 1985; Oxley, 1990)
- decentralized management (Committee for Economic Development, 1987; David, Purkey, & White, 1989; Oxley, 1990; Purkey & Smith, 1983, 1985)
- broad-based decision-making bodies (Boyer, 1983; Comer, 1985; Committee for Economic Development, 1987; Goodlad, 1984; National Coalition of Advocates for Students, 1985; Purkey & Smith, 1985; Sizer, 1984)
- cross-role/discipline collaborative groups (Carnegie Task Force on Teaching as a Profession, 1986; Children's Defense Fund, 1988; Comer, 1985; David et al., 1989; Purkey & Smith, 1985; Sizer, 1984)
- bridges across temporal gaps in schooling (Children's Defense Fund, 1988; Comer, 1985; Oxley, 1990; Ratzki, 1988)
- heterogeneous instructional groups (Goodlad, 1984; National Coalition of Advocates for Students, 1985; Oakes, 1985; Reynolds, Wang, & Walberg, in press; Wang, 1990)

These structures describe an organization composed of small, relatively autonomous, and interdisciplinary groups of staff and students working together
over extended periods of time, guided and supported by parents and supervi-
sors situated at both middle and higher levels of the organization. Because
management responsibilities are shared among a wider group of individuals,
administrators are able to devote some of their time to other functions, such
as instruction and student support, thereby closing the gaps between these functions. Staff–student groups are small enough that informal as well as formal
structures can be used to convey opinions and information. In this way, the
groups remain flexible and responsive. Collaborations among school staff with
varying kinds and levels of expertise help reduce gaps in service delivery, as
well as redundancy.

This team approach allows teachers to instruct mixes of individuals who
are heterogeneous with respect to entry-level abilities, gender, race, and ethnicity. Contrary to the long-standing, pervasive, but discredited (Oakes, 1985)
practice of grouping students with like abilities, the small, intimate, and integrative nature of school communities enables teachers to deal with the unique
needs of each student rather than the presumed shared characteristics of
homogeneously grouped students (Wang, 1990). Students' heterogeneity, their
social and cultural differences, can be made an integral part of the curriculum, and learning to consider issues from different perspectives becomes a
means of furthering cognitive development (New York State Social Studies
Review and Development Committee, 1991).

Cross-role collaborations between school staff and outside agents (such as
universities, parents, health and social services, and businesses) are also key
to a school community. Of special importance is the establishment of linkages
between school districts and universities and colleges, linkages that allow an
ongoing interchange between university trainers and researchers and school
practitioners. Permanent partnerships with universities are needed to eliminate
the cultural discontinuity that exists between schools and universities and creates not only knowledge gaps but outright hostility to the differing areas of
expertise of these two groups.

Current Educational Practices

Haberman (1991) identified a typical, urban style of teaching that he labeled
the *pedagogy of poverty*. It consists of a one-way form of communication between
teachers and students, wherein the teacher issues information, directions, assignments, tests, homework, and grades, and attempts to gain student com-
pliance through close monitoring of student behavior and, if necessary,
punishment. In response to this directive, control-oriented pedagogy, students
spend a great deal of instructional time trying to manipulate and reduce the

power of teachers (Haberman, 1991; Oxley, 1990). Beyond classroom instruction, again one-way communication predominates: Teachers inform parents, and police student behavior throughout the school, while administrators instruct teachers and maintain records on students. The bureaucratic, hierarchical style of education may work efficiently in homogenous communities where one may assume shared points of view. But in the inner city, where important differences exist among the cultural subgroups of school personnel, students, and their families, there is a premium on parent and student involvement (e.g., Comer, 1987).

Processual Features of a School Community

The structural elements of a school community listed here are consistent with and supportive of a set of interdependent management, teaching, and learning activities that have been advanced in the recent school advocacy and research literatures:

- shared decision making (Boyer, 1983; Comer, 1985; Committee for Economic Development, 1987; Goodlad, 1984; National Coalition of Advocates for Students, 1985; Purkey & Smith, 1985; Purkey et al., 1985; Sizer, 1984)
- collaborative planning (Children's Defense Fund, 1988; Comer, 1985; David et al., 1989; Purkey et al., 1985; Purkey & Smith, 1985; Wang, 1992)
- active learning/inquiry (Children's Defense Fund, 1988; McCombs, 1991; Sizer, 1984; Wang & Palincsar, 1989)
- collaborative learning/mentoring (Council of Chief State School Officers, 1990; Newmann & Thompson, 1987)
- social learning/guidance (Children's Defense Fund, 1988; Ratzki, 1988)

Shared decision making and collaborative planning drive the work of a school community. It is significant that these activities are consistent with the predominantly verbal mode in which teachers operate. Teachers also function as inquirers on an ongoing basis, continuing to extend their knowledge and mirroring the learning process for students. Integral to this process are teachers' evaluations of their own and others' performance. Similarly, students function as "workers" (Sizer, 1984), discover answers, produce knowledge, and help one another in the process. Students learn how to work together with other students, teachers, and their parents to achieve their educational objectives (Ratzki, 1988). They have opportunities to participate in school government and social activities as part of the school's explicit social curriculum.

Current Educational Goals

The restricted range of educational goals for which schools are held account-able is reflected in the research on effective schools discussed earlier. Yet, U.S. public education has a long-standing commitment to well-rounded student de-velopment. This commitment has, however, been expressed in terms of the provision of "extras" such as sports programs, student government, and fine arts, participation in which is completely disconnected from mastery of "seri-ous" courses. In the final analysis, the school's responsiveness to inner-city children rests on its embrace of a broadened set of goals that honor the diverse strengths, aptitudes, and needs of these children.

School Community Goals

The school community processes just listed are geared to achieving a wider range of formal social/emotional, physical, and intellectual developmental goals than presently exists:

- mastery of core subjects (Carnegie Foundation for the Advancement of Teaching, 1988; Sizer, 1984; Walberg, 1990; Wang, Haertel, & Wal-berg, 1990)
- higher order intellectual functioning (Children's Defense Fund, 1988; Good & Weinstein, 1986; Segal, Chipman, & Glaser, 1985; Sizer, 1984; Walberg, 1988)
- development of nontraditional intelligences (Children's Defense Fund, 1988; Eisner, 1988; Gardner, 1983)
- social competence (Carnegie Council on Adolescent Development, 1989; Children's Defense Fund, 1988; Comer, 1985; Committee for Economic Development, 1987)
- good health (Carnegie Council on Adolescent Development, 1989)

These educational goals are based on the explicit recognition that intellec-tual growth depends on social and physical development and vice versa. They rest on the philosophy that schools should be devoted to helping students real-ize their full human potential, not just the narrower aims of the society (e.g., employability). The human development perspective figures prominently in the school restructuring literature (Murphy, 1991).

The widespread conviction that educators have pursued too broad and shal-low a curriculum over the past several decades has led to intensified instruc-tion of core academic subjects. This shift need not deter educators from providing opportunities for students (often within basic classes) to develop artistic, musical, mechanical, and other talents, which have meaning in their own right and may give students the confidence to pursue more traditional subjects.

Broadened school goals are coupled with diversified measures of students' progress toward these goals. Demonstrations of student competence in different areas are integrated as much as possible to increase their external validity. Student portfolios containing work products that required collaboration with peers and teachers, initiative, and persistence in carrying out long-term projects, as well as mastery of particular academic skills and facts, are used to offset constrictive standardized tests.

SUMMARY AND CONCLUSIONS

The theory that underpins the framework presented here can best be described as a theory of a communally organized school that both requires and responds constructively to diverse characteristics of students and their families. The theory stipulates that a successful school community depends on the application of a generic, mutually supportive set of structures, processes, and goals at multiple levels of the educational system. It posits causal relationships among the features identified in each dimension; the structures that have been delineated define a context in which it becomes possible to pursue the key educational processes that are considered instrumental to attaining the broad goals of child development. Research in the areas of organizational development, school size, academic tracking, effective schools, program implementation, and so on, provide support for these hypothesized causal linkages.

The heterogeneous school community may find useful application in any locale, but has special relevance to the inner city. School communities offer a means of enculturating diverse social and cultural groups, to the extent that they lead individuals to identify with the values and goals of the school as a whole. At the same time, school communities have a greater-than-ordinary capacity to recognize individual and group differences, and to employ these differences as pedagogical tools. In this way, the school community curriculum represents less a fixed and independent entity than a dynamic transaction between existing knowledge bases and particular community contexts. What students learn is not divorced from how they live.

"Treatments" for racial and cultural diversity are a nearly ubiquitous feature of urban school reform agendas. The "all children can learn" maxim promulgated by school districts, parent outreach, bilingual programs, and linkages with social service agencies give an idea of the range of such treatments. However, approaches to school restructuring seldom stipulate diversity as a necessary ingredient. On the contrary, recent efforts to establish schools that serve and are staffed by African-American males rest on the view that the intellectual development of African-American males is best pursued within a homogeneous social context.

The report of the New York State Social Studies Review and Development Committee (1991) helps turn common responses to cultural diversity on their heads. The Committee concluded, rather controversially, that social studies instruction should cover a broad range of cultures, examine social problems from differing cultural perspectives, and draw upon students' own backgrounds and experience. On that basis, schools with diverse populations of students can offer a learning context that is intellectually rich, whereas schools with homogeneous student bodies must rely on less compelling methods of bringing differing perspectives and experiences into the curriculum. Indeed, the availability of such diverse knowledge and skills remains a unique, though still untapped, resource of inner-city schools.

Finally, while attempting to develop a heterogeneous school community framework that is responsive to the unique qualities of inner cities, I have tried to be consistent with the features of generic, "adaptive models" of school organization put forward by other authors. For example, Louis and Miles (1990) suggested that an adaptive school organization has the following characteristics:

- planning and proactive, not reactive;
- guided by professional judgment, not bureaucratic rules;
- the staff evaluate their performance;
- team-oriented;
- semiautonomous;
- staff perform multiple, not just specialized functions; and
- staff are involved with the whole person.

The framework's alignment with such models is important, because it suggests that heterogeneous school communities are not only well suited to inner cities in their present state, but capable of responding to changing conditions, which is the ultimate measure of a responsive organization.

REFERENCES

Boyd, W. (1990, February). *What makes ghetto schools work or not work?* Paper presented at the Social Science Research Council and Northwestern University Conference on the Truly Disadvantaged, Evanston, IL.

Boyer, E. (1983). *High school: A report on secondary education in America.* New York: Harper & Row.

Bryk, A., & Driscoll, M. (1988). *The high school as community: Contextual influences and consequences for students and teachers.* Madison, WI: University of Wisconsin National Center on Effective Secondary Schools.

Carnegie Council on Adolescent Development. (1989). *Turning points.* Washington, DC: Carnegie Corporation of New York.

Carnegie Foundation for the Advancement of Teaching. (1988). *An imperiled generation: Saving urban schools*. Princeton, NJ: Author.

Carnegie Task Force on Teaching as a Profession. (1986). *A nation prepared: Teachers for the 21st century*. New York: Carnegie Forum on Education and the Economy.

Children's Defense Fund. (1988, September). *Making the middle grades work*. Washington, DC: Author.

Chubb, J. E., & Moe, T. M. (1988). Politics, markets, and the organization of schools. *American Political Science Review, 82*, 1065–1087.

Comer, J. P. (1976). Improving the quality and continuity of relationships in two inner-city schools. *Journal of the American Academy of Child Psychiatry, 15*, 535–545.

Comer, J. P. (1985). The Yale-New Haven primary prevention project: A follow-up study. *Journal of the American Academy of Child Psychiatry, 24*, 154–160.

Comer, J. P. (1987). New Haven's school-community connection. *Educational Leadership, 44*, 13–16.

Committee for Economic Development. (1987). *Children in need: Investment strategies for the educationally disadvantaged*. New York: Author.

Council of Chief State School Officers. (1990, March). *Voices from successful schools: Elements of improved schools serving at-risk students and how state education agencies can support more local school improvement*. Washington, DC: Author.

Cuban, L. (1986, September). Persistent instruction: Another look at constancy in the classroom. *Phi Delta Kappan*, 7–11.

David, J., Purkey, S., & White, P. (1989). *Restructuring in progress: Lessons from pioneering districts*. Washington, DC: National Governors' Association.

Edmonds, R. R. (1979). Effective schools for the urban poor. *Educational Leadership, 37*, 15–27.

Edmonds, R. R. (1981). Making public schools effective. *Social Policy, 12*, 56–60.

Eisner, E. W. (1988, February). The ecology of school imporvement. *Educational Leadership*, pp. 24–29.

Elmore, R. (1988). *Early experience in restructuring schools: Voices from the field*. Washington, DC: National Governors' Association.

Fine, M. (in press). *Chartering urban school reform*. Philadelphia, PA: Philadelphia Schools Collaborative, School District of Philadelphia.

Finn, C. (1990). The biggest reform of all. *Phi Delta Kappan, 71*, 584–592.

Gardner, H. (1983). *Frames of mind: The theory of multiple intelligences*. New York: Basic Books.

Good, T., & Weinstein, R. (1986). Schools make a difference: Evidence, criticisms, and new directions. *American Psychologist, 41*, 1090–1097.

Goodlad, J. I. (1984). *A place called school: Prospects for the future*. New York: McGraw-Hill.

Gregory, T. B., & Smith, G. R. (1987). *High schools as communities: The small school considered*. Bloomington, IN: Phi Delta Kappa Educational Foundation.

Haberman, M. (1991). The pedagogy of poverty versus good teaching. *Phi Delta Kappan, 73*(4), 290–294.

Louis, K., & Miles, M. (1990). *Improving the urban high school: What works and why*. New York: Teachers College Press.

McCombs, B. (1991). Motivation and lifelong learning. *Educational Psychologist, 26*(2), 117–127.

Murphy, J. (1991). *Restructuring schools*. New York: Teachers College Press.

National Coalition of Advocates for Students. (1985). *Barriers to excellence: Our children at risk*. Boston, MA: Author.

Newmann, F. M. (1981). Reducing alienation in high schools: Implications of theory. *Harvard Educational Review, 51*, 546–564.

Newmann, F. M., & Thompson, J. A. (1987, September). *Effects of cooperative learning on achievement in secondary schools: A summary of research*. Madison, WI: University of Wisconsin-Madison.

New York State Social Studies Review and Development Committee. (1991, June). *One nation, many people: A declaration of cultural interdependence*. Albany, NY: New York State Department of Education.

Oakes, J. (1985). *Keeping track: How schools structure inequality*. New Haven, CT: Yale University Press.

Oxley, D. (1989). Smaller is better: How the house plan can make large high schools less anonymous. *American Educator, 13*(1), 28–31, 51–52.

Oxley, D. (1990). *An analysis of house systems in New York City neighborhood high schools*. Philadelphia, PA: Temple University Center for Research in Human Development and Education.

Pittman, R. B., & Haughwout, P. (1987). Influence of high school size on dropout rate. *Educational Evaluation and Policy Analysis, 9*, 337–343.

Purkey, S. C., Rutter, R., & Newmann, F. (1985). U.S. high school improvement programs: A profile from the High School and Beyond Supplemental Survey. *Curriculum Inquiry*.

Purkey, S. C., & Smith, M. S. (1983). Effective schools: A review. *The Elementary School Journal, 83*, 427–452.

Purkey, S. C., & Smith, M. S. (1985). School reform: The district policy implications of the effective schools literature. *The Elementary School Journal, 85*, 353–389.

Ratzki, A. (1988). Creating a school community: One model of how it can be done. *American Educator, 12*(1), 10–17, 38–43.

Reynolds, M. C., Wang, M. C., & Walberg, H. J. (in press). Changing the direction of research and practice in special education: A case of disjointedness. *Exceptional Children*.

Schlechty, P. (1990). *Schools for the twenty-first century: Leadership imperatives for educational reform*. San Francisco: Jossey-Bass.

Segal, J. W., Chipman, S. G., & Glaser, R. (Eds.). (1985). *Thinking and learning skills. Vol. 1: Relating instruction to research*. Hillsdale, NJ: Lawrence Erlbaum Associates.

Sizer, T. (1984). *Horace's compromise: The dilemma of the American high school*. Boston: Houghton-Mifflin.

Walberg, H. J. (1988). Creativity as learning. In R. J. Sternberg (Ed.), *The nature of creativity* (pp. 340–361). New York: Cambridge University Press.

Walberg, H. J. (1990, February). Productive teaching and instruction: Assessing the knowledge base. *Phi Delta Kappan, 71*, 470–478.

Wang, M. C. (1990). *Designing and evaluating school learning environments for effective mainstreaming of special education students: Synthesis, validation, and dissemination of research methods* (Final Report). Philadelphia, PA: Temple University Center for Research in Human Development and Education.

Wang, M. C. (1992). *Adaptive education strategies*. Baltimore: Paul H. Brookes.

Wang, M. C., Haertel, G. D., & Walberg, H. J. (1990). What influences learning? A content analysis of review literature. *Journal of Educational Research, 84*(1), 30–43.

Wang, M. C., & Palincsar, A. S. (1989). Teaching students to assume an active role in their learning. In M. C. Reynolds (Ed.), *Knowledge base for the beginning teacher* (pp. 71–84). Oxford: Pergamon Press.

Weber, M. (1947). *Theory of social and economic organization* (A. M. Henderson & T. Parsons, Trans.). New York: Macmillan.

Wiggins, G. (1991). Standards, not standardization: Evoking quality student work. *Educational Leadership, 48*(5), 18–25.

Epilogue:
Educational Resilience—
Challenges and Prospects

Edmund W. Gordon
Yale University

Margaret C. Wang
Temple University
Center for Research in Human Development and Education

Resilience has recently inspired a multitude of discussions and investigations among researchers involved in studying human development and the life circumstances of children and families, especially those living in urban environments. This intensification of interest in and research devoted to resilience as a human phenomenon has its roots in the work of Garmezy (1974). He was one of the first to use the term to refer either to the human capacity to recover from psychological trauma or to the achievement of successful adaptation despite developmental risk and adversity. But Garmezy's initial use of the construct was more specific; it concentrated on the adaptation and adjustment experiences of children who had faced serious psychopathology and responded well to treatment. He was less concerned with spontaneous recovery than with recoverability under treatment. The implicit assumption of the research was that these children had resources that could be tapped through therapy to enable recovery. Because the natural history of psychosis in children did not make for good prognoses, the successes of these patients were thought to defy the odds favoring failure. This notion of resilience has dominated the field of investigation with which this volume is concerned.

In her seminal review of extant resilience research, Horowitz (1989) identified five categories or foci of investigations, including: (a) infants born prematurely or with prenatal complications, (b) children with serious behavior disorders, (c) children exposed to toxic environmental agents, (d) experiments subjecting nonhuman animals to sensory deprivation during critical periods, and (e) children experiencing stress as a function of psychopathology. In all of the work noted by Horowitz in her review, as in the collection of chapters and research reports included in this book, the Garmezian conceptualization has dominated. However, in the work discussed in this volume the construct has been more broadly applied to include individuals, institutions, and communities. Perhaps even more significant is the paradigm shift evident in the work discussed in the preceding chapters. We see a kind of celebration of the human capacity to overcome the odds. An emerging theme in investigations into this general topic area can be characterized as a search for the mechanisms and strategies of resilient adaptation, such that those mechanisms and strategies might be identified and fostered. We are now able to talk, albeit with a limited research base, about the characteristics of resilient persons and the correlates of resilience. For such a recent psychological construct, resilience seems to have come of age, gaining broader respect and attention from the scientific community.

There are, however, several theoretical and methodological problems, associated with the current conceptualization of resilience, that require further explication. As noted by Sameroff, Seifer, Baracas, Zax, and Greenspan (1987), there are no definite criteria by which a particular variable can be defined as a risk factor. Consequently, there are no clear criteria by which a set of human behaviors or behavioral outcomes can be defined as resilient. The judgment is always made after the fact, and is based on the projection of risk or threat onto the conditions that are thought to have been culpable. In such murky water, is resilience a quality of persons or of their life circumstances? Is resilience an adaptive outcome or should it refer to the quality of adaptive effort? Is resilience a predictable human characteristic or a phenomenon controlled by chance? Despite increasing knowledge of the correlates of resilience, we are hard pressed to describe reliable mechanisms by which resilience might be achieved in persons, institutions, or communities. The core of the problem may reside in the conceptualization of the construct. Instead of a single construct referable to identifiable entities, we are confronted with two or more constructs that are influenced by differential contexts and perspectives.

In one of the possible conceptions resilience may correctly be defined as a human capacity, that is, the capacity to reestablish equilibrium, to maintain homeostasis, to recover. Some people, it seems, have a greater capacity than others. Persons in good physical health seem to recover from injury and physical illness more rapidly than those who begin with poor health. However, in order to define resilience as the capacity to recover, we must first establish the fact of trauma. Because trauma is often an existential and relative phenomenon, resilience defined as recovery from trauma is problematic.

Clearly, another related conception has to do with situation, circumstance, and context. Some environments possess more and better resources for recovery and adaptation. Adjustment and recovery are simply easier under some circumstances, such that resilience may be a function of one's situation. For example, poor swimmers are much more likely to survive in the Great Salt Lake than in any freshwater lake, not because of who they are or what they do but because salt water provides greater buoyancy. From this example, it seems that resilience as a situationally dependent construct is extremely difficult to study with a view to generalization. We simply do not know how to study the dialectics of personal and situational conjoint variance.

There may be yet another construction of resilience. Because human behavior, human conditions, and human efforts are also attributionally determined, resilience is partly an existential phenomenon. If resilience requires that a stressful or traumatic experience be overcome, in the classic use of the resilience construct the situation must first be perceived as stressful or traumatic. If I view an obstacle as a stimulating challenge or opportunity, have I shown resilience in overcoming it? If I do not find a situation stressful, even if others do, have I succeeded in dealing with stress? Currently, resilience is used in most extant research to refer to adaptation under all these circumstances. It is often difficult to determine which of the conceptions is specifically under investigation. The resulting confusion seems to contradict our progress in understanding resilience as a psychological construct.

Several years ago, Hebb (1958) argued for the utilitarian importance of theory development. According to Hebb, a theory need not be correct to be valuable. Rather, a theory is a way of looking at a phenomenon at a particular time and place, given the available information. Its value resides in its capacity to enable human action (i.e., the theory's capacity to enable us to do something or at least think about the issues involved). It is in the nature of theories to be disconfirmed and replaced by more useful theories. The process of confirming and disconfirming theories is intrinsic to the scientific enterprise.

In the several chapters and reports included in this book, scholars have examined resilience in a variety of contexts. That the notion of the construct that has dominated this work may be limited does not obviate the value of the construct or the work. The increasing research into resilience as a construct is an example of Hebb's contention. The Garmezian notion or theory has enabled human effort, both investigations and interventions. We are beginning to formulate better questions and our concept of resilience is expanding. Perhaps of equal importance, we have identified some situations and some variables which, when appropriately managed, appear to foster resilience and capacity for successful adaptation despite risk and adversity. Building a research base for effective human intervention, first to prevent dysfunction and, when necessary, to correct and heal, will be one of our greatest immediate challenges.

REFERENCES

Garmezy, N. (1974). Children at risk: The search for the antecedents of schizophrenia. Part I. Conceptual models and research methods. *Schizophrenia Bulletin, 8*, 14–90.

Hebb, D. (1958). *A textbook of psychology*. London: W. B. Saunders.

Horowitz, F. D. (1989). *The concept of risk: A reevaluation*. Invited address to the Annual Meeting of the Society for Research in Child Development, Kansas City, MO.

Sameroff, A. J., Seifer, R., Barocas, R., Zax, M., & Greenspan, S. I. (1987). Intelligence quotient scores of 4-year-old children: Social environmental risk factors. *Pediatrics, 79*, 343–350.

Author Index

195

I

Ihlanfeldt, K. R., 105, *108*
Ingels, S. J., 75, 76, 80, *84*
Inger, M., 58, *69*
Iverson, B. K., 58, *69*

J

Jacobson, A. M., 12, *23, 25*
James, W., 27, *43*
Jameson, J., 121, *129*
Janes, C. L., 9, *25*
Jankowski, M. S., 103, *108*
Japzon, D. M., 46, 64, *72*
Jason, L. A., 17, *22*
Jenkins, J. R., 65, *69*
Johnson, C. M., 16, *23*
Johnson, J. H., 112, *117*, 121, *130*
Johnson, R. J., 171, *176*
Johnston, P., 65, *67*

K

Kagan, D. M., 151, *165*
Kagan, J., 112, *117*
Kandel, E., 13, *23*
Kaplan, A., 99, 100, 102, *108*
Kaplan, H. B., 171, *176*
Karr, R., 75, 76, 80, *84*
Katz, M., 105, *108*
Kaufman, J., 13, *24*
Kazdin, A. E., 170, 175, *176*
Kellam, S. G., 113, *116*
Keller, G. G., 46, 64, *72*
Kendall, P. C., 17, *22*, 170, *176*
Kestenberg, J., 151, *165*
Kiesler, D. J., 169, *176*
King, L., 121, *130*
Kirby, P., 52, *71*
Kirkegaard-Sorensen, L., 13, *23*
Kirkpatrick, S. L., 57, *69*
Kirst, M. W., 55, *69*
Klein, R., 113, *117*
Klenk, L. J., 61, *70*
Knapp, M. S., 62, 63, 66, *69, 70*
Knop, J., 13, *23*
Kobasa, S. C., 112, 113, *117*
Kokes, R. F., 8, 9, *23*

Kolvin, I., 12, *24*
Kolvin, P. A., 12, *24*
Kontopoulos, K., 88, 91, *94*
Kopp, C. B., 5, *24*
Kostelny, K., 16, *23*
Kottkamp, R. B., 146, *149*
Krehbiel, G., 111, *116*
Kropp, J., 121, *129*

L

Lahey, B., 121, *129*
Langner, R., 121, *129*
Lareau, A., 124, *129*
Lash, A. A., 57, *69*
Laudan, L., 87, *94*
Lee, R. M., 49, 58, *70*, 74, 79, *84*
Lee, V. E., 65, *69*
Lefkowitz, B., 63, *69*
Lempers, J., 121, *129*
Lerner, R. M., 90, 91, *94*, 170, *176*
Levin, H., 153, *165*
Lewis, E. M., 66, *69*
Lewis, J. M., 10, *24*
Liddle, H. A., 58, *69*, 168, 170, *176*
Liem, J., 121, *129*
Liem, R., 121, *129*
Lindenthal, J. J., 112, *117*
Loeber, R., 111, 112, *117*
Long, J. V. F., 10, *24, 69*
Long, L. H., 54, 57, *69*
Longfellow, C., 121, *129*
Looney, J. G., 10, *24*
Lorenz, F. O., 10, *22*
Louis, K., 179, 188, *189*
Lowell, E., 111, *117*
Lowell, R., 161, *164*
Luthar, S. S., 8, *24*, 30, *43*
Lyneis, J. M., 142, *149*

M

Maccoby, E. E., 153, *165*
Madden, N., 51, *71*
Magnusson, D., 19, *24*
Majors, R. G., 125, *129*
Malgady, R. G., 171, *176*
Manicas, P., 91, *94*
Mason, B. J., 51, *72*

Subject Index